S0-AZT-246

Working Papers with Study Guide

Chapters 1-12

to Accompany

College Accounting

Eleventh Edition

Tracie L. Nobles, CPA
Austin Community College

Cathy J. Scott
Navarro College

Douglas J. McQuaig
Wenatchee Valley College, Emeritus

Patricia A. Bille
Wenatchee Valley College

 SOUTH-WESTERN
CENGAGE Learning·

Australia • Brazil • Japan • Korea • Mexico • Singapore • Spain • United Kingdom • United States

SOUTH-WESTERN
CENGAGE Learning·

© 2013, 2010 South-Western, Cengage Learning

ALL RIGHTS RESERVED. No part of this work covered by the copyright herein may be reproduced, transmitted, stored, or used in any form or by any means graphic, electronic, or mechanical, including but not limited to photocopying, recording, scanning, digitizing, taping, Web distribution, information networks, or information storage and retrieval systems, except as permitted under Section 107 or 108 of the 1976 United States Copyright Act, without the prior written permission of the publisher except as may be permitted by the license terms below.

For product information and technology assistance, contact us at **Cengage Learning Academic Resource Center, 1-800-423-0563**.

For permission to use material from this text or product, submit all requests online at **www.cengage.com/permissions**. Further permissions questions can be emailed to **permissionrequest@cengage.com**.

ISBN-13: 978-1-111-53021-1
ISBN-10: 1-111-53021-1

South-Western Cengage Learning
Cengage Learning
2640 Eagan Woods Drive Suite 220
Eagan, MN 55121

Cengage Learning is a leading provider of customized learning solutions with office locations around the globe, including Singapore, the United Kingdom, Australia, Mexico, Brazil, and Japan. Locate your local office at: **international.cengage.com/region**.

Cengage Learning products are represented in Canada by Nelson Education, Ltd.

For your course and learning solutions, visit **www.cengage.com**.

Purchase any of our products at your local college store or at our preferred online store **www.cengagebrain.com**.

Printed in the United States of America
1 2 3 4 5 6 7   15 14 13 12

CONTENTS

To the Student iv
Review of T Account Placement and Representative Transactions v
Review of Business Mathematics xiv
Suggested Abbreviations for Account Titles in Chapters 1–12 xxiii

		Study Guide	Working Papers
Introduction		1	
Chapter 1	Asset, Liability, Owner's Equity, Revenue, and Expense Accounts	1	6
Chapter 2	T Accounts, Debits and Credits, Trial Balance, and Financial Statements	19	25
Chapter 3	The General Journal and the General Ledger	41	50
All About You Spa:			
Chapter 3:	*Journalizing, Posting, and Preparing a Trial Balance*		97
Chapter 4:	*Work Sheet and Adjusting Entries*		108
	Adjustments		110
Chapter 5:	*Closing Entries*		114
Chapter 4	Adjusting Entries and the Work Sheet	117	127
Chapter 5	Closing Entries and the Post-Closing Trial Balance	163	167
Accounting Cycle Review Problem A		209
Accounting Cycle Review Problem B		227
Chapter 6	Bank Accounts, Cash Funds, and Internal Controls	247	252
Chapter 7	Employee Earnings and Deductions	267	270
Chapter 8	Employer Taxes, Payments, and Reports	283	288
Chapter 9	Sales and Purchases	305	325
All About You Spa:			
Chapter 9:	*Sales and Purchases*		363
Chapter 10	Cash Receipts and Cash Payments	389	396
All About You Spa:			
Chapter 10:	*Cash Receipts and Cash Payments*		433
Chapter 10	Appendix		460
Chapter 11	Work Sheet and Adjusting Entries	471	476
All About You Spa:			
Chapter 11:	*Work Sheet and Adjusting Entries*		490
Chapter 12	Financial Statements, Closing Entries, and Reversing Entries	503	509
Comprehensive Review Problem (General Journals)		526
Comprehensive Review Problem (Special Journals)		551
All About You Spa:			
Chapter 12:	*Closing Entries and Financial Statements*		575
Appendix A:	*Methods of Depreciation*		581
Appendix B:	*Bad Debts*		583
Appendix C:	*Inventory Methods*		587
Appendix D:	*The Statement of Cash Flows*		589
Appendix E:	*Departmental Accounting*		595

© 2013 Cengage Learning. All Rights Reserved. May not be scanned, copied, duplicated, or posted to a publicly accessible website, in whole or in part.

To the Student

As you study *College Accounting,* Eleventh Edition, you will find these Working Papers helpful in many ways. The first part of the book contains the following selections to assist you in your study of accounting:

- Review of T Account Placement and Representative Transactions
- Review of Business Mathematics
- Suggested Abbreviations for Account Titles in Chapters 1–12

Then for each chapter in the textbook, the Working Papers with Study Guide provide the following:

- **Learning Objectives and Accounting Language**   The Learning Objectives match your textbook. When you begin your study session, read the objectives and try to recall the text explanations. If you do not feel you can fulfill a learning objective, look for the learning objective in the margin of your textbook and review the corresponding material before trying to complete your homework assignments. Use the list of Accounting Language to test your recall of vocabulary in the end-of-chapter glossaries. Look in the glossary at the end of the chapter in your textbook to find the definition of any term you do not know. If you still don't understand the term, note the page number in the glossary and look for the term itself in the body of the chapter. Each key term is printed in blue type when it is first used and defined. Make sure you understand all the key terms before going on to the next chapter.

- **Study Guide Questions**   After you read each chapter in the textbook, try answering these short questions. They will show how well you have learned the material in the text. Answers are provided at the back of the Working Papers with Study Guide, so you can find out right away whether you are correct. If you missed a few questions, go back to the text and review those areas where your understanding is incomplete. If you have mastered the material, you are ready to move ahead.

- **Demonstration Problem and Solution** Important concepts are illustrated by a self-study problem and its solution. Test yourself by working this sample problem. Next, verify your answer with the solution presented. Also, as you work your homework assignments, you may want to refer to the Demonstration Problem as well as to the text.

- **Accounting Forms** Blank forms are provided for every exercise and problem in the textbook. Sometimes information is provided to help you get started. The pages are perforated so that you can tear them out if the instructor asks for them.

  In addition, all the information you need to complete the All About You Spa Continuing Problem (following Chapter 4), Accounting Cycle Review Problems (following Chapter 5), and the Comprehensive Review Problem (following Chapter 12) is provided in the Working Papers with Study Guide, including the required blank accounting forms.

We hope that the Working Papers will make it easier for you to learn the fundamentals of accounting. Please write to us in care of Cengage Learning if you have suggestions about the text or other learning materials in your course.

   Good luck in your college accounting class!

Tracie L. Nobles
Cathy J. Scott

© 2013 Cengage Learning. All Rights Reserved. May not be scanned, copied, duplicated, or posted to a publicly accessible website, in whole or in part.

Review of T Account Placement and Representative Transactions (Parts I–III)

PART I
CHAPTERS 2 THROUGH 5

Review of T Account Placement

The following display sums up the placement of T accounts covered in Part I, Chapters 2 through 5, in relation to the fundamental accounting equation. Italicized accounts are contra accounts.

	Assets		=	Liabilities		+	Owner's Equity								
							Capital		−	Drawing		+	Revenue		−	Expenses
	+	−		−	+		−	+		+	−		−	+		+	−
	Debit	Credit		Debit	Credit		Debit	Credit		Debit	Credit		Debit	Credit		Debit	Credit

Cash		Accounts Payable		J. Conner, Capital		J. Conner, Drawing		Income from Tours		Wages Expense	
+	−	−	+	−	+	+	−	−	+	+	−

Accounts Receivable		Wages Payable		Income Summary						Rent Expense	
+	−	−	+	Expense	Revenue					+	−

Supplies										Supplies Expense	
+	−									+	−

Prepaid Insurance										Advertising Expense	
+	−									+	−

Equipment										Utilities Expense	
+	−									+	−

Accumulated Depreciation, Equipment										Insurance Expense	
−	+									+	−

										Depreciation Expense, Equipment	
										+	−

© 2013 Cengage Learning. All Rights Reserved. May not be scanned, copied, duplicated, or posted to a publicly accessible website, in whole or in part.

Review of Representative Transactions

The following table summarizes the recording of the various transactions described in Part I,
Chapters 2 through 5, and the classification of the accounts involved.

TRANSACTION	ACCOUNTS INVOLVED	CLASS.	INCREASE OR DECREASE	THEREFORE DEBIT OR CREDIT	FINANCIAL STATEMENT
Owner invested cash in business	Cash J. Conner, Capital	A OE	I I	Debit Credit	Balance Sheet and Statement of Owner's Equity
Bought equipment for cash	Equipment Cash	A A	I D	Debit Credit	Balance Sheet Balance Sheet
Bought equipment on account	Equipment Accounts Payable	A L	I I	Debit Credit	Balance Sheet Balance Sheet
Paid creditor on account	Accounts Payable Cash	L A	D D	Debit Credit	Balance Sheet Balance Sheet
Owner invested equipment in business	Equipment J. Conner, Capital	A OE	I I	Debit Credit	Balance Sheet and Statement of Owner's Equity
Sold services for cash	Cash Income from Tours	A R	I I	Debit Credit	Balance Sheet Income Statement
Paid rent for month	Rent Expense Cash	E A	I D	Debit Credit	Income Statement Balance Sheet
Bought supplies on account	Supplies Accounts Payable	A L	I I	Debit Credit	Balance Sheet Balance Sheet
Paid premium for insurance policy	Prepaid Insurance Cash	A A	I D	Debit Credit	Balance Sheet Balance Sheet
Sold services on account	Accounts Receivable Income from Tours	A R	I I	Debit Credit	Balance Sheet Income Statement
Paid wages to employees	Wages Expense Cash	E A	I D	Debit Credit	Income Statement Balance Sheet
Bought equipment, paying a down payment with the remainder on account	Equipment Cash Accounts Payable	A A L	I D I	Debit Credit Credit	Balance Sheet Balance Sheet Balance Sheet
Received cash from charge customer to apply on account	Cash Accounts Receivable	A A	I D	Debit Credit	Balance Sheet Balance Sheet

© 2013 Cengage Learning. All Rights Reserved. May not be scanned, copied, duplicated, or posted to a publicly accessible website, in whole or in part.

Review of Representative Transactions

(Part I, Chapters 2–5, concluded)

TRANSACTION	ACCOUNTS INVOLVED	CLASS.	INCREASE OR DECREASE	THEREFORE DEBIT OR CREDIT	FINANCIAL STATEMENT
Owner withdrew cash for personal use	J. Conner, Drawing	OE	I	Debit	Statement of Owner's Equity
	Cash	A	D	Credit	Balance Sheet
Adjusting entry for supplies used	Supplies Expense	E	I	Debit	Income Statement
	Supplies	A	D	Credit	Balance Sheet
Adjusting entry for insurance expired	Insurance Expense	E	I	Debit	Income Statement
	Prepaid Insurance	A	D	Credit	Balance Sheet
Adjusting entry for depreciation of assets	Depreciation Expense	E	I	Debit	Income Statement
	Accumulated Depreciation	A	I	Credit	Balance Sheet
Adjusting entry for accrued wages	Wages Expense	E	I	Debit	Income Statement
	Wages Payable	L	I	Credit	Balance Sheet
Closing entry for revenue accounts	Revenue accounts	R	D	Debit	Income Statement
	Income Summary	OE	—	Credit	—
Closing entry for expense accounts	Income Summary	OE	—	Debit	—
	Expense accounts	E	D	Credit	Income Statement
Closing entry for Income Summary account (Net Income)	Income Summary	OE	—	Debit	—
	J. Conner, Capital	OE	I	Credit	Balance Sheet and Statement of Owner's Equity
Closing entry for Drawing account	J. Conner, Capital	OE	D	Debit	Balance Sheet and Statement of Owner's Equity
	J. Conner, Drawing	OE	D	Credit	

© 2013 Cengage Learning. All Rights Reserved. May not be scanned, copied, duplicated, or posted to a publicly accessible website, in whole or in part.

PART II
CHAPTERS 6 THROUGH 8

Review of T Account Placement

The following display sums up the placement of T accounts covered in Part II, Chapters 6 through 8, in relation to the fundamental accounting equation.

						Owner's Equity					
Assets	=	**Liabilities**	+	**Capital**	–	**Drawing**	+	**Revenue**	–	**Expenses**	
+ | –		– | +		– | +		+ | –		– | +		+ | –	
Debit | Credit		Debit | Credit		Debit | Credit		Debit | Credit		Debit | Credit		Debit | Credit	

Assets

Notes Receivable
+ | –

Petty Cash Fund
+ | –

Change Fund
+ | –

Cash–Payroll Bank Account
+ | –

Prepaid Insurance, Workers' Compensation
+ | –

Liabilities

Employees' Income Tax Payable
– | +

FICA Taxes Payable
– | +

Employees' United Way Payable
– | +

State Unemployment Tax Payable
– | +

Federal Unemployment Tax Payable
– | +

Workers' Compensation Insurance Payable
– | +

Revenue

Interest Income
– | +

Cash Short and Over
| Credit balance

Expenses

Cash Short and Over
Debit balance |

Payroll Tax Expense
+ | –

Workers' Compensation Insurance Expense
+ | –

© 2013 Cengage Learning. All Rights Reserved. May not be scanned, copied, duplicated, or posted to a publicly accessible website, in whole or in part.

Review of Representative Transactions

The following table summarizes the recording of transactions covered in Part II, Chapters 6 through 8, along with a classification of the accounts involved.

TRANSACTION	ACCOUNTS INVOLVED	CLASS.	INCREASE OR DECREASE	THEREFORE DEBIT OR CREDIT	FINANCIAL STATEMENT
Recorded non-interest-bearing note receivable collected by our bank	Cash Notes Receivable	A A	I D	Debit Credit	Balance Sheet Balance Sheet
Recorded service charge on bank account	Miscellaneous Expense Cash	E A	I D	Debit Credit	Income Statement Balance Sheet
Recorded interest-bearing note receivable collected by bank	Cash Notes Receivable Interest Income	A A R	I D I	Debit Credit Credit	Balance Sheet Balance Sheet Income Statement
Recorded NSF check received from customer	Accounts Receivable Cash	A A	I D	Debit Credit	Balance Sheet Balance Sheet
Established a Petty Cash Fund	Petty Cash Fund Cash	A A	I D	Debit Credit	Balance Sheet Balance Sheet
Reimbursed Petty Cash Fund	Expenses or Assets or Drawing Cash	E A OE A	I D	Debit Debit Debit Credit	Income Statement Balance Sheet Statement of Owner's Equity Balance Sheet
Established a Change Fund	Change Fund Cash	A A	I D	Debit Credit	Balance Sheet Balance Sheet
Recorded cash sales (amount on cash register tape was greater than cash count)	Cash Cash Short and Over Income from Services	A E R	I — I	Debit Debit Credit	Balance Sheet Income Statement Income Statement
Recorded cash sales (amount on cash register tape was less than cash count)	Cash Income from Services Cash Short and Over	A R R	I I —	Debit Credit Credit	Balance Sheet Income Statement Income Statement

© 2013 Cengage Learning. All Rights Reserved. May not be scanned, copied, duplicated, or posted to a publicly accessible website, in whole or in part.

Review of Representative Transactions

(Part II, Chapters 6–8, concluded)

TRANSACTION	ACCOUNTS INVOLVED	CLASS.	INCREASE OR DECREASE	THEREFORE DEBIT OR CREDIT	FINANCIAL STATEMENT
Recorded the payroll entry from the payroll register	Sales Wages Expense	E	I	Debit	Income Statement
	Office Wages Expense	E	I	Debit	Income Statement
	Employees' Income Tax Payable	L	I	Credit	Balance Sheet
	FICA Taxes Payable	L	I	Credit	Balance Sheet
	Employees' United Way Payable	L	I	Credit	Balance Sheet
	Wages Payable	L	I	Credit	Balance Sheet
Issued check payable to Cash to pay payroll	Wages Payable	L	D	Debit	Balance Sheet
	Cash	A	D	Credit	Balance Sheet
Issued check to transfer cash to the Payroll Bank Account	Cash–Payroll Bank Account	A	I	Debit	Balance Sheet
	Cash	A	D	Credit	Balance Sheet
Recorded employer's payroll taxes	Payroll Tax Expense	E	I	Debit	Income Statement
	FICA Taxes Payable	L	I	Credit	Balance Sheet
	State Unemployment Tax Payable	L	I	Credit	Balance Sheet
	Federal Unemployment Tax Payable	L	I	Credit	Balance Sheet
Recorded deposit of FICA taxes and employees' income tax withheld	Employees' Income Tax Payable	L	D	Debit	Balance Sheet
	FICA Taxes Payable	L	D	Debit	Balance Sheet
	Cash	A	D	Credit	Balance Sheet
Paid state unemployment tax	State Unemployment Tax Payable	L	D	Debit	Balance Sheet
	Cash	A	D	Credit	Balance Sheet
Recorded deposit of federal unemployment tax	Federal Unemployment Tax Payable	L	D	Debit	Balance Sheet
	Cash	A	D	Credit	Balance Sheet
Paid for workers' compensation insurance in advance	Prepaid Insurance, Workers' Compensation	A	I	Debit	Balance Sheet
	Cash	A	D	Credit	Balance Sheet
Adjusting entry for workers' compensation insurance, assuming an additional amount is owed	Workers' Compensation Insurance Expense	E	I	Debit	Income Statement
	Prepaid Insurance, Workers' Compensation	A	D	Credit	Balance Sheet
	Workers' Compensation Insurance Payable	L	I	Credit	Balance Sheet

© 2013 Cengage Learning. All Rights Reserved. May not be scanned, copied, duplicated, or posted to a publicly accessible website, in whole or in part.

PART III
CHAPTERS 9 THROUGH 12

Review of T Account Placement

The following sums up the placement of T accounts covered in Part III, Chapters 9 through 12, in relation to the fundamental accounting equation. Italics indicates those accounts that are treated as deductions from the related accounts above them.

					Owner's Equity						
Assets	=	**Liabilities**	+	**Capital**	−	**Drawing**	+	**Revenue**	−	**Expenses**	
+ | −		− | +		− | +		+ | −		− | +		+ | −	
Debit | Credit		Debit | Credit		Debit | Credit		Debit | Credit		Debit | Credit		Debit | Credit	

Merchandise Inventory	**Sales Tax Payable**				**Sales**	**Purchases**
+ | −	− | +				− | +	+ | −

	Notes Payable				*Sales Returns and Allowances*	*Purchases Returns and Allowances*
	− | +				+ | −	− | +

	Unearned Course Fees				*Sales Discounts*	*Purchases Discounts*
	− | +				+ | −	− | +

					Course Fees Income	**Freight In**
					− | +	+ | −

						Credit Card Expense
						+ | −

Review of T Account Placement

The following table summarizes the recording of transactions covered in Part III, Chapters 9 through 12, along with a classification of the accounts involved.

Classifications

Balance Sheet		**Income Statement**	
CA	Current Assets	S	Revenue from Sales
P&E	Property and Equipment	CGS	Cost of Goods Sold
CL	Current Liabilities	SE	Selling Expense
LTL	Long-Term Liabilities	GE	General Expenses
		OI	Other Income
		OE	Other Expenses

© 2013 Cengage Learning. All Rights Reserved. May not be scanned, copied, duplicated, or posted to a publicly accessible website, in whole or in part.

Review of Representative Transactions

(Part III, Chapters 9–12, continued)

TRANSACTION	ACCOUNTS INVOLVED	CLASS.	INCREASE OR DECREASE	THEREFORE DEBIT OR CREDIT	FINANCIAL STATEMENT
Sold merchandise on account	Accounts Receivable Sales	CA S	I I	Debit Credit	Balance Sheet Income Statement
Sold merchandise on account involving sales tax	Accounts Receivable Sales Sales Tax Payable	CA S CL	I I I	Debit Credit Credit	Balance Sheet Income Statement Balance Sheet
Issued credit memo to customer for merchandise returned	Sales Returns and Allowances Accounts Receivable	S CA	I D	Debit Credit	Income Statement Balance Sheet
Issued credit memo to customer for merchandise returned with sales tax	Sales Returns and Allowances Sales Tax Payable Accounts Receivable	S CL CA	I D D	Debit Debit Credit	Income Statement Balance Sheet Balance Sheet
Bought merchandise on account	Purchases Accounts Payable	CGS CL	I I	Debit Credit	Income Statement Balance Sheet
Bought merchandise on account with freight prepaid as a convenience to the buyer	Purchases Freight In Accounts Payable	CGS CGS CL	I I I	Debit Debit Credit	Income Statement Income Statement Balance Sheet
Received credit memo from supplier for merchandise returned	Accounts Payable Purchases Returns and Allowances	CL CGS	D I	Debit Credit	Balance Sheet Income Statement
Paid for transportation charges on incoming merchandise	Freight In Cash	CGS CA	I D	Debit Credit	Income Statement Balance Sheet
Sold merchandise, involving sales tax, for cash	Cash Sales Sales Tax Payable	CA S CL	I I I	Debit Credit Credit	Balance Sheet Income Statement Balance Sheet
Sold merchandise involving sales tax and the customer used a bank charge card	Cash Credit Card Expense Sales Sales Tax Payable	CA SE S CL	I I I I	Debit Debit Credit Credit	Balance Sheet Income Statement Income Statement Balance Sheet
Charge customer paid bill within the discount period	Cash Sales Discounts Accounts Receivable	CA S CA	I I D	Debit Debit Credit	Balance Sheet Income Statement Balance Sheet

© 2013 Cengage Learning. All Rights Reserved. May not be scanned, copied, duplicated, or posted to a publicly accessible website, in whole or in part.

Review of Representative Transactions

(Part III, Chapters 9–12, concluded)

TRANSACTION	ACCOUNTS INVOLVED	CLASS.	INCREASE OR DECREASE	THEREFORE DEBIT OR CREDIT	FINANCIAL STATEMENT
Paid invoice for the purchase of merchandise within the discount period	Accounts Payable Cash Purchases Discounts	CL CA CGS	D D I	Debit Credit Credit	Balance Sheet Balance Sheet Income Statement
First adjusting entry for merchandise inventory— periodic	Income Summary Merchandise Inventory	— CA & CGS	— D	Debit Credit	— Balance Sheet and Income Statement
Second adjusting entry for merchandise inventory— periodic	Merchandise Inventory Income Summary	CA & CGS —	I —	Debit Credit	Balance Sheet and Income Statement —
Adjusting entry for course fees earned (Course Fees Income)	Unearned Course Fees Course Fees Income	CL OI	D I	Debit Credit	Balance Sheet Income Statement
Adjusting entry for merchandise inventory— perpetual, if physical count is less than ledger balance of merchandise inventory	Costs of Goods Sold Merchandise Inventory	CGS CA	I D	Debit Credit	Income Statement Balance Sheet
Adjusting entry for merchandise inventory— perpetual, if physical count is greater than ledger balance of merchandise inventory	Merchandise Inventory Cost of Goods Sold	CA CGS	I D	Debit Credit	Balance Sheet Income Statement
Reversing entry for adjustment for accrued wages	Wages Payable Wages Expense	CL SE or GE	D D	Debit Credit	Balance Sheet Income Statement

© 2013 Cengage Learning. All Rights Reserved. May not be scanned, copied, duplicated, or posted to a publicly accessible website, in whole or in part.

Review of Business Mathematics

People assume that anyone who is an accountant is good at mathematics. But accountants are like anyone else; they can make simple errors in arithmetic that cause them hours of searching later on. The thing that slows down the beginning accountant more than any other single factor is not being really sure about certain common mathematical processes. For example, how do you convert from fractions to percentages? What do you do with the decimal point when you are dividing?

Of course, we all agree that a calculator capable of performing the arithmetic functions is an invaluable aid in accounting. However, even with a calculator, you still need to know what to divide by what, what to multiply by what, and so forth. The calculator will do only what you tell it to do, so you will always need a knowledge of basic business mathematics.

The following short review of business mathematics, which has items labeled so that you can better identify them, is designed to help you recall what you learned about mathematics long ago. In other words, it's a mathematical booster shot.

Decimals

Examples of terms:

Whole number	12
Decimal	0.62
Mixed decimal	4.15

Addition

When adding decimals or mixed decimals, keep the decimal points lined up, one under the other. Fill in any blank places to the right with zeros so that all the addends have the same number of decimal places.

Example Add 4.2, 16.53, 0.004, and 322.

$$
\left.\begin{array}{r}
4.200 \\
16.530 \\
0.004 \\
+\ \ 322.000 \\
\hline
342.734
\end{array}\right\} \text{Addends}
$$

Example Add 16.02, 4.035, 40, and 0.06.

$$
\begin{array}{r}
16.020 \\
4.035 \\
40.000 \\
+\ \ \ \ 0.060 \\
\hline
60.115
\end{array}
$$

Subtraction

When subtracting decimals or mixed decimals, keep the decimal points lined up, one under the other. Fill in any blank places to the right with zeros so that all the numbers have the same number of decimal places.

Example 5.378 minus 0.8421.

$$
\begin{array}{rl}
5.3780 & \text{Minuend} \\
-\ \ \ 0.8421 & \text{Subtrahend} \\
\hline
4.5359 &
\end{array}
$$

Example 624.1 minus 16.003.

$$
\begin{array}{r}
624.100 \\
-\ \ \ 16.003 \\
\hline
608.097
\end{array}
$$

© 2013 Cengage Learning. All Rights Reserved. May not be scanned, copied, duplicated, or posted to a publicly accessible website, in whole or in part.

Multiplication

When multiplying decimals or mixed decimals, find the position of the decimal point in the product (answer) by adding the number of decimal places in the multiplicand (number to be multiplied) and in the multiplier (number of times to multiply), and count off the same number of places from right to left in the product.

Example Multiply 0.62 by 0.4.

$$
\begin{array}{r}
0.62 \quad \text{Multiplicand} \\
\times \quad 0.4 \quad \text{Multiplier} \\
\hline
0.248 \quad \text{Product}
\end{array}
$$

Example Multiply 626.231 by 2.87.

$$
\begin{array}{r}
626.231 \\
\times \quad 2.87 \\
\hline
43\ 83617 \\
500\ 9848 \\
1252\ 462 \\
\hline
1{,}797.28297
\end{array}
$$

When the number of decimal places required is greater than the number of places in the product, add as many zeros to the left of the product as necessary.

Example Multiply 0.049 by 0.02.

$$
\begin{array}{r}
0.049 \\
\times \quad 0.02 \\
\hline
0.00098
\end{array}
$$

Example Multiply 0.26 by 0.0091.

$$
\begin{array}{r}
0.26 \\
\times \quad 0.0091 \\
\hline
26 \\
234 \\
\hline
0.002366
\end{array}
$$

© 2013 Cengage Learning. All Rights Reserved. May not be scanned, copied, duplicated, or posted to a publicly accessible website, in whole or in part.

Division

When the divisor (dividing number) is a whole number and the dividend (number to be divided) is a mixed decimal, place the decimal point in the quotient (answer) directly above the decimal point in the dividend.

Example Divide 172.64 by 4.

```
                    43.16     Quotient
    Divisor    4 ) 172.64     Dividend
                   16
                   12
                   12
                    6
                    4
                    24
                    24
```

Example Divide 6.39 by 15.

```
                  0.426
           15 ) 6.390
                6 0
                  39
                  30
                   90
                   90
```

When the divisor is a decimal, move the decimal point in the divisor as many places to the right as necessary to make the divisor a whole number, and move the decimal point in the dividend to the right also, the same number of places.

Example Divide 14.406 by 0.007.

```
                   2,058
      0.007 ) 14.406
                14
                  40
                  35
                   56
                   56
```

Example Divide 8.3927 by 0.943.

```
                    8.9
      0.943 ) 8.392 7
               7 544
               8487
               8487
```

© 2013 Cengage Learning. All Rights Reserved. May not be scanned, copied, duplicated, or posted to a publicly accessible website, in whole or in part.

FRACTIONS

Examples of terms:

Numerator ⟶ 6
Denominator ⟶ 39

Proper fraction: 8/9

Improper fraction: 13/6

Mixed number: 2 3/8

Like fractions: 2/5, 3/5, 4/5

Unlike fractions: 1/2, 1/4, 5/6

Addition of Fractions

To add like fractions, add their numerators.

Example Add 1/5 and 3/5.

$$
\begin{array}{r}
1/5 \\
+\quad 3/5 \\
\hline
4/5
\end{array}
$$

To add unlike fractions, you must convert them to like fractions. First, find the least common denominator (the smallest number that is exactly divisible by each denominator).

Next, divide the least common denominator by the denominator of each original fraction. Then multiply both the numerator and the denominator of each original fraction by this number. Add the numerators of the like fractions and, if necessary, reduce the sum to lowest terms.

Example Add 3/4 and 2/3. The least common denominator is 12.

$$
4\overline{)12}^{\,3} \quad \frac{3}{4} = \frac{3 \times 3}{4 \times 3} = \frac{9}{12}
$$

$$
3\overline{)12}^{\,4} \quad \frac{2}{3} = \frac{2 \times 4}{3 \times 4} = +\frac{8}{12}
$$

$$
\frac{17}{12} = 1\frac{5}{12}
$$

Example Add 1/3, 1/6, and 3/8. The least common denominator is 24.

$$
3\overline{)24}^{\,8} \quad \frac{1}{3} = \frac{1 \times 8}{3 \times 8} = \frac{8}{24}
$$

$$
6\overline{)24}^{\,4} \quad \frac{1}{6} = \frac{1 \times 4}{6 \times 4} = \frac{4}{24}
$$

$$
8\overline{)24}^{\,3} \quad \frac{3}{8} = \frac{3 \times 3}{8 \times 3} = +\frac{9}{24}
$$

$$
\frac{21}{24} = \frac{7}{8}
$$

© 2013 Cengage Learning. All Rights Reserved. May not be scanned, copied, duplicated, or posted to a publicly accessible website, in whole or in part.

Subtraction of Fractions

To subtract like fractions, subtract their numerators.

Example 7/8 minus 3/8.

$$
\begin{array}{r}
7/8 \\
- \quad 3/8 \\
\hline
4/8 = 1/2
\end{array}
$$

To subtract unlike fractions, you must convert them to like fractions. First, find the least common denominator and divide it by the denominator of each original fraction. Then multiply both the numerator and the denominator of each original fraction by this number and subtract. When subtracting mixed numbers, change each mixed number to an improper like fraction.

Example 8/9 minus 5/12. The common denominator is 36.

$$
9 \overline{)36} = 4 \qquad \frac{8}{9} = \frac{8 \times 4}{9 \times 4} = \frac{32}{36}
$$

$$
12 \overline{)36} = 3 \qquad \frac{5}{12} = \frac{5 \times 3}{12 \times 3} = -\frac{15}{36}
$$

$$
\frac{17}{36}
$$

Example 4 1/6 minus 2 3/8. The common denominator is 24.

$$
6 \overline{)24} = 4 \qquad 4\frac{1}{6} = \frac{25 \times 4}{6 \times 4} = \frac{100}{24}
$$

$$
8 \overline{)24} = 3 \qquad 2\frac{3}{8} = \frac{19 \times 3}{8 \times 3} = -\frac{57}{24}
$$

$$
\frac{43}{24} = 1\frac{19}{24}
$$

Multiplication of Fractions

When multiplying fractions, first simplify by canceling (dividing one numerator and one denominator, regardless of their positions, by the same number). Next multiply the numerators, multiply the denominators, and reduce the results to the lowest terms.

Example 5/16 × 1/5 × 9/8.

$$
\frac{\overset{1}{\cancel{5}}}{16} \times \frac{1}{\underset{1}{\cancel{5}}} \times \frac{9}{8} = \frac{1 \times 1 \times 9}{16 \times 1 \times 8} = \frac{9}{128}
$$

Example 140 × 4/25 × 5/18.

$$
\frac{\overset{14}{\cancel{\overset{28}{\cancel{140}}}}}{1} \times \frac{4}{\underset{5}{\cancel{25}}} \times \frac{\overset{1}{\cancel{5}}}{\underset{9}{\cancel{18}}} = \frac{14 \times 4 \times 1}{1 \times 1 \times 9} = \frac{56}{9} = 6\frac{2}{9}
$$

© 2013 Cengage Learning. All Rights Reserved. May not be scanned, copied, duplicated, or posted to a publicly accessible website, in whole or in part.

Division of Fractions

When dividing fractions, invert the divisor (turn the fraction upside down) and multiply.

Example Divide 7/16 by 3/4.

$$\frac{7}{16} \div \frac{3}{4} = \frac{7}{\overset{}{\underset{4}{\cancel{16}}}} \times \frac{\overset{1}{\cancel{4}}}{3} = \frac{7 \times 1}{4 \times 3} = \frac{7}{12}$$

Example Divide 36 by 2/3.

$$36 \div \frac{2}{3} = \frac{\overset{18}{\cancel{36}}}{1} \times \frac{3}{\underset{1}{\cancel{2}}} = 54$$

Changing a Fraction to a Decimal

Divide the numerator by the denominator.

Example Change 7/8 to a decimal.

```
      0.875
  8 ) 7.000
      6 4
        60
        56
        40
        40
```

Example Change 146/42 to a decimal.

$$\frac{146}{42} = \frac{146 \div 2}{42 \div 2} = \frac{73}{21}$$

```
         3.476 +
  21 ) 73.000
        63
        10 0
         8 4
         1 60
         1 47
           130
           126
             4
```

Changing a Decimal to a Fraction

Draw a line under the decimal. Write a 1 immediately below the decimal point and a 0 below each number in the decimal. Then drop the decimal point. Reduce to lowest terms.

Example Change 0.72 to a fraction.

$$0.72 = \frac{72}{100} = \frac{72 \div 4}{100 \div 4} = \frac{18}{25}$$

Example Change 0.8125 to a fraction.

$$0.8125 = \frac{8,125}{10,000} = \frac{8,125 \div 625}{10,000 \div 625} = \frac{13}{16}$$

© 2013 Cengage Learning. All Rights Reserved. May not be scanned, copied, duplicated, or posted to a publicly accessible website, in whole or in part.

Common Decimal Equivalents

The following equivalents are rounded off at the fourth decimal place.

1/2 = 0.5	1/6 = 0.1667	1/10 = 0.1
1/3 = 0.3333	1/7 = 0.1429	1/11 = 0.0909
2/3 = 0.6667	1/8 = 0.125	1/12 = 0.0833
1/4 = 0.25	3/8 = 0.375	1/15 = 0.0667
3/4 = 0.75	5/8 = 0.625	1/16 = 0.0625
1/5 = 0.2	7/8 = 0.875	1/20 = 0.05
3/5 = 0.6	1/9 = 0.1111	1/25 = 0.04

PERCENTAGES

Percentages are fractions that have 100 for their denominators.

Changing a Percentage to a Decimal

Drop the percent sign and move the decimal point two places to the left. If the percentage consists of only one digit, add a 0 to the left of the digit.

Example Change 36 percent to a decimal.

$$36\% = 36. = 0.36$$

Example Change 5.85 percent to a decimal.

$$5.85\% = 05.85 = 0.0585$$

Changing a Decimal to a Percentage

Move the decimal point two places to the right and add the percent sign.

Example Change 0.48 to a percentage.

$$0.48 = 0.48 = 48\%$$

Example Change 1.495 to a percentage.

$$1.495 = 1.495 = 149.5\%$$

Changing a Percentage to a Fraction

Drop the percent sign, make a fraction with the percentage as numerator and 100 as denominator, and reduce to lowest terms.

Example Change 25 percent to a fraction.

$$25\% = \frac{25}{100} = \frac{25 \div 25}{100 \div 25} = \frac{1}{4}$$

Example Change 31.5% to a fraction.

$$31.5\% = \frac{31.5}{100} = \frac{315}{1,000} = \frac{315 \div 5}{1,000 \div 5} = \frac{63}{200}$$

© 2013 Cengage Learning. All Rights Reserved. May not be scanned, copied, duplicated, or posted to a publicly accessible website, in whole or in part.

Changing a Fraction to a Percentage

Reduce to lowest terms. Divide the numerator by the denominator, move the decimal point two places to the right, and add the percent sign.

Example Change 5/8 to a percentage.

$$
\begin{array}{r}
0.625 \\
8 \overline{)\ 5.000} \\
4\ 8 \\
\overline{20} \\
16 \\
\overline{40} \\
40 \\
\overline{}
\end{array}
\quad = \quad 0.625 \quad = \quad 62.5\%
$$

Example Change 46/8 to a percentage.

$$
\frac{46}{8} = \frac{46 \div 2}{8 \div 2} = \frac{23}{4}
$$

$$
\begin{array}{r}
5.75 \\
4 \overline{)\ 23.00} \\
20 \\
\overline{3\ 0} \\
2\ 8 \\
\overline{20} \\
20 \\
\overline{}
\end{array}
\quad = \quad 5.75 \quad = \quad 575\%
$$

Finding the Ratio of … to …

This is the same thing as finding the percentage that one thing is of another. Write the "of…" amount in the numerator and the "to…" amount in the denominator. Reduce to lowest terms and divide the numerator by the denominator.

Example Find the ratio of current assets ($69,000) to current liabilities ($27,000).

$$
\frac{69,000}{27,000} = \frac{69,000 \div 3,000}{27,000 \div 3,000} = \frac{23}{9}
$$

$$
\begin{array}{r}
2.555 \\
9 \overline{)\ 23.000} \\
18 \\
\overline{5\ 0} \\
4\ 5 \\
\overline{50} \\
45 \\
\overline{50} \\
45 \\
\overline{5}
\end{array}
\quad = \quad 2.555 \quad \text{or} \quad 2.56
$$

© 2013 Cengage Learning. All Rights Reserved. May not be scanned, copied, duplicated, or posted to a publicly accessible website, in whole or in part.

Example Find the ratio of salesroom floor space (6,000 square feet) to office floor space (900 square feet).

$$\frac{6,000}{900} = \frac{6,000 \div 300}{900 \div 300} = \frac{20}{3}$$

$$
\begin{array}{r}
6.666 \\
3,000 \overline{\smash{)}\ 20.000} \\
\underline{18} \\
2\,0 \\
\underline{1\,8} \\
20 \\
\underline{18} \\
20 \\
\underline{18} \\
2
\end{array}
$$

= 6.666   or 6.67

Finding the Percentage of Increase or Decrease

Divide the amount of the change by the base (starting figure). Change the decimal to a percentage.

Example Moore's income increased from $12,000 to $15,000. Find the percentage of increase.

Amount of change   = 15,000 − 12,000 = 3,000

$$
\begin{array}{r}
0.25 \\
12,000 \overline{\smash{)}\ 3,000.00} \\
\underline{2\,400\,0} \\
600\,00 \\
\underline{600\,00}
\end{array}
$$

= 0.25 = 25%

Example Arnold's grade-point average decreased from 3.6 to 3.1. Find the percentage of decrease.

Amount of change   = 3.6 − 3.1 = 0.5

$$
\begin{array}{r}
0.1388 \\
3.6 \overline{\smash{)}\ 0.50000} \\
\underline{36} \\
140 \\
\underline{108} \\
320 \\
\underline{288} \\
320 \\
\underline{288} \\
32
\end{array}
$$

= 0.1388 = 0.139 = 13.9%

ROUNDING OFF

If the last number in a decimal is 5 or greater, drop it and add one to the next number on the left. If the last number in a decimal is less than 5, drop it and let the other number stay the same.

Example Round off to two decimal places.

1.825 = 1.83

Example Round off to three decimal places.

0.6923 = 0.692

© 2013 Cengage Learning. All Rights Reserved. May not be scanned, copied, duplicated, or posted to a publicly accessible website, in whole or in part.

Suggested Abbreviations for Account Titles in Chapters 1–12

Because traditional accounting methods have called for the use of full account titles in journal entries and financial statements, the text and solutions keep abbreviations to a minimum. However, computerized accounting programs and working papers present significant space constraints, and students' handwriting differs considerably in size. As a result, many instructors have requested a list of suggested abbreviations for account titles. Please bear in mind that there is no standard list of abbreviations; these are suggestions only. Account titles that are not included in this list are generally short enough to be written out in full.

Accounts Payable	Accts. Pay. or A/P
Accounts Receivable	Accts. Rec. or A/R
Accumulated Depreciation, Equipment	Accum. Depr., Equip.
Depreciation Expense, Equipment	Depr. Exp., Equip.
J. Conner, Capital	J. Conner, Cap.
J. Conner, Drawing	J. Conner, Draw.
Employees' Bond Deduction Payable	Empl. Bond Ded. Pay.
Employees' Federal Income Tax Payable	Empl. Fed. Inc. Tax Pay.
Employees' Union Dues Payable	Empl. Union Dues Pay.
Federal Unemployment Tax Payable	Fed. Unemp. Tax Pay.
FICA Taxes Payable	FICA Taxes Pay.
Interest Expense	Int. Exp.
Interest Income	Int. Inc.
Interest Payable	Int. Pay.
Merchandise Inventory	Merch. Inv.
Miscellaneous General Expense	Misc. Gen. Exp.
Miscellaneous Selling Expense	Misc. Sell. Exp.
Notes Payable	Notes Pay.
Notes Receivable	Notes Rec.
Prepaid Workers' Compensation Insurance	Prepaid Workers' Comp. Ins.
Purchases Discount	Purch. Dist.
Purchases Returns and Allowances	Purch. Ret. and Allow.
Sales Commissions Expense	Sales Comm. Exp.
Sales Discount	Sales Dist.
Sales Returns and Allowances	Sales Ret. and Allow.
State Unemployment Tax Payable	State Unemp. Tax Pay.
Workers' Compensation Insurance Expense	Workers' Comp. Ins. Exp.

© 2013 Cengage Learning. All Rights Reserved. May not be scanned, copied, duplicated, or posted to a publicly accessible website, in whole or in part.

Introduction to Accounting

LEARNING OBJECTIVES

1. Define *accounting*.

2. Explain the importance of accounting information.

3. Describe the various career opportunities in accounting.

4. Define *ethics*.

ACCOUNTING LANGUAGE

Accountant

Accounting

Economic unit

Ethics

Financial Accounting Standards
  Board (FASB)

Generally accepted accounting
  principles (GAAP)

International Accounting Standards Board (IASB)

International Financial Reporting Standards (IFRS)

Paraprofessional accountants

Sarbanes-Oxley Act

Securities and Exchange Commission (SEC)

Transaction

1

Asset, Liability, Owner's Equity, Revenue, and Expense Accounts

LEARNING OBJECTIVES

1. Define and identify *asset, liability,* and *owner's equity* accounts.

2. Record, in column form, a group of business transactions involving changes in assets, liabilities, and owner's equity.

3. Define and identify *revenue* and *expense* accounts.

4. Record, in column form, a group of business transactions involving all five elements of the fundamental accounting equation.

ACCOUNTING LANGUAGE

Account numbers

Accounts

Accounts Payable

Accounts Receivable

Assets

Business entity

Capital

Chart of accounts

Creditor

Double-entry accounting

Equity

Expenses

Fair market value

Fundamental accounting equation

Liabilities

Owner's equity

Revenues

Separate entity concept

Sole proprietorship

Withdrawal

1

© 2013 Cengage Learning. All Rights Reserved. May not be scanned, copied, duplicated, or posted to a publicly accessible website, in whole or in part.

STUDY GUIDE QUESTIONS

PART 1   True/False

For each of the following statements, circle T if the statement is true and F if the statement is false.

T	F	1.	The term *owner's equity* means the owner's investment.
T	F	2.	When an asset is purchased for cash, the owner's equity account is decreased.
T	F	3.	People who loan money to a company are considered the company's creditors.
T	F	4.	A business entity is considered an economic unit.
T	F	5.	Equipment is considered an asset.
T	F	6.	Expenses have the effect of decreasing owner's equity.
T	F	7.	The amounts owed by charge customers are recorded in the Accounts Receivable account.
T	F	8.	Withdrawals by the owner decrease owner's equity.
T	F	9.	When a business receives a payment from a charge customer, the revenue account is not affected.
T	F	10.	An accountant keeps a separate record for each asset, liability, owner's equity, revenue, and expense account.

PART 2   Completion—Accounting Language

Complete each of the following statements by writing the appropriate words in the spaces provided.

1. A one-owner business is called a(n) _____.
2. Debts owed by a business are called _____.
3. A person or business to whom money is owed is called a(n) _____.
4. The categories listed under the classifications Assets, Liabilities, Owner's Equity, Revenues, and Expenses are called _____.
5. An event affecting a business that can be expressed in terms of money and that must be recorded in the accounting records is called a(n) _____.
6. The owner's investment or equity in an enterprise is called _____.
7. The equation expressing the relationship of assets, liabilities, and owner's equity is called the _____.
8. The _____ is the official list of account titles to be used to record the transactions of a business.
9. A financial interest in or claim to an asset is called _____.
10. _____ represents the amount a business earns by providing or performing a service for a customer.
11. If the owner takes cash out of the business each month, this is called a(n) _____.
12. The account used to record the amounts owed by charge customers is _____.
13. _____ are the costs related to the earning of revenue.
14. The numbers preceding the account titles are the _____.
15. The account used to record the amounts owed to creditors is _____.

© 2013 Cengage Learning. All Rights Reserved. May not be scanned, copied, duplicated, or posted to a publicly accessible website, in whole or in part.

PART 3   Classifying Accounts

The office of financial consultant T. Acosta has the following accounts:

Income from Services   Wages Expense
Office Equipment   Mortgage Payable
Supplies   Land
Accounts Payable   T. Acosta, Capital
Building   Prepaid Insurance
Cash   Neon Sign
Rent Expense   T. Acosta, Drawing

List each account under the appropriate heading.

Assets   **Owner's Equity**

_____   _____

_____   _____

_____

_____   **Revenue**

_____   _____

_____

                                              Expenses

Liabilities   _____

_____   _____

_____   _____

© 2013 Cengage Learning. All Rights Reserved. May not be scanned, copied, duplicated, or posted to a publicly accessible website, in whole or in part.

PART 4   Analyzing Transactions

Here are some typical transactions of Bartlett Insect Control Service. For each transaction, indicate the increase (+) or the decrease (−) in Assets (A), Liabilities (L), Owner's Equity (OE), Revenue (R), or Expenses (E) by placing the appropriate sign(s) in the appropriate column(s). A column can have a (+) and a (−) for the same transaction.

		A	L	OE	R	E
0.	Example: Owner invested cash	+		+		
1.	Payment of rent					
2.	Sales of services for cash					
3.	Investment of equipment by owner					
4.	Payment of insurance premium for two years					
5.	Payment of wages					
6.	Sales of services on account					
7.	Withdrawal of cash by owner					
8.	Purchase of supplies on account					
9.	Collection from charge customer previously billed					
10.	Payment made to creditor on account					

DEMONSTRATION PROBLEM

During November of this year, James Kirkland opened an accounting practice called James Kirkland, CPA. The following transactions were completed during the first month.

a.   Deposited $13,500 in a bank account in the name of James Kirkland, CPA.

b.   Paid rent for the month, $1,600 (Rent Expense).

c.   Bought office equipment, including a computer and a printer, for $9,500 from Bingham Company. Paid $6,700 in cash, with the balance due in 30 days.

d.   Purchased office supplies and announcements for $970 from City Stationers. Payment is due in 30 days.

e.   Billed clients $5,500 for services rendered (Client Fees).

f.   Paid $1,450 salary to secretary/assistant for the month.

g.   Paid telephone bill of $210 (Telephone Expense).

h.   Received cash from clients previously billed on account, $2,450.

i.   Paid Bingham Company $970 to apply on account.

j.   Paid $275 for continuing education course (Miscellaneous Expense).

k.   Kirkland withdrew $2,200 for personal use.

Instructions

1.   Record the transactions and the balance after each transaction, using the following headings.

Assets	=	Liabilities	+	Owner's Equity				
Cash + Receivable + Supplies + Equip. =		Payable	+	Accounts J. Kirkland, Capital −	J. Kirkland, Drawing +	Revenue −	Expenses

2.   Demonstrate that the total of one side of the equation equals the total of the other side of the equation.

© 2013 Cengage Learning. All Rights Reserved. May not be scanned, copied, duplicated, or posted to a publicly accessible website, in whole or in part.

SOLUTION

	Cash	+ Accounts Receivable	+ Supplies	+ Equipment	=	Accounts Payable	+ J. Kirkland, Capital	− J. Kirkland, Drawing	+ Revenue	− Expenses
(a) +	13,500				=		13,500			
(b) −	1,600				=					+ 1,600 (Rent Expense)
Bal.	11,900				=		13,500			1,600 (Rent Expense)
(c) −	6,700			+ 9,500	=	+ 2,800				
Bal.	5,200			9,500	=	2,800	13,500			1,600
(d)			+ 970		=	+ 970				
Bal.	5,200		970	9,500	=	3,770	13,500			1,600
(e)		+ 5,500			=				+ 5,500 (Client Fees)	
Bal.	5,200	5,500	970	9,500	=	3,770	13,500		5,500	1,600
(f) −	1,450				=					+ 1,450 (Salary Expense)
Bal.	3,750	5,500	970	9,500	=	3,770	13,500		5,500	3,050
(g) −	210				=					+ 210 (Telephone Expense)
Bal.	3,540	5,500	970	9,500	=	3,770	13,500		5,500	3,260
(h) +	2,450	− 2,450			=					
Bal.	5,990	3,050	970	9,500	=	3,770	13,500		5,500	3,260
(i) −	970				=	− 970				
Bal.	5,020	3,050	970	9,500	=	2,800	13,500		5,500	3,260
(j) −	275				=					+ 275 (Misc. Expense)
Bal.	4,745	3,050	970	9,500	=	2,800	13,500		5,500	3,535
(k) −	2,200				=			+ 2,200		
Bal.	2,545	3,050	970	9,500	=	2,800	13,500	2,200	5,500	3,535

(Header groupings: Assets = [Cash + Accounts Receivable + Supplies + Equipment]; = Liabilities [Accounts Payable]; + Owner's Equity [J. Kirkland, Capital − J. Kirkland, Drawing + Revenue − Expenses])

Left Side of Equals Sign:

Cash	$ 2,545
Accounts Receivable	3,050
Supplies	970
Equipment	9,500
	$16,065

Right Side of Equals Sign:

Accounts Payable	$ 2,800
J. Kirkland, Capital	13,500
J. Kirkland, Drawing	− 2,200
Revenue	5,500
Expenses	− 3,535
	$16,065

5

© 2013 Cengage Learning. All Rights Reserved. May not be scanned, copied, duplicated, or posted to a publicly accessible website, in whole or in part.

EXERCISES AND PROBLEMS

Exercise 1-1

a. $22,800   A – L = _____ $40,000 – $17,200 = _____
b. _____ _____ = _____   _____ = _____
c. _____ _____ = _____   _____ = _____

Exercise 1-2

a. _____ _____ = _____   _____ = _____
b. _____ _____ = _____   _____ = _____
c. _____ _____ = _____   _____ = _____

Exercise 1-3

Assets = _____ + _____

Assets = _____ + _____ + _____

Liabilities = _____ + _____

_____ – _____ = Owner's Equity

Thus,

Assets _____ = Liabilities _____ + Owner's Equity _____

Exercise 1-4

a. _____
b. _____
c. _____
d. _____
e. _____
f. _____

Exercise 1-5

a. _____
b. _____
c. _____
d. _____
e. _____

© 2013 Cengage Learning. All Rights Reserved. May not be scanned, copied, duplicated, or posted to a publicly accessible website, in whole or in part.

Exercise 1-6

a. _____   f. _____
b. _____   g. _____
c. _____   h. _____
d. _____   i. _____
e. _____   j. _____

Exercise 1-7

a. _____
   _____

b. _____
   _____

c. _____
   _____

d. _____
   _____

e. _____
   _____

f. _____
   _____

Exercise 1-8

a. _____
   _____

b. _____
   _____

c. _____
   _____

d. _____
   _____

e. _____
   _____

© 2013 Cengage Learning. All Rights Reserved. May not be scanned, copied, duplicated, or posted to a publicly accessible website, in whole or in part.

Asset, Liability, Owner's Equity, Revenue, and Expense Accounts

Problem 1-1A or 1-1B

	Assets				=	Liabilities	+	Owner's Equity						
	Cash	+	Supplies	+	Office Equipment	=	Accounts Payable	+	Capital	–	Drawing	+	Revenue	–	Expenses
(a)															
(b)															
Bal.	+	+	+		=	+		+	–		+		–		
(c)															
Bal.	+	+	+		=	+		+	–		+		–		
(d)															
Bal.	+	+	+		=	+		+	–		+		–		
(e)															
Bal.	+	+	+		=	+		+	–		+		–		
(f)															
Bal.	+	+	+		=	+		+	–		+		–		
(g)															
Bal.	+	+	+		=	+		+	–		+		–		
(h)															
Bal.	+	+	+		=	+		+	–		+		–		
(i)															
Bal.	+	+	+		=	+		+	–		+		–		
(j)															
Bal.	+	+	+		=	+		+	–		+		–		
(k)															
Bal.	+	+	+		=	+		+	–		+		–		

Complete the summary of accounts on the next page.

© 2013 Cengage Learning. All Rights Reserved. May not be scanned, copied, duplicated, or posted to a publicly accessible website, in whole or in part.

Problem 1-1A or 1-1B (concluded)

Left Side of Equals Sign: *Right Side of Equals Sign:*

Cash   _____   **Accounts Payable**   _____

Supplies   _____   _____ **, Capital**   _____

Office Equipment   _____   _____ **, Drawing**   − _____

                                                     Revenue   _____

                                                     Expenses   − _____

                                  ═══════════   ═══════════

© 2013 Cengage Learning. All Rights Reserved. May not be scanned, copied, duplicated, or posted to a publicly accessible website, in whole or in part.

Problem 1-2A or 1-2B

	Cash		Supplies		Office Equipment		Professional Equipment	=	Accounts Payable	+	Capital	−	Drawing	+	Revenue	−	Expenses
									Liabilities				Owner's Equity				
(a)		+		+		+		=		+		−		+		−	
(b)																	
Bal.		+		+		+		=		+		−		+		−	
(c)		+		+		+		=		+		−		+		−	
Bal.		+		+		+		=		+		−		+		−	
(d)		+		+		+		=		+		−		+		−	
Bal.		+		+		+		=		+		−		+		−	
(e)		+		+		+		=		+		−		+		−	
Bal.		+		+		+		=		+		−		+		−	
(f)		+		+		+		=		+		−		+		−	
Bal.		+		+		+		=		+		−		+		−	
(g)		+		+		+		=		+		−		+		−	
Bal.		+		+		+		=		+		−		+		−	
(h)		+		+		+		=		+		−		+		−	
Bal.		+		+		+		=		+		−		+		−	
(i)		+		+		+		=		+		−		+		−	
Bal.		+		+		+		=		+		−		+		−	
(j)		+		+		+		=		+		−		+		−	
Bal.		+		+		+		=		+		−		+		−	
(k)		+		+		+		=		+		−		+		−	
Bal.		+		+		+		=		+		−		+		−	

Complete the summary of accounts on the next page.

© 2013 Cengage Learning. All Rights Reserved. May not be scanned, copied, duplicated, or posted to a publicly accessible website, in whole or in part.

Problem 1-2A or 1-2B (concluded)

Left Side of Equals Sign:

Cash   _____

Supplies   _____

Office Equipment   _____

Professional Equipment   _____

_____

Right Side of Equals Sign:

Accounts Payable   _____

_____, Capital   _____

_____, Drawing   – _____

Revenue   _____

Expenses   – _____

_____

© 2013 Cengage Learning. All Rights Reserved. May not be scanned, copied, duplicated, or posted to a publicly accessible website, in whole or in part.

Problem 1-3A or 1-3B

	Assets					=	Liabilities	+	Owner's Equity				
Cash	+	Supplies	+	Prepaid Insurance	+	Office Equipment	+ _____	=	Accounts Payable	+	Capital	–	Drawing	+	Revenue	–	Expenses

(rows a through m, each followed by "Bal.", with +, +, +, +, =, +, –, –, +, – column markers)

Complete the summary of accounts on the next page.

© 2013 Cengage Learning. All Rights Reserved. May not be scanned, copied, duplicated, or posted to a publicly accessible website, in whole or in part.

Problem 1-3A or 1-3B (concluded)

Left Side of Equals Sign:			*Right Side of Equals Sign:*	
Cash	_____		Accounts Payable	_____
Supplies	_____		_____ , Capital	_____
Prepaid Insurance	_____		_____ , Drawing	– _____
Office Equipment	_____		Revenue	_____
_____	_____		Expenses	– _____
	_____			_____

© 2013 Cengage Learning. All Rights Reserved. May not be scanned, copied, duplicated, or posted to a publicly accessible website, in whole or in part.

Problem 1-4A or 1-4B

	Assets					=	Liabilities	+	Owner's Equity				
	Cash	+ Accounts Receivable	+ Supplies	+ Prepaid Insurance	+ Truck	=	Accounts Payable	+	Capital	– Drawing	+ Revenue	– Expenses
(a)												
(b)												
Bal.	+	+	+	+	=	+	–	+	–		
(c)												
Bal.	+	+	+	+	=	+	–	+	–		
(d)												
Bal.	+	+	+	+	=	+	–	+	–		
(e)												
Bal.	+	+	+	+	=	+	–	+	–		
(f)												
Bal.	+	+	+	+	=	+	–	+	–		
(g)												
Bal.	+	+	+	+	=	+	–	+	–		
(h)												
Bal.	+	+	+	+	=	+	–	+	–		
(i)												
Bal.	+	+	+	+	=	+	–	+	–		
(j)												
Bal.	+	+	+	+	=	+	–	+	–		
(k)												
Bal.	+	+	+	+	=	+	–	+	–		
(l)												
Bal.	+	+	+	+	=	+	–	+	–		
(m)												
Bal.	+	+	+	+	=	+					

Complete the summary of accounts on the next page.

14

© 2013 Cengage Learning. All Rights Reserved. May not be scanned, copied, duplicated, or posted to a publicly accessible website, in whole or in part.

Problem 1-4A or 1-4B (concluded)

Left Side of Equals Sign:

Cash _____

Accounts Receivable _____

Supplies _____

Prepaid Insurance _____

Truck _____

_____ _____

_____

Right Side of Equals Sign:

Accounts Payable _____

_____ , Capital _____

_____ , Drawing – _____

Revenue _____

Expenses – _____

_____

© 2013 Cengage Learning. All Rights Reserved. May not be scanned, copied, duplicated, or posted to a publicly accessible website, in whole or in part.

Problem 1-5A or 1-5B

			Assets				=	Liabilities	+			Owner's Equity		
	Cash	+ Accounts Receivable	+ Supplies	+ Prepaid Insurance	+ Truck	+ Office Equipment	=	Accounts Payable	+	Capital	− Drawing	+	Revenue	− Expenses
(a)														
(b)														
Bal.	+	+	+	+	+	+	=	+	+	+	−	+		−
(c)														
Bal.	+	+	+	+	+	+	=	+	+	+	−	+		−
(d)														
Bal.	+	+	+	+	+	+	=	+	+	+	−	+		−
(e)														
Bal.	+	+	+	+	+	+	=	+	+	+	−	+		−
(f)														
Bal.	+	+	+	+	+	+	=	+	+	+	−	+		−
(g)														
Bal.	+	+	+	+	+	+	=	+	+	+	−	+		−
(h)														
Bal.	+	+	+	+	+	+	=	+	+	+	−	+		−
(i)														
Bal.	+	+	+	+	+	+	=	+	+	+	−	+		−
(j)														
Bal.	+	+	+	+	+	+	=	+	+	+	−	+		−
(k)														
Bal.	+	+	+	+	+	+	=	+	+	+	−	+		−
(l)														
Bal.	+	+	+	+	+	+	=	+	+	+	−	+		−
(m)														
Bal.	+	+	+	+	+	+	=	+	+	+	−	+		−

Complete the summary of accounts on the next page.

16

© 2013 Cengage Learning. All Rights Reserved. May not be scanned, copied, duplicated, or posted to a publicly accessible website, in whole or in part.

Problem 1-5A or 1-5B (concluded)

Left Side of Equals Sign	*Amount*	*Right Side of Equals Sign*	*Amount*
Cash	_____	**Accounts Payable**	_____
Accounts Receivable	_____	_____ , Capital	_____
Supplies	_____	_____ , Drawing	– _____
Prepaid Insurance	_____	**Revenue**	_____
Truck	_____	**Expenses**	– _____
Office Equipment	_____		
	_____		_____

© 2013 Cengage Learning. All Rights Reserved. May not be scanned, copied, duplicated, or posted to a publicly accessible website, in whole or in part.

Answers to Study Guide Questions

CHAPTER 1

PART 1   True/False

1.	T	5.	T	9.	T
2.	F	6.	T	10.	T
3.	T	7.	T		
4.	T	8.	T		

PART 2   Completion—Accounting Language

1. sole proprietorship
2. liabilities
3. creditor
4. accounts
5. transaction
6. capital
7. fundamental accounting equation
8. chart of accounts
9. equity
10. Revenue
11. withdrawal
12. Accounts Receivable
13. Expenses
14. account numbers
15. Accounts Payable

PART 3   Classifying Accounts

Assets
Office Equipment
Supplies
Building
Cash
Land
Prepaid Insurance
Neon Sign

Liabilities
Accounts Payable
Mortgage Payable

Owner's Equity
T. Acosta, Capital
T. Acosta, Drawing

Revenue
Income from Services

Expenses
Rent Expense
Wages Expense

PART 4   Analyzing Transactions

Here are some typical transactions of Bartlett Insect Control Service. For each transaction, indicate the increase (+) or the decrease (−) in Assets (A), Liabilities (L), Owner's Equity (OE), Revenue (R), or Expenses (E) by placing the appropriate sign(s) in the appropriate column(s). A column can have a (+) and a (−) for the same transaction.

		A	L	OE	R	E
0.	*Example: Owner invested cash*	+		+		
1.	Payment of rent	−				+
2.	Sales of services for cash	+			+	
3.	Investment of equipment by owner	+		+		
4.	Payment of insurance premium for two years	+ −				
5.	Payment of wages	−				+
6.	Sales of services on account	+			+	
7.	Withdrawal of cash by owner	−		−		
8.	Purchase of supplies on account	+	+			
9.	Collection from charge customer previously billed	+ −				
10.	Payment made to creditor on account	−	−			

© 2013 Cengage Learning. All Rights Reserved. May not be scanned, copied, duplicated, or posted to a publicly accessible website, in whole or in part.

T Accounts, Debits and Credits, Trial Balance, and Financial Statements

LEARNING OBJECTIVES

1. Determine balances of T accounts.

2. Present the fundamental accounting equation using the T account form, and label the plus and minus sides.

3. Present the fundamental accounting equation using the T account form, and label the debit and credit sides.

4. Record directly in T accounts a group of business transactions involving changes in asset, liability, owner's equity, revenue, and expense accounts for a service business.

5. Prepare a trial balance.

6. Prepare (a) an income statement, (b) a statement of owner's equity, and (c) a balance sheet.

7. Recognize the effect of errors on account balances.

ACCOUNTING LANGUAGE

Balance sheet	Net loss
Compound entry	Normal balance
Credit	Report form
Debit	Slide
Financial position	Statement of owner's equity
Financial statement	T account form
Footings	Transposition
Income statement	Trial balance
Net income	

STUDY GUIDE QUESTIONS

PART 1   True/False

For each of the following statements, circle T if the statement is true and F if the statement is false.

T   F   1. Expenses have the effect of increasing owner's equity.

T   F   2. A summary of assets, liabilities, and owner's equity shows the financial position of an economic unit.

T   F   3. The third line in the heading of a balance sheet indicates one specific date.

T   F   4. The amounts owed by credit customers are recorded in the Accounts Payable account.

T   F   5. The net income for a given financial period is found on both the income statement and the statement of owner's equity.

© 2013 Cengage Learning. All Rights Reserved. May not be scanned, copied, duplicated, or posted to a publicly accessible website, in whole or in part.

T   F   6. To prepare the financial statements for a business, you should prepare the balance sheet first, followed by the income statement, and then the statement of owner's equity.

T   F   7. The net income is the connecting link between the income statement and the balance sheet.

T   F   8. An income statement is prepared at the end of the financial period to show the results of operations.

T   F   9. In the report form of the balance sheet, the elements in the accounting equation are presented one on top of the other.

T   F   10. If the owner withdraws more than the amount of the net income, there will be an increase in owner's equity.

PART 2   Completion—Accounting Language

Complete each of the following statements by writing the appropriate words in the spaces provided.

1. The left-hand side of any account is the _____ side.

2. The small, penciled-in figures showing the totals of each side of a T account in a manual system are called _____.

3. If the digits are switched around when you record a number, the error is called a(n) _____.

4. The report used to prove that the total of all the debit balances equals the total of all the credit balances is called a(n) _____.

5. A(n) _____ is used to record a transaction that has more than one debit and/or more than one credit.

6. The right-hand side of any account is called the _____ side.

© 2013 Cengage Learning. All Rights Reserved. May not be scanned, copied, duplicated, or posted to a publicly accessible website, in whole or in part.

PART 3   Accounting Entries

The following transactions were completed by B. T. House, Physical Therapist. Using appropriate account titles, record the transactions in pairs of T accounts, and show plus and minus signs with each T account. List accounts to be debited in the left-hand T account column and accounts to be credited in the right-hand T account column.

0.   Example: Paid electric bill, $92.

Utilities Expense		Cash	
+	−	+	−
(0) 92			(0) 92

a.   Bought professional equipment on account, $560.

b.   Billed patients for services performed, $870.

c.   Paid rent for the month, $1,000.

d.   Bought supplies on account, $220.

e.   Paid telephone bill, $110.

f.   Collected $920 from patients previously billed.

g.   Paid creditors on account, $700.

h.   Paid salary of assistant, $900.

i.   Bought office equipment for cash, $452.

© 2013 Cengage Learning. All Rights Reserved. May not be scanned, copied, duplicated, or posted to a publicly accessible website, in whole or in part.

DEMONSTRATION PROBLEM

Dr. Christy Rene maintains an office for the practice of veterinary medicine. The account balances as of September 1 follow. All are normal balances.

Assets		**Revenue**	
Cash	$ 2,459	Professional Fees	$72,118
Accounts Receivable	18,120		
Supplies	840	**Expenses**	
Prepaid Insurance	980	Salary Expense	14,380
Automobile	20,650	Rent Expense	10,320
Furniture and Equipment	5,963	Automobile Expense	859
		Utilities Expense	1,213
Liabilities			
Accounts Payable	1,590		
Owner's Equity			
C. Rene, Capital	42,076		
C. Rene, Drawing	40,000		

The following transactions occurred during September of this year.

a.   Paid rent for the month, $1,290.

b.   Paid $1,800 for one year's coverage of liability insurance.

c.   Bought medical equipment on account from Bennett Surgical Supply, $849, paying $200 down with the balance due in 30 days.

d.   Billed patients for services performed, $9,015.

e.   Paid employee salaries, $1,797.

f.   Received and paid gas and electric bill, $112.

g.   Received cash from patients previously billed, $11,060.

h.   Received bill for gasoline for car, used only in the professional practice, from Garza Fuel Company, $116.

i.   Paid creditors on account, $1,590.

j.   Dr. Rene withdrew cash for personal use, $5,000.

Instructions

1.   Correctly place plus and minus signs under each T account and label the sides of the T accounts as debit or credit in the fundamental accounting equation. Record the account balances as of September 1.

2.   Record the September transactions in the T accounts. Key each transaction to the letter that identifies the transaction.

3.   Foot the columns and determine the balance in the T accounts.

4.   Prepare a trial balance dated September 30, 20—.

5.   Prepare an income statement for two months ended September 30, 20—.

6.   Prepare a statement of owner's equity for two months ended September 30, 20—.

7.   Prepare a balance sheet as of September 30, 20—.

© 2013 Cengage Learning. All Rights Reserved. May not be scanned, copied, duplicated, or posted to a publicly accessible website, in whole or in part.

SOLUTION

Assets = Liabilities + (Capital / Drawing / Revenue / Expenses)

Cash

Debit (+)		Credit (−)	
Bal.	2,459	(a)	1,290
(g)	11,060	(b)	1,800
	13,519	(c)	200
		(e)	1,797
		(f)	112
		(i)	1,590
		(j)	5,000
			11,789
Bal.	1,730		

Accounts Receivable

Debit (+)		Credit (−)	
Bal.	18,120	(g)	11,060
(d)	9,015		
	27,135		
Bal.	16,075		

Supplies

Debit (+)		Credit (−)
Bal.	840	

Prepaid Insurance

Debit (+)		Credit (−)
Bal.	980	
(b)	1,800	
	2,780	
Bal.	2,780	

Automobile

Debit (+)		Credit (−)
Bal.	20,650	

Furniture and Equipment

Debit (+)		Credit (−)
Bal.	5,963	
(c)	849	
Bal.	6,812	

Liabilities — Accounts Payable

Debit (−)		Credit (+)	
(i)	1,590	Bal.	1,590
		(c)	649
		(h)	116
			2,355
		Bal.	765

Capital — C. Rene, Capital

Debit (−)	Credit (+)	
	Bal.	42,076

Drawing — C. Rene, Drawing

Debit (+)		Credit (−)
Bal.	40,000	
(j)	5,000	
Bal.	45,000	

Revenue — Professional Fees

Debit (−)	Credit (+)	
	Bal.	72,118
	(d)	9,015
	Bal.	81,133

Expenses — Salary Expense

Debit (+)		Credit (−)
Bal.	14,380	
(e)	1,797	
Bal.	16,177	

Rent Expense

Debit (+)		Credit (−)
Bal.	10,320	
(a)	1,290	
Bal.	11,610	

Automobile Expense

Debit (+)		Credit (−)
Bal.	859	
(h)	116	
Bal.	975	

Utilities Expense

Debit (+)		Credit (−)
Bal.	1,213	
(f)	112	
Bal.	1,325	

Dr. Christy Rene
Trial Balance
September 30, 20—

ACCOUNT NAME	DEBIT	CREDIT
Cash	1,730	
Accounts Receivable	16,075	
Supplies	840	
Prepaid Insurance	2,780	
Automobile	20,650	
Furniture and Equipment	6,812	
Accounts Payable		765
C. Rene, Capital		42,076
C. Rene, Drawing	45,000	
Professional Fees		81,133
Salary Expense	16,177	
Rent Expense	11,610	
Automobile Expense	975	
Utilities Expense	1,325	
	123,974	123,974

© 2013 Cengage Learning. All Rights Reserved. May not be scanned, copied, duplicated, or posted to a publicly accessible website, in whole or in part.

SOLUTION (concluded)

Dr. Christy Rene
Income Statement
For Two Months Ended September 30, 20—

Revenue:		
Professional Fees		$81,133
Expenses:		
Salary Expense	$16,177	
Rent Expense	11,610	
Automobile Expense	975	
Utilities Expense	1,325	
Total Expenses		30,087
Net Income		$51,046

Dr. Christy Rene
Statement of Owner's Equity
For Two Months Ended September 30, 20—

C. Rene, Capital, September 1, 20—		$42,076
Investments during August and September	$ 0	
Net Income for August and September	51,046	
Subtotal	$51,046	
Less Withdrawals for August and September	45,000	
Increase in Capital		6,046
C. Rene, Capital, September 30, 20 —		$48,122

Dr. Christy Rene
Balance Sheet
September 30, 20—

Assets		
Cash	$ 1,730	
Accounts Receivable	16,075	
Supplies	840	
Prepaid Insurance	2,780	
Automobile	20,650	
Furniture and Equipment	6,812	
Total Assets		$48,887
Liabilities		
Accounts Payable		765
Owner's Equity		
C. Rene, Capital		48,122
Total Liabilities and Owner's Equity		$48,887

© 2013 Cengage Learning. All Rights Reserved. May not be scanned, copied, duplicated, or posted to a publicly accessible website, in whole or in part.

EXERCISES AND PROBLEMS

Exercise 2-1

Assets	=	Liabilities	+	Capital	–	Drawing	+	Revenue	–	Expenses

+	–
Debit	**Credit**

Exercise 2-2

ACCOUNT	CLASSIFICATION	INCREASE SIDE	NORMAL BALANCE SIDE	DECREASE SIDE
0. Cash	*A*	*Debit*	*Debit*	*Credit*
1. Wages Expense				
2. Equipment				
3. L. Cross, Capital				
4. Service Revenue				
5. L. Cross, Drawing				
6. Accounts Receivable				
7. Rent Expense				
8. Fees Earned				
9. Accounts Payable				

© 2013 Cengage Learning. All Rights Reserved. May not be scanned, copied, duplicated, or posted to a publicly accessible website, in whole or in part.

Exercise 2-3

a.

+	−
Debit	Credit

+	−
Debit	Credit

f.

+	−
Debit	Credit

−	+
Debit	Credit

b.

+	−
Debit	Credit

−	+
Debit	Credit

g.

+	−
Debit	Credit

+	−
Debit	Credit

c.

+	−
Debit	Credit

+	−
Debit	Credit

h.

+	−
Debit	Credit

+	−
Debit	Credit

d.

−	+
Debit	Credit

+	−
Debit	Credit

i.

+	−
Debit	Credit

+	−
Debit	Credit

e.

+	−
Debit	Credit

+	−
Debit	Credit

© 2013 Cengage Learning. All Rights Reserved. May not be scanned, copied, duplicated, or posted to a publicly accessible website, in whole or in part.

Exercise 2-4

a. _____

b. _____

c. _____

d. _____

e. _____

f. _____

_____

g. _____

_____

h. _____

i. _____

j. _____

k. _____

Exercise 2-5

ACCOUNT NAME	DEBIT	CREDIT

© 2013 Cengage Learning. All Rights Reserved. May not be scanned, copied, duplicated, or posted to a publicly accessible website, in whole or in part.

Exercise 2-6

	Cash		
(a)	8,200	(b)	350
(c)	8,400	(d)	1,600
(i)	7,580	(f)	175
		(g)	3,400
		(h)	2,200

	Accounts Payable	
	(k)	2,800
	(j)	82

	Salary Expense
(g)	3,400

	Rent Expense
(d)	1,600

	Accounts Receivable
(e)	2,600

	R. Landish, Capital	
	(a)	8,200

	Utilities Expense
(f)	175

	Supplies
(j)	82

	R. Landish, Drawing
(h)	2,200

	Office Furniture
(b)	350

	Modeling Fees	
	(c)	8,400
	(e)	2,600
	(i)	7,580

	Office Equipment
(k)	2,800

ACCOUNT NAME	DEBIT	CREDIT

© 2013 Cengage Learning. All Rights Reserved. May not be scanned, copied, duplicated, or posted to a publicly accessible website, in whole or in part.

Exercise 2-6 *(concluded)*

© 2013 Cengage Learning. All Rights Reserved. May not be scanned, copied, duplicated, or posted to a publicly accessible website, in whole or in part.

Exercise 2-7

	DESCRIPTION	AMOUNT OF DIFFERENCE	DEBIT OR CREDIT COLUMN OF TRIAL BALANCE UNDERSTATED OR OVERSTATED
0.	*Example: A $149 debit to Accounts Receivable was not recorded.*	*$149*	*Debit column understated*
a.	A $42 debit to Supplies was recorded as $420.		
b.	A $155 debit to Accounts Receivable was recorded twice.		
c.	A $179 debit to Prepaid Insurance was not recorded.		
d.	A $65 credit to Cash was not recorded.		
e.	A $190 debit to Equipment was recorded twice.		
f.	A $57 debit to Utilities Expense was recorded as $75.		

Exercise 2-8

a. _____
   _____
   _____
   _____

b. _____
   _____
   _____
   _____

c. _____
   _____
   _____
   _____

d. _____
   _____
   _____
   _____

© 2013 Cengage Learning. All Rights Reserved. May not be scanned, copied, duplicated, or posted to a publicly accessible website, in whole or in part.

Problem 2-1A or 2-1B

Assets =

Debit +	Credit −

Cash

Debit +	Credit −
(a)	(b)

© 2013 Cengage Learning. All Rights Reserved. May not be scanned, copied, duplicated, or posted to a publicly accessible website, in whole or in part.

Problem 2-2A or 2-2B

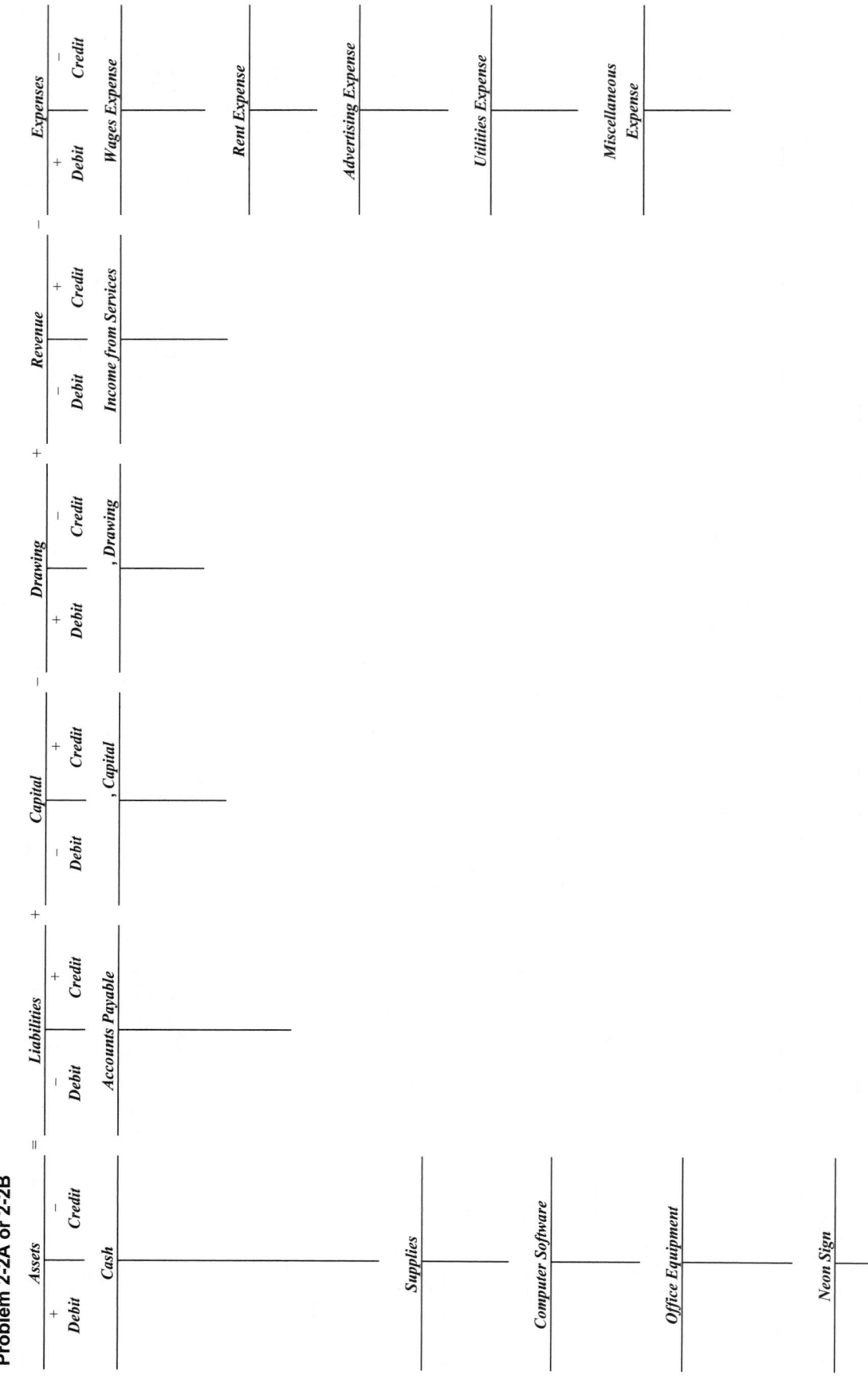

© 2013 Cengage Learning. All Rights Reserved. May not be scanned, copied, duplicated, or posted to a publicly accessible website, in whole or in part.

Problem 2-2A or 2-2B (concluded)

ACCOUNT NAME	DEBIT	CREDIT

© 2013 Cengage Learning. All Rights Reserved. May not be scanned, copied, duplicated, or posted to a publicly accessible website, in whole or in part.

Problem 2-3A or 2-3B

Assets			=	Liabilities			+	Capital			+	Drawing			+	Revenue			–	Expenses		
+		–		–		+		–		+		+		–		–		+		+		–
Debit		Credit		Debit		Credit		Debit		Credit		Debit		Credit		Debit		Credit		Debit		Credit

Cash

Accounts Payable

, Capital

, Drawing

Professional Fees

Salary Expense

Accounts Receivable

Rent Expense

Office Equipment

Utilities Expense

Office Furniture

Miscellaneous Expense

© 2013 Cengage Learning. All Rights Reserved. May not be scanned, copied, duplicated, or posted to a publicly accessible website, in whole or in part.

Problem 2-3A or 2-3B (continued)

ACCOUNT NAME	DEBIT	CREDIT

© 2013 Cengage Learning. All Rights Reserved. May not be scanned, copied, duplicated, or posted to a publicly accessible website, in whole or in part.

Problem 2-3A or 2-3B (concluded)

© 2013 Cengage Learning. All Rights Reserved. May not be scanned, copied, duplicated, or posted to a publicly accessible website, in whole or in part.

Problem 2-4A or 2-4B

Assets = Liabilities + Capital

Assets					Liabilities		Capital			Drawing			Revenue			Expenses	
+	–				–	+	–	+		+	–		–	+		+	–
Debit	Credit				Debit	Credit	Debit	Credit		Debit	Credit		Debit	Credit		Debit	Credit

Cash

Accounts Payable

_____, Capital

_____, Drawing

Revenue

Wages Expense

Supplies

Rent Expense

Prepaid Insurance

Utilities Expense

Equipment

Miscellaneous Expense

Furniture and Fixtures

© 2013 Cengage Learning. All Rights Reserved. May not be scanned, copied, duplicated, or posted to a publicly accessible website, in whole or in part.

Problem 2-4A or 2-4B (continued)

ACCOUNT NAME	DEBIT	CREDIT

© 2013 Cengage Learning. All Rights Reserved. May not be scanned, copied, duplicated, or posted to a publicly accessible website, in whole or in part.

Problem 2-4A or 2-4B (concluded)

Problem 2-5A or 2-5B

(a) _____

(b) _____

(c) _____

(d) _____

(e) _____

(f) _____

(g) _____

(h) _____

(i) _____

(j) _____

(k) _____

© 2013 Cengage Learning. All Rights Reserved. May not be scanned, copied, duplicated, or posted to a publicly accessible website, in whole or in part.

Answers to Study Guide Questions

CHAPTER 2

PART 1   True/False

1.	F	5.	T	9.	T
2.	T	6.	F	10.	F
3.	T	7.	F		
4.	F	8.	T		

PART 2   Completion—Accounting Language

1. debit
2. footings
3. transposition
4. trial balance
5. compound entry
6. credit

PART 3   Accounting Entries

Professional Equipment			*Accounts Payable*	
+	−		−	+
(a) 560				(a) 560

Accounts Receivable			*Professional Fees*	
+	−		−	+
(b) 870				(b) 870

Rent Expense			*Cash*	
+	−		+	−
(c) 1,000				(c) 1,000

Supplies			*Accounts Payable*	
+	−		−	+
(d) 220				(d) 220

Utilities Expense			*Cash*	
+	−		+	−
(e) 110				(e) 110

Cash			*Accounts Receivable*	
+	−		+	−
(f) 920				(f) 920

Accounts Payable			*Cash*	
−	+		+	−
(g) 700				(g) 700

Salary Expense			*Cash*	
+	−		+	−
(h) 900				(h) 900

Office Equipment			*Cash*	
+	−		+	−
(i) 452				(i) 452

© 2013 Cengage Learning. All Rights Reserved. May not be scanned, copied, duplicated, or posted to a publicly accessible website, in whole or in part.

The General Journal and the General Ledger

LEARNING OBJECTIVES

1. Record a group of transactions pertaining to a service business in a two-column general journal.
2. Post entries from a two-column general journal to general ledger accounts.
3. Prepare a trial balance from the ledger accounts.
4. Explain the importance of source documents.
5. Correct entries using the ruling or correcting entry method.

ACCOUNTING LANGUAGE

Cost principle	Ledger account
Cross-reference	Posting
General ledger	Source documents
Journal	Two-column general journal
Journalizing	

STUDY GUIDE QUESTIONS

PART 1   True/False

For each of the following statements, circle T if the statement is true and F if the statement is false.

T   F   1.   The credit part of a journal entry always comes first.

T   F   2.   Dollar signs are required in all journal entries.

T   F   3.   A transaction must be posted before it is journalized.

T   F   4.   In a journal entry, if two accounts are debited, two accounts must be credited.

T   F   5.   The first step in the posting process is to write the date of the transaction.

T   F   6.   In the presentation of a general journal in the text, the title of the account credited is indented approximately one-half inch.

T   F   7.   A number in the Post. Ref. column in the ledger account indicates that the balance has been recorded in the trial balance.

T   F   8.   Failure to post an entire transaction from the journal to the ledger will cause an error in the trial balance.

T   F   9.   Having a running balance is an advantage of a four-column ledger account form.

T   F   10.   A trial balance is prepared directly from the journal.

T   F   11.   The method for correcting errors depends on how and when the errors were made.

© 2013 Cengage Learning. All Rights Reserved. May not be scanned, copied, duplicated, or posted to a publicly accessible website, in whole or in part.

PART 2   Completion—Accounting Language

Complete each of the following statements by writing the appropriate words in the spaces provided.

1.   A book or file containing the accounts of a business is called a(n) _____

_____ .

2.   The process of transferring information from the journal to the ledger is called

_____ .

3.   The information about transactions comes from _____

_____ such as checks, invoices, receipts, letters, and memos.

4.   The _____ states that the purchase of an asset

should be recorded at the agreed amount of the transaction.

5.   The process of recording a business transaction in a book of original entry is called

_____ .

6.   A cross-reference exists when the journal page number is recorded in the Post. Ref.

column of the ledger and the ledger account number is recorded in the _____

_____ .

7.   If the transaction was journalized incorrectly and the amounts were posted, you should use the

_____ for correcting journal entries.

PART 3   Completing a Journal Entry

Here are a partially completed journal entry and the Cash ledger account. Complete the entry, including the explanation, using the data given. The entry represents the first entry on page 33 and occurred during October of the current year.

GENERAL JOURNAL   PAGE _____

	DATE		DESCRIPTION	POST. REF.	DEBIT	CREDIT	
1	20 —						1
2	Oct.	29	Cash		1,100.00		2
3			Accounts Receivable	113			3
4			Income from Services	411		1,700.00	4
5							5
6							6

© 2013 Cengage Learning. All Rights Reserved. May not be scanned, copied, duplicated, or posted to a publicly accessible website, in whole or in part.

GENERAL LEDGER

ACCOUNT __*Cash*__   ACCOUNT NO. ____ *111*

DATE		ITEM	POST. REF.	DEBIT	CREDIT	BALANCE DEBIT	BALANCE CREDIT
20—							
Oct.	1	Balance	√			2,900.00	
	6		30	600.00		3,500.00	
	6		30		700.00	2,800.00	
	12		32	1,100.00		3,900.00	
	14		32		400.00	3,500.00	
	27		32		200.00	3,300.00	
	29		33	1,100.00		4,400.00	

1. What is the missing amount in the journal entry? _____
2. What is the total cash received during October? _____
3. What is the total cash paid out during October? _____
4. The journal entry is an example of a(n) _____ journal entry.

DEMONSTRATION PROBLEM

C. Bela, a fitness enthusiast, buys an existing exercise center, Body Firm. The chart of accounts is shown below, followed by transactions for the month of April.

Assets
111   Cash
124   Land
126   Building
128   Equipment

Liabilities
221   Accounts Payable
223   Mortgage Payable

Owner's Equity
311   C. Bela, Capital
312   C. Bela, Drawing

Revenue
411   Income from Services

Expenses
511   Wages Expense
512   Utilities Expense
513   Advertising Expense
514   Repair Expense
519   Miscellaneous Expense

© 2013 Cengage Learning. All Rights Reserved. May not be scanned, copied, duplicated, or posted to a publicly accessible website, in whole or in part.

DEMONSTRATION PROBLEM (continued)

Apr. 16   Bela deposited $100,000 in a bank account for the purpose of buying Body Firm.

   17   Bought the assets of Body Firm for a total price of $188,000. The assets include equipment, $28,000; building, $96,000; and land, $64,000. Made a down payment of $89,000 and signed a mortgage note for the remainder.

   17   Bought additional equipment from Fitness Supply Co. on account for $3,550, paying $710 down, with balance due in 30 days.

   29   Celebrated the grand opening of Body Firm. Advertising expenses were paid in cash for the following:

Advertising in newspaper	$314
Announcements mailed to local residents	85
Postage	125
Balloons, ribbons, flowers	126
Food and refreshments	58

   30   Received fees for daily use of the facilities, $1,152.

   30   Paid wages for the period April 17 through April 30, $833.

   30   Received and paid electric bill, $129.

   30   Received and paid repair bill, $96.

   30   Bela withdrew $600 for personal use.

Instructions

1.   Record the transactions in the general journal.

2.   Post the transactions to the general ledger.

3.   Prepare a trial balance as of April 30.

© 2013 Cengage Learning. All Rights Reserved. May not be scanned, copied, duplicated, or posted to a publicly accessible website, in whole or in part.

SOLUTION

GENERAL JOURNAL   PAGE _____1_____

	DATE		DESCRIPTION	POST. REF.	DEBIT	CREDIT	
1	20—						1
2	Apr.	16	Cash	111	100,000.00		2
3			C. Bela, Capital	311		100,000.00	3
4			Invested cash in the business.				4
5							5
6		17	Equipment	128	28,000.00		6
7			Building	126	96,000.00		7
8			Land	124	64,000.00		8
9			Cash	111		89,000.00	9
10			Mortgage Payable	223		99,000.00	10
11			Bought Body Firm.				11
12							12
13		17	Equipment	128	3,550.00		13
14			Cash	111		710.00	14
15			Accounts Payable	221		2,840.00	15
16			Bought equipment on account from				16
17			Fitness Supply Co., with balance				17
18			due in 30 days.				18
19							19
20		29	Advertising Expense	513	708.00		20
21			Cash	111		708.00	21
22			Grand opening expenses.				22
23							23
24		30	Cash	111	1,152.00		24
25			Income from Services	411		1,152.00	25
26			Received fees.				26
27							27
28		30	Wages Expense	511	833.00		28
29			Cash	111		833.00	29
30			Paid wages for period April 17				30
31			through April 30.				31
32							32
33		30	Utilities Expense	512	129.00		33
34			Cash	111		129.00	34
35			Paid electric bill.				35
36							36
37		30	Repair Expense	514	96.00		37
38			Cash	111		96.00	38
39			Paid repair bill.				39
40							40
41		30	C. Bela, Drawing	312	600.00		41
42			Cash	111		600.00	42
43			Withdrawal for personal use.				43
44							44

45

© 2013 Cengage Learning. All Rights Reserved. May not be scanned, copied, duplicated, or posted to a publicly accessible website, in whole or in part.

SOLUTION (continued)

GENERAL LEDGER

ACCOUNT *Cash*   ACCOUNT NO. *111*

DATE		ITEM	POST. REF.	DEBIT	CREDIT	BALANCE	
						DEBIT	CREDIT
20—							
Apr.	*16*		*1*	*100,000.00*		*100,000.00*	
	17		*1*		*89,000.00*	*11,000.00*	
	17		*1*		*710.00*	*10,290.00*	
	29		*1*		*708.00*	*9,582.00*	
	30		*1*	*1,152.00*		*10,734.00*	
	30		*1*		*833.00*	*9,901.00*	
	30		*1*		*129.00*	*9,772.00*	
	30		*1*		*96.00*	*9,676.00*	
	30		*1*		*600.00*	*9,076.00*	

ACCOUNT *Land*   ACCOUNT NO. *124*

DATE		ITEM	POST. REF.	DEBIT	CREDIT	BALANCE	
						DEBIT	CREDIT
20—							
Apr.	*17*		*1*	*64,000.00*		*64,000.00*	

ACCOUNT *Building*   ACCOUNT NO. *126*

DATE		ITEM	POST. REF.	DEBIT	CREDIT	BALANCE	
						DEBIT	CREDIT
20—							
Apr.	*17*		*1*	*96,000.00*		*96,000.00*	

ACCOUNT *Equipment*   ACCOUNT NO. *128*

DATE		ITEM	POST. REF.	DEBIT	CREDIT	BALANCE	
						DEBIT	CREDIT
20—							
Apr.	*17*		*1*	*28,000.00*		*28,000.00*	
	17		*1*	*3,550.00*		*31,550.00*	

© 2013 Cengage Learning. All Rights Reserved. May not be scanned, copied, duplicated, or posted to a publicly accessible website, in whole or in part.

SOLUTION (continued)

ACCOUNT *Accounts Payable*   ACCOUNT NO. 221

DATE		ITEM	POST. REF.	DEBIT	CREDIT	BALANCE DEBIT	BALANCE CREDIT
20—							
Apr.	17		1		2,840.00		2,840.00

ACCOUNT *Mortgage Payable*   ACCOUNT NO. 223

DATE		ITEM	POST. REF.	DEBIT	CREDIT	BALANCE DEBIT	BALANCE CREDIT
20—							
Apr.	17		1		99,000.00		99,000.00

ACCOUNT *C. Bela, Capital*   ACCOUNT NO. 311

DATE		ITEM	POST. REF.	DEBIT	CREDIT	BALANCE DEBIT	BALANCE CREDIT
20—							
Apr.	16		1		100,000.00		100,000.00

ACCOUNT *C. Bela, Drawing*   ACCOUNT NO. 312

DATE		ITEM	POST. REF.	DEBIT	CREDIT	BALANCE DEBIT	BALANCE CREDIT
20—							
Apr.	30		1	600.00		600.00	

ACCOUNT *Income from Services*   ACCOUNT NO. 411

DATE		ITEM	POST. REF.	DEBIT	CREDIT	BALANCE DEBIT	BALANCE CREDIT
20—							
Apr.	30		1		1,152.00		1,152.00

© 2013 Cengage Learning. All Rights Reserved. May not be scanned, copied, duplicated, or posted to a publicly accessible website, in whole or in part.

SOLUTION (continued)

ACCOUNT   *Wages Expense*   ACCOUNT NO.   *511*

DATE		ITEM	POST. REF.	DEBIT	CREDIT	BALANCE	
						DEBIT	CREDIT
20—							
Apr.	30		1	833.00		833.00	

ACCOUNT   *Utilities Expense*   ACCOUNT NO.   *512*

DATE		ITEM	POST. REF.	DEBIT	CREDIT	BALANCE	
						DEBIT	CREDIT
20—							
Apr.	30		1	129.00		129.00	

ACCOUNT   *Advertising Expense*   ACCOUNT NO.   *513*

DATE		ITEM	POST. REF.	DEBIT	CREDIT	BALANCE	
						DEBIT	CREDIT
20—							
Apr.	29		1	708.00		708.00	

ACCOUNT   *Repair Expense*   ACCOUNT NO.   *514*

DATE		ITEM	POST. REF.	DEBIT	CREDIT	BALANCE	
						DEBIT	CREDIT
20—							
Apr.	30		1	96.00		96.00	

ACCOUNT   *Miscellaneous Expense*   ACCOUNT NO.   *519*

DATE		ITEM	POST. REF.	DEBIT	CREDIT	BALANCE	
						DEBIT	CREDIT

© 2013 Cengage Learning. All Rights Reserved. May not be scanned, copied, duplicated, or posted to a publicly accessible website, in whole or in part.

SOLUTION (continued)

Body Firm

Trial Balance

April 30, 20—

ACCOUNT NAME	DEBIT	CREDIT
Cash	9,076	
Land	64,000	
Building	96,000	
Equipment	31,550	
Accounts Payable		2,840
Mortgage Payable		99,000
C. Bela, Capital		100,000
C. Bela, Drawing	600	
Income from Services		1,152
Wages Expense	833	
Utilities Expense	129	
Advertising Expense	708	
Repair Expense	96	
	202,992	202,992

© 2013 Cengage Learning. All Rights Reserved. May not be scanned, copied, duplicated, or posted to a publicly accessible website, in whole or in part.

EXERCISES AND PROBLEMS

Exercise 3-1

1. _____   5. _____
2. _____   6. _____
3. _____   7. _____
4. _____   8. _____

Exercise 3-2

GENERAL JOURNAL   PAGE _____

	DATE		DESCRIPTION	POST. REF.	DEBIT	CREDIT	
1							1
2							2
3							3
4							4
5							5
6							6
7							7
8							8
9							9
10							10
11							11
12							12
13							13
14							14
15							15
16							16
17							17
18							18
19							19
20							20
21							21
22							22
23							23
24							24
25							25
26							26
27							27
28							28

© 2013 Cengage Learning. All Rights Reserved. May not be scanned, copied, duplicated, or posted to a publicly accessible website, in whole or in part.

Exercise 3-3

GENERAL JOURNAL   PAGE _____

	DATE		DESCRIPTION	POST. REF.	DEBIT	CREDIT	
1							1
2							2
3							3
4							4
5							5
6							6
7							7
8							8
9							9
10							10
11							11
12							12
13							13
14							14
15							15
16							16
17							17
18							18
19							19
20							20
21							21
22							22
23							23
24							24
25							25
26							26
27							27
28							28

© 2013 Cengage Learning. All Rights Reserved. May not be scanned, copied, duplicated, or posted to a publicly accessible website, in whole or in part.

Exercise 3-4

GENERAL LEDGER

ACCOUNT   *Cash*   ACCOUNT NO.   *111*

DATE		ITEM	POST. REF.	DEBIT	CREDIT	BALANCE	
						DEBIT	CREDIT

Exercise 3-5

© 2013 Cengage Learning. All Rights Reserved. May not be scanned, copied, duplicated, or posted to a publicly accessible website, in whole or in part.

Exercise 3-6

ACCOUNT NAME	DEBIT	CREDIT

Notes: **a.** _____

b. _____

c. _____

d. _____

Exercise 3-7

DESCRIPTION	TOTAL REVENUE	TOTAL EXPENSES	NET INCOME
0. Example: A check for $325 was written to pay on account. The accountant debited Rent Expense for $325 and credited Cash for $325.	NA	O	U
a. $420 was received on account from customers. The accountant debited Cash for $420 and credited Professional Fees for $420.			
b. The owner withdrew $1,200 for personal use. The accountant debited Wages Expense for $1,200 and credited Cash for $1,200.			
c. A check was written for $1,250 to pay the rent. The accountant debited Rent Expense for $1,520 and credited Cash for $1,520.			
d. $1,800 was received on account from customers. The accountant debited Cash for $1,800 and credited the Capital account for $1,800.			
e. A check was written for $225 to pay the phone bill received and recorded earlier in the month. The accountant debited Phone Expense for $225 and Cash for $225.			

© 2013 Cengage Learning. All Rights Reserved. May not be scanned, copied, duplicated, or posted to a publicly accessible website, in whole or in part.

Exercise 3-8

GENERAL JOURNAL

PAGE _____

	DATE		DESCRIPTION	POST. REF.	DEBIT	CREDIT	
1							1
2							2
3							3
4							4
5							5
6							6
7							7
8							8
9							9
10							10
11							11
12							12
13							13
14							14
15							15
16							16
17							17
18							18
19							19
20							20
21							21
22							22
23							23
24							24
25							25
26							26
27							27
28							28
29							29
30							30
31							31
32							32
33							33
34							34
35							35
36							36
37							37
38							38
39							39
40							40
41							41
42							42
43							43
44							44

© 2013 Cengage Learning. All Rights Reserved. May not be scanned, copied, duplicated, or posted to a publicly accessible website, in whole or in part.

Problem 3-1A or 3-1B

GENERAL JOURNAL   PAGE _____

	DATE		DESCRIPTION	POST. REF.	DEBIT	CREDIT	
1							1
2							2
3							3
4							4
5							5
6							6
7							7
8							8
9							9
10							10
11							11
12							12
13							13
14							14
15							15
16							16
17							17
18							18
19							19
20							20
21							21
22							22
23							23
24							24
25							25
26							26
27							27
28							28
29							29
30							30
31							31
32							32
33							33
34							34
35							35
36							36
37							37
38							38
39							39
40							40
41							41
42							42
43							43
44							44

© 2013 Cengage Learning. All Rights Reserved. May not be scanned, copied, duplicated, or posted to a publicly accessible website, in whole or in part.

Problem 3-1A or 3-1B (concluded)

GENERAL JOURNAL   PAGE _____

	DATE		DESCRIPTION	POST. REF.	DEBIT	CREDIT	
1							1
2							2
3							3
4							4
5							5
6							6
7							7
8							8
9							9
10							10
11							11
12							12
13							13
14							14
15							15
16							16
17							17
18							18
19							19
20							20
21							21
22							22
23							23
24							24
25							25
26							26
27							27
28							28
29							29
30							30
31							31
32							32
33							33
34							34
35							35
36							36
37							37
38							38
39							39
40							40
41							41
42							42
43							43
44							44

© 2013 Cengage Learning. All Rights Reserved. May not be scanned, copied, duplicated, or posted to a publicly accessible website, in whole or in part.

Problem 3-2A

GENERAL JOURNAL   PAGE ____5____

	DATE		DESCRIPTION	POST. REF.	DEBIT	CREDIT	
1	20—						1
2	Aug.	1	Rent Expense		1,200.00		2
3			Cash			1,200.00	3
4			Paid rent for August, Ck. No. 145.				4
5							5
6		5	Cash		36.00		6
7			Accounts Receivable			36.00	7
8			Paid Bill's Deli on account, Inv. No. 316.				8
9							9
10		8	Cash		3,690.00		10
11			Income from Services			3,690.00	11
12			Week of August 2.				12
13							13
14		10	Accounts Payable		612.00		14
15			Cash			612.00	15
16			Paid Ashbey Equipment Co.,				16
17			on account, Ck. No. 146.				17
18							18
19		15	Cash		3,254.00		19
20			Income from Services			3,254.00	20
21			Week of August 9.				21
22							22
23		16	Wages Expense		1,586.00		23
24			Cash			1,586.00	24
25			Paid wages, August 1–15, Ck. No. 147.				25
26							26
27		18	Accounts Receivable		830.00		27
28			Income from Services			830.00	28
29			Billed Central Transit for services				29
30			rendered, Inv. No. 317.				30
31							31
32		20	Supplies		795.00		32
33			Accounts Payable			795.00	33
34			Bought supplies from General Supply				34
35			Company, Inv. No. 6165.				35
36							36
37							37
38							38

© 2013 Cengage Learning. All Rights Reserved. May not be scanned, copied, duplicated, or posted to a publicly accessible website, in whole or in part.

Problem 3-2A (continued)

GENERAL JOURNAL   PAGE _____ 6 _____

	DATE		DESCRIPTION	POST. REF.	DEBIT	CREDIT	
1	20—						1
2	Aug.	22	Cash		3,679.00		2
3			Income from Services			3,679.00	3
4			Week of August 16.				4
5							5
6		24	Utilities Expense		695.00		6
7			Cash			695.00	7
8			Paid utilities bill, Ck. No. 148.				8
9							9
10		25	Accounts Payable		400.00		10
11			Cash			400.00	11
12			Paid General Supply Company on				12
13			account, Ck. No. 149.				13
14							14
15		29	Cash		3,125.00		15
16			Income from Services			3,125.00	16
17			Week of August 23.				17
18							18
19		31	Wages Expense		1,465.00		19
20			Cash			1,465.00	20
21			Paid wages, August 16–31, Ck.				21
22			No. 150.				22
23							23
24		31	Cash		400.00		24
25			Accounts Receivable			400.00	25
26			Received from Central Transit to				26
27			apply on account, Inv. No. 317.				27
28							28
29		31	Advertising Expense		620.00		29
30			Accounts Payable			620.00	30
31			Received advertising bill from				31
32			Metro News, Inv. No. D1694.				32
33							33
34		31	M. Carley, Drawing		1,800.00		34
35			Cash			1,800.00	35
36			Withdrawal for personal use,				36
37			Ck. No. 151.				37
38							38

© 2013 Cengage Learning. All Rights Reserved. May not be scanned, copied, duplicated, or posted to a publicly accessible website, in whole or in part.

Problem 3-2A (continued)

GENERAL LEDGER

ACCOUNT *Cash*   ACCOUNT NO. *111*

DATE		ITEM	POST. REF.	DEBIT	CREDIT	BALANCE	
						DEBIT	CREDIT
20—							
July	31	Balance	✓			24,113.00	

ACCOUNT *Accounts Receivable*   ACCOUNT NO. *113*

DATE		ITEM	POST. REF.	DEBIT	CREDIT	BALANCE	
						DEBIT	CREDIT
20—							
July	31	Balance	✓			150.00	

ACCOUNT *Supplies*   ACCOUNT NO. *115*

DATE		ITEM	POST. REF.	DEBIT	CREDIT	BALANCE	
						DEBIT	CREDIT
20—							
July	31	Balance	✓			320.00	

ACCOUNT *Prepaid Insurance*   ACCOUNT NO. *117*

DATE		ITEM	POST. REF.	DEBIT	CREDIT	BALANCE	
						DEBIT	CREDIT
20—							
July	31	Balance	✓			840.00	

© 2013 Cengage Learning. All Rights Reserved. May not be scanned, copied, duplicated, or posted to a publicly accessible website, in whole or in part.

Problem 3-2A (continued)

ACCOUNT   *Equipment*   ACCOUNT NO.   *124*

| DATE | | ITEM | POST. REF. | DEBIT | CREDIT | BALANCE | |
						DEBIT	CREDIT
20—							
July	31	Balance	✓			18,950.00	

ACCOUNT   *Accounts Payable*   ACCOUNT NO.   *221*

| DATE | | ITEM | POST. REF. | DEBIT | CREDIT | BALANCE | |
						DEBIT	CREDIT
20—							
July	31	Balance	✓				4,236.00

ACCOUNT   *M. Carley, Capital*   ACCOUNT NO.   *311*

| DATE | | ITEM | POST. REF. | DEBIT | CREDIT | BALANCE | |
						DEBIT	CREDIT
20—							
July	31	Balance	✓				42,000.00

ACCOUNT   *M. Carley, Drawing*   ACCOUNT NO.   *312*

| DATE | | ITEM | POST. REF. | DEBIT | CREDIT | BALANCE | |
						DEBIT	CREDIT
20—							
July	31	Balance	✓			4,500.00	

ACCOUNT   *Income from Services*   ACCOUNT NO.   *411*

| DATE | | ITEM | POST. REF. | DEBIT | CREDIT | BALANCE | |
						DEBIT	CREDIT
20—							
July	31	Balance	✓				6,800.00

© 2013 Cengage Learning. All Rights Reserved. May not be scanned, copied, duplicated, or posted to a publicly accessible website, in whole or in part.

Problem 3-2A (continued)

ACCOUNT **Wages Expense**   ACCOUNT NO. **511**

DATE		ITEM	POST. REF.	DEBIT	CREDIT	BALANCE	
						DEBIT	CREDIT
20—							
July	31	Balance	✓			2,395.00	

ACCOUNT **Rent Expense**   ACCOUNT NO. **512**

DATE		ITEM	POST. REF.	DEBIT	CREDIT	BALANCE	
						DEBIT	CREDIT
20—							
July	31	Balance	✓			900.00	

ACCOUNT **Advertising Expense**   ACCOUNT NO. **513**

DATE		ITEM	POST. REF.	DEBIT	CREDIT	BALANCE	
						DEBIT	CREDIT
20—							
July	31	Balance	✓			487.00	

ACCOUNT **Utilities Expense**   ACCOUNT NO. **514**

DATE		ITEM	POST. REF.	DEBIT	CREDIT	BALANCE	
						DEBIT	CREDIT
20—							
July	31	Balance	✓			381.00	

© 2013 Cengage Learning. All Rights Reserved. May not be scanned, copied, duplicated, or posted to a publicly accessible website, in whole or in part.

Problem 3-2A (continued)

ACCOUNT NAME	DEBIT	CREDIT

© 2013 Cengage Learning. All Rights Reserved. May not be scanned, copied, duplicated, or posted to a publicly accessible website, in whole or in part.

Problem 3-2A (concluded)

© 2013 Cengage Learning. All Rights Reserved. May not be scanned, copied, duplicated, or posted to a publicly accessible website, in whole or in part.

Problem 3-2B

GENERAL JOURNAL   PAGE ____4____

	DATE		DESCRIPTION	POST. REF.	DEBIT	CREDIT	
1	20—						1
2	May	1	Rent Expense		1,050.00		2
3			Cash			1,050.00	3
4			Paid rent for May, Ck. No. 148.				4
5							5
6		5	Cash		1,035.00		6
7			Accounts Receivable			1,035.00	7
8			Paid Jay Company on account,				8
9			Inv. No. 125.				9
10							10
11		7	Cash		3,560.00		11
12			Income from Services			3,560.00	12
13			Week of May 1.				13
14							14
15		8	Accounts Payable		425.00		15
16			Cash			425.00	16
17			Paid Tofer Equipment Co.,				17
18			on account, Ck. No. 149.				18
19							19
20		14	Cash		3,490.00		20
21			Income from Services			3,490.00	21
22			Week of May 8.				22
23							23
24		15	Wages Expense		1,845.00		24
25			Cash			1,845.00	25
26			Paid wages, May 1–May 15,				26
27			Ck. No. 150.				27
28							28
29		17	Accounts Receivable		2,280.00		29
30			Income from Services			2,280.00	30
31			Paid Leggit Company on account,				31
32			Inv. No. 126.				32
33							33
34		18	Supplies		355.00		34
35			Accounts Payable			355.00	35
36			Bought supplies on account from				36
37			Everyday Supply Company, Inv.				37
38			No. 3160.				38
39							39

© 2013 Cengage Learning. All Rights Reserved. May not be scanned, copied, duplicated, or posted to a publicly accessible website, in whole or in part.

Problem 3-2B (continued)

GENERAL JOURNAL   PAGE ____5____

	DATE		DESCRIPTION	POST. REF.	DEBIT	CREDIT	
1	20—						1
2	May	21	Cash		3,694.00		2
3			Income from Services			3,694.00	3
4			Week of May 15.				4
5							5
6		23	Utilities Expense		398.00		6
7			Cash			398.00	7
8			Paid telephone bill, Ck. No. 151.				8
9							9
10		25	Accounts Payable		355.00		10
11			Cash			355.00	11
12			Paid Everyday Supply Company on				12
13			account, Inv. No. 3160, Ck. No. 152.				13
14							14
15		28	Cash		3,250.00		15
16			Income from Services			3,250.00	16
17			Week of May 22.				17
18							18
19		31	Wages Expense		1,688.00		19
20			Cash			1,688.00	20
21			Paid wages, May 16–May 31, Ck.				21
22			No. 153.				22
23							23
24		31	Cash		250.00		24
25			Accounts Receivable			250.00	25
26			Received from Leggit Company on				26
27			account, Inv. No. 126.				27
28							28
29		31	Advertising Expense		560.00		29
30			Accounts Payable			560.00	30
31			Received advertising bill from				31
32			Neighborhood News, Inv. No. 316.				32
33							33
34		31	R. Ramirez, Drawing		1,200.00		34
35			Cash			1,200.00	35
36			Withdrawal for personal use, Ck.				36
37			No. 154.				37
38							38
39							39

© 2013 Cengage Learning. All Rights Reserved. May not be scanned, copied, duplicated, or posted to a publicly accessible website, in whole or in part.

Problem 3-2B (continued)

GENERAL LEDGER

ACCOUNT   *Cash*   ACCOUNT NO.   *111*

DATE		ITEM	POST. REF.	DEBIT	CREDIT	BALANCE DEBIT	BALANCE CREDIT
20—							
Apr.	30	Balance	✓			12,980.00	

ACCOUNT   *Accounts Receivable*   ACCOUNT NO.   *113*

DATE		ITEM	POST. REF.	DEBIT	CREDIT	BALANCE DEBIT	BALANCE CREDIT
20—							
Apr.	30	Balance	✓			1,560.00	

ACCOUNT   *Supplies*   ACCOUNT NO.   *115*

DATE		ITEM	POST. REF.	DEBIT	CREDIT	BALANCE DEBIT	BALANCE CREDIT
20—							
Apr.	30	Balance	✓			180.00	

ACCOUNT   *Prepaid Insurance*   ACCOUNT NO.   *117*

DATE		ITEM	POST. REF.	DEBIT	CREDIT	BALANCE DEBIT	BALANCE CREDIT
20—							
Apr.	30	Balance	✓			460.00	

© 2013 Cengage Learning. All Rights Reserved. May not be scanned, copied, duplicated, or posted to a publicly accessible website, in whole or in part.

Problem 3-2B (continued)

ACCOUNT *Equipment*   ACCOUNT NO. *124*

DATE		ITEM	POST. REF.	DEBIT	CREDIT	BALANCE DEBIT	BALANCE CREDIT
20—							
Apr.	30	Balance	✓			8,500.00	

ACCOUNT *Accounts Payable*   ACCOUNT NO. *221*

DATE		ITEM	POST. REF.	DEBIT	CREDIT	BALANCE DEBIT	BALANCE CREDIT
20—							
Apr.	30	Balance	✓				2,080.00

ACCOUNT *R. Ramirez, Capital*   ACCOUNT NO. *311*

DATE		ITEM	POST. REF.	DEBIT	CREDIT	BALANCE DEBIT	BALANCE CREDIT
20—							
Apr.	30	Balance	✓				21,572.00

ACCOUNT *R. Ramirez, Drawing*   ACCOUNT NO. *312*

DATE		ITEM	POST. REF.	DEBIT	CREDIT	BALANCE DEBIT	BALANCE CREDIT
20—							
Apr.	30	Balance	✓			1,500.00	

ACCOUNT *Income from Services*   ACCOUNT NO. *411*

DATE		ITEM	POST. REF.	DEBIT	CREDIT	BALANCE DEBIT	BALANCE CREDIT
20—							
Apr.	30	Balance	✓				4,236.00

© 2013 Cengage Learning. All Rights Reserved. May not be scanned, copied, duplicated, or posted to a publicly accessible website, in whole or in part.

Problem 3-2B (continued)

ACCOUNT   *Wages Expense*   ACCOUNT NO. _____ *511*

DATE		ITEM	POST. REF.	DEBIT	CREDIT	BALANCE	
						DEBIT	CREDIT
20—							
Apr.	30	Balance	✓			1,050.00	

ACCOUNT   *Rent Expense*   ACCOUNT NO. _____ *512*

DATE		ITEM	POST. REF.	DEBIT	CREDIT	BALANCE	
						DEBIT	CREDIT
20—							
Apr.	30	Balance	✓			850.00	

ACCOUNT   *Advertising Expense*   ACCOUNT NO. _____ *513*

DATE		ITEM	POST. REF.	DEBIT	CREDIT	BALANCE	
						DEBIT	CREDIT
20—							
Apr.	30	Balance	✓			423.00	

ACCOUNT   *Utilities Expense*   ACCOUNT NO. _____ *514*

DATE		ITEM	POST. REF.	DEBIT	CREDIT	BALANCE	
						DEBIT	CREDIT
20—							
Apr.	30	Balance	✓			385.00	

© 2013 Cengage Learning. All Rights Reserved. May not be scanned, copied, duplicated, or posted to a publicly accessible website, in whole or in part.

Problem 3-2B (continued)

ACCOUNT NAME	DEBIT	CREDIT

© 2013 Cengage Learning. All Rights Reserved. May not be scanned, copied, duplicated, or posted to a publicly accessible website, in whole or in part.

Problem 3-2B (concluded)

© 2013 Cengage Learning. All Rights Reserved. May not be scanned, copied, duplicated, or posted to a publicly accessible website, in whole or in part.

Problem 3-3A

GENERAL JOURNAL   PAGE _____

	DATE		DESCRIPTION	POST. REF.	DEBIT	CREDIT	
1							1
2							2
3							3
4							4
5							5
6							6
7							7
8							8
9							9
10							10
11							11
12							12
13							13
14							14
15							15
16							16
17							17
18							18
19							19
20							20
21							21
22							22
23							23
24							24
25							25
26							26
27							27
28							28
29							29
30							30
31							31
32							32
33							33
34							34
35							35
36							36
37							37
38							38
39							39
40							40
41							41

© 2013 Cengage Learning. All Rights Reserved. May not be scanned, copied, duplicated, or posted to a publicly accessible website, in whole or in part.

Problem 3-3A (continued)

GENERAL JOURNAL   PAGE _____

	DATE		DESCRIPTION	POST. REF.	DEBIT	CREDIT	
1							1
2							2
3							3
4							4
5							5
6							6
7							7
8							8
9							9
10							10
11							11
12							12
13							13
14							14
15							15
16							16
17							17
18							18
19							19
20							20
21							21
22							22
23							23
24							24
25							25
26							26
27							27
28							28
29							29
30							30
31							31
32							32
33							33
34							34
35							35
36							36
37							37
38							38
39							39
40							40
41							41

© 2013 Cengage Learning. All Rights Reserved. May not be scanned, copied, duplicated, or posted to a publicly accessible website, in whole or in part.

Problem 3-3A (continued)

GENERAL LEDGER

ACCOUNT *Cash*   ACCOUNT NO. *111*

DATE		ITEM	POST. REF.	DEBIT	CREDIT	BALANCE	
						DEBIT	CREDIT
20—							
June	30	Balance	✓			25,312.00	

ACCOUNT *Accounts Receivable*   ACCOUNT NO. *113*

DATE		ITEM	POST. REF.	DEBIT	CREDIT	BALANCE	
						DEBIT	CREDIT
20—							
June	30	Balance	✓			560.00	

ACCOUNT *Supplies*   ACCOUNT NO. *115*

DATE		ITEM	POST. REF.	DEBIT	CREDIT	BALANCE	
						DEBIT	CREDIT
20—							

ACCOUNT *Prepaid Insurance*   ACCOUNT NO. *117*

DATE		ITEM	POST. REF.	DEBIT	CREDIT	BALANCE	
						DEBIT	CREDIT
20—							
June	30	Balance	✓			450.00	

© 2013 Cengage Learning. All Rights Reserved. May not be scanned, copied, duplicated, or posted to a publicly accessible website, in whole or in part.

Problem 3-3A (continued)

ACCOUNT   *Equipment*   ACCOUNT NO.   *124*

DATE		ITEM	POST. REF.	DEBIT	CREDIT	BALANCE	
						DEBIT	CREDIT
20—							
June	30	Balance	✓			16,500.00	

ACCOUNT   *Accounts Payable*   ACCOUNT NO.   *221*

DATE		ITEM	POST. REF.	DEBIT	CREDIT	BALANCE	
						DEBIT	CREDIT
20—							
June	30	Balance	✓				2,976.00

ACCOUNT   *C. Lucern, Capital*   ACCOUNT NO.   *311*

DATE		ITEM	POST. REF.	DEBIT	CREDIT	BALANCE	
						DEBIT	CREDIT
20—							
June	30	Balance	✓				39,846.00

ACCOUNT   *C. Lucern, Drawing*   ACCOUNT NO.   *312*

DATE		ITEM	POST. REF.	DEBIT	CREDIT	BALANCE	
						DEBIT	CREDIT
20—							

ACCOUNT   *Professional Fees*   ACCOUNT NO.   *411*

DATE		ITEM	POST. REF.	DEBIT	CREDIT	BALANCE	
						DEBIT	CREDIT
20—							

© 2013 Cengage Learning. All Rights Reserved. May not be scanned, copied, duplicated, or posted to a publicly accessible website, in whole or in part.

Problem 3-3A (continued)

ACCOUNT   *Salary Expense*   ACCOUNT NO.   *511*

DATE	ITEM	POST. REF.	DEBIT	CREDIT	BALANCE	
					DEBIT	CREDIT
20—						

ACCOUNT   *Rent Expense*   ACCOUNT NO.   *512*

DATE	ITEM	POST. REF.	DEBIT	CREDIT	BALANCE	
					DEBIT	CREDIT
20—						

ACCOUNT   *Laboratory Expense*   ACCOUNT NO.   *513*

DATE	ITEM	POST. REF.	DEBIT	CREDIT	BALANCE	
					DEBIT	CREDIT
20—						

ACCOUNT   *Utilities Expense*   ACCOUNT NO.   *514*

DATE	ITEM	POST. REF.	DEBIT	CREDIT	BALANCE	
					DEBIT	CREDIT
20—						

© 2013 Cengage Learning. All Rights Reserved. May not be scanned, copied, duplicated, or posted to a publicly accessible website, in whole or in part.

Problem 3-3A (concluded)

ACCOUNT NAME	DEBIT	CREDIT	

© 2013 Cengage Learning. All Rights Reserved. May not be scanned, copied, duplicated, or posted to a publicly accessible website, in whole or in part.

Problem 3-3B

GENERAL JOURNAL   PAGE _____

	DATE		DESCRIPTION	POST. REF.	DEBIT	CREDIT	
1							1
2							2
3							3
4							4
5							5
6							6
7							7
8							8
9							9
10							10
11							11
12							12
13							13
14							14
15							15
16							16
17							17
18							18
19							19
20							20
21							21
22							22
23							23
24							24
25							25
26							26
27							27
28							28
29							29
30							30
31							31
32							32
33							33
34							34
35							35
36							36
37							37
38							38
39							39
40							40
41							41
42							42

© 2013 Cengage Learning. All Rights Reserved. May not be scanned, copied, duplicated, or posted to a publicly accessible website, in whole or in part.

Problem 3-3B (continued)

GENERAL JOURNAL   PAGE _____

	DATE		DESCRIPTION	POST. REF.	DEBIT	CREDIT	
1							1
2							2
3							3
4							4
5							5
6							6
7							7
8							8
9							9
10							10
11							11
12							12
13							13
14							14
15							15
16							16
17							17
18							18
19							19
20							20
21							21
22							22
23							23
24							24
25							25
26							26
27							27
28							28
29							29
30							30
31							31
32							32
33							33
34							34
35							35
36							36
37							37
38							38
39							39
40							40
41							41
42							42

© 2013 Cengage Learning. All Rights Reserved. May not be scanned, copied, duplicated, or posted to a publicly accessible website, in whole or in part.

Problem 3-3B (continued)

GENERAL LEDGER

ACCOUNT **Cash**   ACCOUNT NO. **111**

DATE		ITEM	POST. REF.	DEBIT	CREDIT	BALANCE	
						DEBIT	CREDIT
20—							
June	30	Balance	✓			4,568.00	

ACCOUNT **Accounts Receivable**   ACCOUNT NO. **113**

DATE		ITEM	POST. REF.	DEBIT	CREDIT	BALANCE	
						DEBIT	CREDIT
20—							
June	30	Balance	✓			3,045.00	

ACCOUNT **Supplies**   ACCOUNT NO. **115**

DATE		ITEM	POST. REF.	DEBIT	CREDIT	BALANCE	
						DEBIT	CREDIT
20—							

ACCOUNT **Prepaid Insurance**   ACCOUNT NO. **117**

DATE		ITEM	POST. REF.	DEBIT	CREDIT	BALANCE	
						DEBIT	CREDIT
20—							
June	30	Balance	✓			2,185.00	

© 2013 Cengage Learning. All Rights Reserved. May not be scanned, copied, duplicated, or posted to a publicly accessible website, in whole or in part.

Problem 3-3B (continued)

ACCOUNT   *Equipment*   ACCOUNT NO.   *124*

DATE		ITEM	POST. REF.	DEBIT	CREDIT	BALANCE	
						DEBIT	CREDIT
20—							
June	30	Balance	✓			16,850.00	

ACCOUNT   *Accounts Payable*   ACCOUNT NO.   *221*

DATE		ITEM	POST. REF.	DEBIT	CREDIT	BALANCE	
						DEBIT	CREDIT
20—							
June	30	Balance	✓				2,804.00

ACCOUNT   *J. Vance , Capital*   ACCOUNT NO.   *311*

DATE		ITEM	POST. REF.	DEBIT	CREDIT	BALANCE	
						DEBIT	CREDIT
20—							
June	30	Balance	✓				23,844.00

ACCOUNT   *J. Vance, Drawing*   ACCOUNT NO.   *312*

DATE		ITEM	POST. REF.	DEBIT	CREDIT	BALANCE	
						DEBIT	CREDIT
20—							

ACCOUNT   *Professional Fees*   ACCOUNT NO.   *411*

DATE		ITEM	POST. REF.	DEBIT	CREDIT	BALANCE	
						DEBIT	CREDIT
20—							

© 2013 Cengage Learning. All Rights Reserved. May not be scanned, copied, duplicated, or posted to a publicly accessible website, in whole or in part.

Problem 3-3B (continued)

ACCOUNT   *Salary Expense*   ACCOUNT NO. ___*511*___

DATE	ITEM	POST. REF.	DEBIT	CREDIT	BALANCE	
					DEBIT	CREDIT
20—						

ACCOUNT   *Rent Expense*   ACCOUNT NO. ___*512*___

DATE	ITEM	POST. REF.	DEBIT	CREDIT	BALANCE	
					DEBIT	CREDIT
20—						

ACCOUNT   *Laboratory Expense*   ACCOUNT NO. ___*513*___

DATE	ITEM	POST. REF.	DEBIT	CREDIT	BALANCE	
					DEBIT	CREDIT
20—						

ACCOUNT   *Utilities Expense*   ACCOUNT NO. ___*514*___

DATE	ITEM	POST. REF.	DEBIT	CREDIT	BALANCE	
					DEBIT	CREDIT
20—						

© 2013 Cengage Learning. All Rights Reserved. May not be scanned, copied, duplicated, or posted to a publicly accessible website, in whole or in part.

Problem 3-3B (concluded)

ACCOUNT NAME	DEBIT	CREDIT	

© 2013 Cengage Learning. All Rights Reserved. May not be scanned, copied, duplicated, or posted to a publicly accessible website, in whole or in part.

Problem 3-4A or 3-4B

GENERAL JOURNAL   PAGE _____

	DATE		DESCRIPTION	POST. REF.	DEBIT	CREDIT	
1							1
2							2
3							3
4							4
5							5
6							6
7							7
8							8
9							9
10							10
11							11
12							12
13							13
14							14
15							15
16							16
17							17
18							18
19							19
20							20
21							21
22							22
23							23
24							24
25							25
25							25
26							26
27							27
28							28
29							29
30							30
31							31
32							32
33							33
34							34
35							35
36							36
37							37
38							38
39							39
40							40
41							41
42							42
43							43
44							44
45							45

© 2013 Cengage Learning. All Rights Reserved. May not be scanned, copied, duplicated, or posted to a publicly accessible website, in whole or in part.

Problem 3-4A or 3-4B (continued)

GENERAL JOURNAL   PAGE _____

	DATE		DESCRIPTION	POST. REF.	DEBIT	CREDIT	
1							1
2							2
3							3
4							4
5							5
6							6
7							7
8							8
9							9
10							10
11							11
12							12
13							13
14							14
15							15
16							16
17							17
18							18
19							19
20							20
21							21
22							22
23							23
24							24
25							25
26							26
27							27
28							28
29							29
30							30
31							31
32							32
33							33
34							34
35							35
36							36
37							37
38							38
39							39
40							40
41							41
42							42
43							43
44							44
45							45

© 2013 Cengage Learning. All Rights Reserved. May not be scanned, copied, duplicated, or posted to a publicly accessible website, in whole or in part.

Problem 3-4A or 3-4B (continued)

GENERAL LEDGER

ACCOUNT _Cash_   ACCOUNT NO. _111_

DATE		ITEM	POST. REF.	DEBIT	CREDIT	BALANCE	
						DEBIT	CREDIT

ACCOUNT _Accounts Receivable_   ACCOUNT NO. _113_

DATE		ITEM	POST. REF.	DEBIT	CREDIT	BALANCE	
						DEBIT	CREDIT

ACCOUNT _Supplies_   ACCOUNT NO. _115_

DATE		ITEM	POST. REF.	DEBIT	CREDIT	BALANCE	
						DEBIT	CREDIT

ACCOUNT _Prepaid Insurance_   ACCOUNT NO. _117_

DATE		ITEM	POST. REF.	DEBIT	CREDIT	BALANCE	
						DEBIT	CREDIT

© 2013 Cengage Learning. All Rights Reserved. May not be scanned, copied, duplicated, or posted to a publicly accessible website, in whole or in part.

Problem 3-4A or 3-4B (continued)

ACCOUNT *Equipment*   ACCOUNT NO. *124*

DATE		ITEM	POST. REF.	DEBIT	CREDIT	BALANCE	
						DEBIT	CREDIT

ACCOUNT *Accounts Payable*   ACCOUNT NO. *221*

DATE		ITEM	POST. REF.	DEBIT	CREDIT	BALANCE	
						DEBIT	CREDIT

ACCOUNT   *, Capital*   ACCOUNT NO. *311*

DATE		ITEM	POST. REF.	DEBIT	CREDIT	BALANCE	
						DEBIT	CREDIT

ACCOUNT   *, Drawing*   ACCOUNT NO. *312*

DATE		ITEM	POST. REF.	DEBIT	CREDIT	BALANCE	
						DEBIT	CREDIT

ACCOUNT *Landscaping Income*   ACCOUNT NO. *411*

DATE		ITEM	POST. REF.	DEBIT	CREDIT	BALANCE	
						DEBIT	CREDIT

© 2013 Cengage Learning. All Rights Reserved. May not be scanned, copied, duplicated, or posted to a publicly accessible website, in whole or in part.

Problem 3-4A or 3-4B (continued)

ACCOUNT   *Salary Expense*   ACCOUNT NO.   *511*

DATE	ITEM	POST. REF.	DEBIT	CREDIT	BALANCE	
					DEBIT	CREDIT

ACCOUNT   *Rent Expense*   ACCOUNT NO.   *512*

DATE	ITEM	POST. REF.	DEBIT	CREDIT	BALANCE	
					DEBIT	CREDIT

ACCOUNT   *Gas and Oil Expense*   ACCOUNT NO.   *513*

DATE	ITEM	POST. REF.	DEBIT	CREDIT	BALANCE	
					DEBIT	CREDIT

ACCOUNT   *Utilities Expense*   ACCOUNT NO.   *514*

DATE	ITEM	POST. REF.	DEBIT	CREDIT	BALANCE	
					DEBIT	CREDIT

© 2013 Cengage Learning. All Rights Reserved. May not be scanned, copied, duplicated, or posted to a publicly accessible website, in whole or in part.

Problem 3-4A or 3-4B (concluded)

ACCOUNT NAME	DEBIT	CREDIT	

© 2013 Cengage Learning. All Rights Reserved. May not be scanned, copied, duplicated, or posted to a publicly accessible website, in whole or in part.

Problem 3-5A or 3-5B

GENERAL JOURNAL   PAGE _____

	DATE		DESCRIPTION	POST. REF.	DEBIT	CREDIT	
1							1
2							2
3							3
4							4
5							5
6							6
7							7
8							8
9							9
10							10
11							11
12							12
13							13
14							14
15							15
16							16
17							17
18							18
19							19
20							20
21							21
22							22
23							23
24							24
25							25
26							26
27							27
28							28
29							29
30							30
31							31
32							32
33							33
34							34
35							35
36							36
37							37
38							38
39							39
40							40
41							41

© 2013 Cengage Learning. All Rights Reserved. May not be scanned, copied, duplicated, or posted to a publicly accessible website, in whole or in part.

Problem 3-5A or 3-5B (continued)

GENERAL JOURNAL   PAGE _____

	DATE		DESCRIPTION	POST. REF.	DEBIT	CREDIT	
1							1
2							2
3							3
4							4
5							5
6							6
7							7
8							8
9							9
10							10
11							11
12							12
13							13
14							14
15							15
16							16
17							17
18							18
19							19
20							20
21							21
22							22
23							23
24							24
25							25
26							26
27							27
28							28
29							29
30							30
31							31
32							32
33							33
34							34
35							35
36							36
37							37
38							38
39							39
40							40
41							41

© 2013 Cengage Learning. All Rights Reserved. May not be scanned, copied, duplicated, or posted to a publicly accessible website, in whole or in part.

Problem 3-5A or 3-5B (continued)

GENERAL LEDGER

ACCOUNT _Cash_   ACCOUNT NO. _111_

DATE	ITEM	POST. REF.	DEBIT	CREDIT	BALANCE DEBIT	BALANCE CREDIT

ACCOUNT _Accounts Receivable_   ACCOUNT NO. _113_

DATE	ITEM	POST. REF.	DEBIT	CREDIT	BALANCE DEBIT	BALANCE CREDIT

ACCOUNT _Supplies_   ACCOUNT NO. _115_

DATE	ITEM	POST. REF.	DEBIT	CREDIT	BALANCE DEBIT	BALANCE CREDIT

ACCOUNT _Prepaid Insurance_   ACCOUNT NO. _117_

DATE	ITEM	POST. REF.	DEBIT	CREDIT	BALANCE DEBIT	BALANCE CREDIT

© 2013 Cengage Learning. All Rights Reserved. May not be scanned, copied, duplicated, or posted to a publicly accessible website, in whole or in part.

Problem 3-5A or 3-5B (continued)

ACCOUNT   *Office Furniture*   ACCOUNT NO.   *124*

DATE	ITEM	POST. REF.	DEBIT	CREDIT	BALANCE DEBIT	BALANCE CREDIT

ACCOUNT   *Accounts Payable*   ACCOUNT NO.   *221*

DATE	ITEM	POST. REF.	DEBIT	CREDIT	BALANCE DEBIT	BALANCE CREDIT

ACCOUNT   *, Capital*   ACCOUNT NO.   *311*

DATE	ITEM	POST. REF.	DEBIT	CREDIT	BALANCE DEBIT	BALANCE CREDIT

ACCOUNT   *, Drawing*   ACCOUNT NO.   *312*

DATE	ITEM	POST. REF.	DEBIT	CREDIT	BALANCE DEBIT	BALANCE CREDIT

ACCOUNT   *Professional Fees*   ACCOUNT NO.   *411*

DATE	ITEM	POST. REF.	DEBIT	CREDIT	BALANCE DEBIT	BALANCE CREDIT

© 2013 Cengage Learning. All Rights Reserved. May not be scanned, copied, duplicated, or posted to a publicly accessible website, in whole or in part.

Problem 3-5A or 3-5B (continued)

ACCOUNT ___Salary Expense_____   ACCOUNT NO. ___511___

DATE	ITEM	POST. REF.	DEBIT	CREDIT	BALANCE	
					DEBIT	CREDIT

ACCOUNT ___Rent Expense_____   ACCOUNT NO. ___512___

DATE	ITEM	POST. REF.	DEBIT	CREDIT	BALANCE	
					DEBIT	CREDIT

ACCOUNT ___Advertising Expense_____   ACCOUNT NO. ___513___

DATE	ITEM	POST. REF.	DEBIT	CREDIT	BALANCE	
					DEBIT	CREDIT

ACCOUNT ___Utilities Expense_____   ACCOUNT NO. ___514___

DATE	ITEM	POST. REF.	DEBIT	CREDIT	BALANCE	
					DEBIT	CREDIT

© 2013 Cengage Learning. All Rights Reserved. May not be scanned, copied, duplicated, or posted to a publicly accessible website, in whole or in part.

Problem 3-5A or 3-5B (continued)

ACCOUNT NAME	DEBIT	CREDIT

© 2013 Cengage Learning. All Rights Reserved. May not be scanned, copied, duplicated, or posted to a publicly accessible website, in whole or in part.

Problem 3-5A or 3-5B (concluded)

© 2013 Cengage Learning. All Rights Reserved. May not be scanned, copied, duplicated, or posted to a publicly accessible website, in whole or in part.

ALL ABOUT YOU SPA: Journalizing, Posting, and Preparing a Trial Balance

GENERAL JOURNAL   PAGE _____

	DATE		DESCRIPTION	POST. REF.	DEBIT	CREDIT	
1							1
2							2
3							3
4							4
5							5
6							6
7							7
8							8
9							9
10							10
11							11
12							12
13							13
14							14
15							15
16							16
17							17
18							18
19							19
20							20
21							21
22							22
23							23
24							24
25							25
26							26
27							27
28							28
29							29
30							30
31							31
32							32
33							33
34							34
35							35
36							36
37							37
38							38
39							39
40							40
41							41
42							42
43							43
44							44
45							45
46							46
47							47
48							48
49							49
50							50

© 2013 Cengage Learning. All Rights Reserved. May not be scanned, copied, duplicated, or posted to a publicly accessible website, in whole or in part.

ALL ABOUT YOU SPA (continued)

GENERAL JOURNAL   PAGE _____

	DATE	DESCRIPTION	POST. REF.	DEBIT	CREDIT	
1						1
2						2
3						3
4						4
5						5
6						6
7						7
8						8
9						9
10						10
11						11
12						12
13						13
14						14
15						15
16						16
17						17
18						18
19						19
20						20
21						21
22						22
23						23
24						24
25						25
26						26
27						27
28						28
29						29
30						30
31						31
32						32
33						33
34						34
35						35
36						36
37						37
38						38
39						39
40						40
41						41
42						42
43						43
44						44
45						45
46						46
47						47
48						48
49						49
50						50

© 2013 Cengage Learning. All Rights Reserved. May not be scanned, copied, duplicated, or posted to a publicly accessible website, in whole or in part.

ALL ABOUT YOU SPA (continued)

GENERAL JOURNAL   PAGE _____

	DATE	DESCRIPTION	POST. REF.	DEBIT	CREDIT	
1						1
2						2
3						3
4						4
5						5
6						6
7						7
8						8
9						9
10						10
11						11
12						12
13						13
14						14
15						15
16						16
17						17
18						18
19						19
20						20
21						21
22						22
23						23
24						24
25						25
26						26
27						27
28						28
29						29
30						30
31						31
32						32
33						33
34						34
35						35
36						36
37						37
38						38
39						39
40						40
41						41
42						42
43						43
44						44
45						45
46						46
47						47
48						48
49						49
50						50

© 2013 Cengage Learning. All Rights Reserved. May not be scanned, copied, duplicated, or posted to a publicly accessible website, in whole or in part.

ALL ABOUT YOU SPA (continued)

GENERAL LEDGER

ACCOUNT _Cash_   ACCOUNT NO. _111_

DATE	ITEM	POST. REF.	DEBIT	CREDIT	BALANCE DEBIT	CREDIT

ACCOUNT _Accounts Receivable_   ACCOUNT NO. _113_

DATE	ITEM	POST. REF.	DEBIT	CREDIT	BALANCE DEBIT	CREDIT

ACCOUNT _Office Supplies_   ACCOUNT NO. _114_

DATE	ITEM	POST. REF.	DEBIT	CREDIT	BALANCE DEBIT	CREDIT

© 2013 Cengage Learning. All Rights Reserved. May not be scanned, copied, duplicated, or posted to a publicly accessible website, in whole or in part.

ALL ABOUT YOU SPA (continued)

ACCOUNT   *Spa Supplies*   ACCOUNT NO.   *115*

DATE	ITEM	POST. REF.	DEBIT	CREDIT	BALANCE DEBIT	BALANCE CREDIT

ACCOUNT   *Prepaid Insurance*   ACCOUNT NO.   *117*

DATE	ITEM	POST. REF.	DEBIT	CREDIT	BALANCE DEBIT	BALANCE CREDIT

ACCOUNT   *Office Equipment*   ACCOUNT NO.   *124*

DATE	ITEM	POST. REF.	DEBIT	CREDIT	BALANCE DEBIT	BALANCE CREDIT

ACCOUNT   *Accumulated Depreciation, Office Equipment*   ACCOUNT NO.   *125*

DATE	ITEM	POST. REF.	DEBIT	CREDIT	BALANCE DEBIT	BALANCE CREDIT

ACCOUNT   *Spa Equipment*   ACCOUNT NO.   *128*

DATE	ITEM	POST. REF.	DEBIT	CREDIT	BALANCE DEBIT	BALANCE CREDIT

© 2013 Cengage Learning. All Rights Reserved. May not be scanned, copied, duplicated, or posted to a publicly accessible website, in whole or in part.

ALL ABOUT YOU SPA (continued)

ACCOUNT *Accumulated Depreciation, Spa Equipment*   ACCOUNT NO. *129*

DATE	ITEM	POST. REF.	DEBIT	CREDIT	BALANCE DEBIT	CREDIT

ACCOUNT *Accounts Payable*   ACCOUNT NO. *211*

DATE	ITEM	POST. REF.	DEBIT	CREDIT	BALANCE DEBIT	CREDIT

ACCOUNT *Wages Payable*   ACCOUNT NO. *212*

DATE	ITEM	POST. REF.	DEBIT	CREDIT	BALANCE DEBIT	CREDIT

ACCOUNT *A. Valli, Capital*   ACCOUNT NO. *311*

DATE	ITEM	POST. REF.	DEBIT	CREDIT	BALANCE DEBIT	CREDIT

ACCOUNT *A. Valli, Drawing*   ACCOUNT NO. *312*

DATE	ITEM	POST. REF.	DEBIT	CREDIT	BALANCE DEBIT	CREDIT

© 2013 Cengage Learning. All Rights Reserved. May not be scanned, copied, duplicated, or posted to a publicly accessible website, in whole or in part.

ALL ABOUT YOU SPA (continued)

ACCOUNT *Income Summary*   ACCOUNT NO.   *313*

DATE		ITEM	POST. REF.	DEBIT	CREDIT	BALANCE	
						DEBIT	CREDIT

ACCOUNT *Income from Services*   ACCOUNT NO.   *411*

DATE		ITEM	POST. REF.	DEBIT	CREDIT	BALANCE	
						DEBIT	CREDIT

ACCOUNT *Wages Expense*   ACCOUNT NO.   *611*

DATE		ITEM	POST. REF.	DEBIT	CREDIT	BALANCE	
						DEBIT	CREDIT

ACCOUNT *Rent Expense*   ACCOUNT NO.   *612*

DATE		ITEM	POST. REF.	DEBIT	CREDIT	BALANCE	
						DEBIT	CREDIT

© 2013 Cengage Learning. All Rights Reserved. May not be scanned, copied, duplicated, or posted to a publicly accessible website, in whole or in part.

ALL ABOUT YOU SPA (continued)

ACCOUNT *Office Supplies Expense*   ACCOUNT NO. *613*

DATE	ITEM	POST. REF.	DEBIT	CREDIT	BALANCE DEBIT	BALANCE CREDIT

ACCOUNT *Spa Supplies Expense*   ACCOUNT NO. *614*

DATE	ITEM	POST. REF.	DEBIT	CREDIT	BALANCE DEBIT	BALANCE CREDIT

ACCOUNT *Laundry Expense*   ACCOUNT NO. *615*

DATE	ITEM	POST. REF.	DEBIT	CREDIT	BALANCE DEBIT	BALANCE CREDIT

ACCOUNT *Advertising Expense*   ACCOUNT NO. *616*

DATE	ITEM	POST. REF.	DEBIT	CREDIT	BALANCE DEBIT	BALANCE CREDIT

ACCOUNT *Utilities Expense*   ACCOUNT NO. *617*

DATE	ITEM	POST. REF.	DEBIT	CREDIT	BALANCE DEBIT	BALANCE CREDIT

© 2013 Cengage Learning. All Rights Reserved. May not be scanned, copied, duplicated, or posted to a publicly accessible website, in whole or in part.

ALL ABOUT YOU SPA (continued)

ACCOUNT   *Insurance Expense*   ACCOUNT NO.   *618*

DATE	ITEM	POST. REF.	DEBIT	CREDIT	BALANCE	
					DEBIT	CREDIT

ACCOUNT   *Depreciation Expense, Office Equipment*   ACCOUNT NO.   *619*

DATE	ITEM	POST. REF.	DEBIT	CREDIT	BALANCE	
					DEBIT	CREDIT

ACCOUNT   *Depreciation Expense, Spa Equipment*   ACCOUNT NO.   *620*

DATE	ITEM	POST. REF.	DEBIT	CREDIT	BALANCE	
					DEBIT	CREDIT

ACCOUNT   *Miscellaneous Expense*   ACCOUNT NO.   *630*

DATE	ITEM	POST. REF.	DEBIT	CREDIT	BALANCE	
					DEBIT	CREDIT

© 2013 Cengage Learning. All Rights Reserved. May not be scanned, copied, duplicated, or posted to a publicly accessible website, in whole or in part.

ALL ABOUT YOU SPA (continued)

ACCOUNT NAME	DEBIT	CREDIT

© 2013 Cengage Learning. All Rights Reserved. May not be scanned, copied, duplicated, or posted to a publicly accessible website, in whole or in part.

ALL ABOUT YOU SPA (concluded)

© 2013 Cengage Learning. All Rights Reserved. May not be scanned, copied, duplicated, or posted to a publicly accessible website, in whole or in part.

Continuing Problem: Chapter 4

ALL ABOUT YOU SPA: Work Sheet and Adjusting Entries

	ACCOUNT NAME	TRIAL BALANCE		ADJUSTMENTS	
		DEBIT	CREDIT	DEBIT	CREDIT
1					
2					
3					
4					
5					
6					
7					
8					
9					
10					
11					
12					
13					
14					
15					
16					
17					
18					
19					
20					
21					
22					
23					
24					
25					
26					
27					
28					
29					
30					
31					
32					
33					
34					
35					
36					
37					
38					
39					
40					
41					

© 2013 Cengage Learning. All Rights Reserved. May not be scanned, copied, duplicated, or posted to a publicly accessible website, in whole or in part.

ALL ABOUT YOU SPA (continued)

		ADJUSTED TRIAL BALANCE		INCOME STATEMENT		BALANCE SHEET		
		DEBIT	CREDIT	DEBIT	CREDIT	DEBIT	CREDIT	

(Lines numbered 1 through 41, all blank)

© 2013 Cengage Learning. All Rights Reserved. May not be scanned, copied, duplicated, or posted to a publicly accessible website, in whole or in part.

ALL ABOUT YOU SPA: Adjustments

GENERAL JOURNAL   PAGE _____

	DATE		DESCRIPTION	POST. REF.	DEBIT	CREDIT	
1							1
2							2
3							3
4							4
5							5
6							6
7							7
8							8
9							9
10							10
11							11
12							12
13							13
14							14
15							15
16							16
17							17
18							18
19							19
20							20
21							21
22							22
23							23
24							24
25							25
26							26
27							27
28							28
29							29
30							30
31							31

© 2013 Cengage Learning. All Rights Reserved. May not be scanned, copied, duplicated, or posted to a publicly accessible website, in whole or in part.

ALL ABOUT YOU SPA (continued)

ACCOUNT NAME	DEBIT	CREDIT	

© 2013 Cengage Learning. All Rights Reserved. May not be scanned, copied, duplicated, or posted to a publicly accessible website, in whole or in part.

ALL ABOUT YOU SPA (continued)

© 2013 Cengage Learning. All Rights Reserved. May not be scanned, copied, duplicated, or posted to a publicly accessible website, in whole or in part.

ALL ABOUT YOU SPA (concluded)

© 2013 Cengage Learning. All Rights Reserved. May not be scanned, copied, duplicated, or posted to a publicly accessible website, in whole or in part.

ALL ABOUT YOU SPA: Closing Entries

GENERAL JOURNAL   PAGE _____

	DATE		DESCRIPTION	POST. REF.	DEBIT	CREDIT	
1							1
2							2
3							3
4							4
5							5
6							6
7							7
8							8
9							9
10							10
11							11
12							12
13							13
14							14
15							15
16							16
17							17
18							18
19							19
20							20
21							21
22							22
23							23
24							24
25							25
26							26

© 2013 Cengage Learning. All Rights Reserved. May not be scanned, copied, duplicated, or posted to a publicly accessible website, in whole or in part.

ALL ABOUT YOU SPA (concluded)

ACCOUNT NAME	DEBIT	CREDIT

© 2013 Cengage Learning. All Rights Reserved. May not be scanned, copied, duplicated, or posted to a publicly accessible website, in whole or in part.

Answers to Study Guide Questions

CHAPTER 3

PART 1   True/False

1.	F	7.	F
2.	F	8.	T
3.	F	9.	T
4.	F	10.	F
5.	T	11.	T
6.	T		

PART 2   Completion—Accounting Language

1. general ledger
2. posting
3. source documents
4. cost principle
5. journalizing
6. Post. Ref. column of the journal
7. correcting entry method

PART 3   Completing a Journal Entry

GENERAL JOURNAL   PAGE ____*33*____

	DATE		DESCRIPTION	POST. REF.	DEBIT	CREDIT	
1	*20—*						1
2	*Oct.*	*29*	*Cash*	*111*	*1,100.00*		2
3			*Accounts Receivable*	*113*	*600.00*		3
4			*Income from Services*	*411*		*1,700.00*	4
5			*Received partial payment for*				5
6			*services performed.*				6
7							7
8							8
9							9

1. $600 ($1,700 − $1,100)
2. $2,800 ($600 + $1,100 + $1,100)
3. $1,300 ($700 + $400 + $200)
4. compound

© 2013 Cengage Learning. All Rights Reserved. May not be scanned, copied, duplicated, or posted to a publicly accessible website, in whole or in part.

Adjusting Entries and the Work Sheet

LEARNING OBJECTIVES

1. Define *fiscal period* and *fiscal year* and explain the accounting cycle.

2. List the classifications of the accounts that occupy each column of a ten-column work sheet.

3. Complete a work sheet for a service enterprise, involving adjustments for supplies, expired insurance, depreciation, and accrued wages.

4. Journalize and post the adjusting entries.

5. Prepare an income statement, a statement of owner's equity, and a balance sheet for a service business directly from the work sheet.

6. Prepare (a) an income statement involving more than one revenue account and a net loss, (b) a statement of owner's equity with an additional investment and either a net income or a net loss, and (c) a balance sheet for a business having more than one accumulated depreciation account.

ACCOUNTING LANGUAGE

Accounting cycle	Depreciation
Accrual	Fiscal period
Accrued wages	Fiscal year
Adjusting entries	Matching principle
Adjustments	Mixed accounts
Book value (carrying value)	Straight-line depreciation
Contra account	Work sheet

STUDY GUIDE QUESTIONS

PART 1   True/False

For each of the following statements, circle T if the statement is true and F if the statement is false.

T   F   1. Adjusting entries recorded on a work sheet also must be journalized.

T   F   2. Each adjusting entry involves both an income statement account and a balance sheet account.

T   F   3. The book value of an asset is always equal to the asset's true market value.

T   F   4. The purpose of a work sheet is to enable the accountant to prepare the financial statements.

T   F   5. The cost of insurance used will appear in the Adjustments Debit column, the Adjusted Trial Balance Debit column, and the Income Statement Debit column.

© 2013 Cengage Learning. All Rights Reserved. May not be scanned, copied, duplicated, or posted to a publicly accessible website, in whole or in part.

T   F   6.   The normal balance of Accumulated Depreciation, Equipment, is on the credit side.

T   F   7.   The purpose of depreciating an asset is to spread out the cost of the asset over its useful life.

T   F   8.   The purpose of adjustments is to correct account amounts that do not reflect such things as depreciation, wages payable, or insurance expired.

T   F   9.   If the total of the Income Statement Debit column is larger than the total of the Income Statement Credit column, the company must have a net income.

T   F   10. Accrued wages represent wages that have been incurred but have not yet been recorded.

PART 2   Completion—Accounting Language

Complete each of the following statements by writing the appropriate words in the spaces provided.

1.   The cost of an asset less the accumulated depreciation is called the _____

_____.

2.   The time span that covers a company's accounting cycle is called its _____

_____.

3.   Since the plus and minus signs on Accumulated Depreciation, Equipment, are the opposite of the signs on Equipment, the Accumulated Depreciation, Equipment, account is called a(n) _____ account.

4.   Internal transactions that are used to bring the ledger accounts up to date are called

_____.

5.   The amount of unpaid wages owed to employees for the time between the last payday and the end of the fiscal period is called _____.

6.   The _____ represents the steps in the accounting process that are completed during the fiscal period.

7.   The Prepaid Insurance account is called a(n) _____ because its balance in the Trial Balance column of a work sheet consists partly of an income statement amount and partly of a balance sheet amount.

8.   The _____ requires that the expenses of one period must be related to the revenue of the same period.

9.   The term representing loss in usefulness of assets is _____.

10. _____ allocates the cost of an asset, less any trade-in value, evenly over the useful life of the asset.

© 2013 Cengage Learning. All Rights Reserved. May not be scanned, copied, duplicated, or posted to a publicly accessible website, in whole or in part.

PART 3   Adjusting Entries

Record the adjusting entries directly in the T accounts, and label the other account.

1. Accrued wages, $550.

	Wages Expense				
Bal.	8,100				

2. Additional depreciation, $1,500.

	Accumulated Depreciation, Equipment				
		Bal.	6,750		

3. Insurance expired, $310.

	Prepaid Insurance				
Bal.	950				

4. Supplies used, $900.

	Supplies				
Bal.	3,000				

© 2013 Cengage Learning. All Rights Reserved. May not be scanned, copied, duplicated, or posted to a publicly accessible website, in whole or in part.

PART 4   Analyzing the Work Sheet

Carry the balances forward from the Trial Balance columns to the appropriate column.
The first account is provided as an example.

ACCOUNT NAME	TRIAL BALANCE		ADJUSTMENTS		ADJUSTED TRIAL BALANCE		INCOME STATEMENT		BALANCE SHEET	
	DEBIT	CREDIT	DEBIT	CREDIT	DEBIT	CREDIT	DEBIT	CREDIT	DEBIT	CREDIT
0. *Equipment*	X				X				X	
1. Cash	X									
2. C. Tumi, Capital		X								
3. Advertising Expense	X									
4. Accounts Receivable	X									
5. Wages Expense	X									
6. Accumulated Depreciation, Equipment		X								
7. Wages Payable										
8. C. Tumi, Drawing	X									
9. Service Revenue		X								
10. Supplies	X									
11. Depreciation Expense, Equipment										

© 2013 Cengage Learning. All Rights Reserved. May not be scanned, copied, duplicated, or posted to a publicly accessible website, in whole or in part.

DEMONSTRATION PROBLEM

The general ledger of Rose Carpenters contains the following account balances for the year ended December 31.

Cash	$ 2,560	H. Rose, Drawing	$60,000
Accounts Receivable	7,428	Income from Services	89,845
Supplies	1,218	Wages Expense	21,500
Prepaid Insurance	960	Rent Expense	4,800
Equipment	4,270	Supplies Expense	0
Accumulated Depreciation, Equipment	1,230	Advertising Expense	1,216
Truck	21,550	Utilities Expense	1,344
Accumulated Depreciation, Truck	4,310	Insurance Expense	0
Accounts Payable	426	Depreciation Expense, Equipment	0
Wages Payable	0	Depreciation Expense, Truck	0
H. Rose, Capital	31,314	Miscellaneous Expense	279

Since the firm has been in operation for longer than a year, Accumulated Depreciation, Equipment, and Accumulated Depreciation, Truck, have balances that should be included on the trial balance.

Data for the year-end adjustments are as follows:

a. Wages accrued at December 31, $448.

b. Insurance expired during the year, $768.

c. Depreciation of equipment during the year, $854.

d. Depreciation of truck during the year, $4,310.

e. Supplies remaining at the end of the year, $430.

Instructions

1. Prepare the year-end work sheet for Rose Carpenters.

2. Journalize the adjusting entries.

3. Prepare the financial statements.

© 2013 Cengage Learning. All Rights Reserved. May not be scanned, copied, duplicated, or posted to a publicly accessible website, in whole or in part.

SOLUTION

		TRIAL BALANCE		ADJUSTMENTS	
		DEBIT	CREDIT	DEBIT	CREDIT
	Rose Carpenters				
	Work Sheet				
	For Year Ended December 31, 20—				

	ACCOUNT NAME	DEBIT	CREDIT	DEBIT	CREDIT
7	Cash	2,560.00			
8	Accounts Receivable	7,428.00			
9	Supplies	1,218.00			(e) 788.00
10	Prepaid Insurance	960.00			(b) 768.00
11	Equipment	4,270.00			
12	Accumulated Depreciation, Equipment		1,230.00		(c) 854.00
13	Truck	21,550.00			
14	Accumulated Depreciation, Truck		4,310.00		(d) 4,310.00
15	Accounts Payable		426.00		
16	H. Rose, Capital		31,314.00		
17	H. Rose, Drawing	60,000.00			
18	Income from Services		89,845.00		
19	Wages Expense	21,500.00		(a) 448.00	
20	Rent Expense	4,800.00			
21	Advertising Expense	1,216.00			
22	Utilities Expense	1,344.00			
23	Miscellaneous Expense	279.00			
24		127,125.00	127,125.00		
25	Wages Payable				(a) 448.00
26	Insurance Expense			(b) 768.00	
27	Depreciation Expense, Equipment			(c) 854.00	
28	Depreciation Expense, Truck			(d) 4,310.00	
29	Supplies Expense			(e) 788.00	
30				7,168.00	7,168.00
31	Net Income				
32					
33					
34					
35					
36					
37					
38					
39					
40					
41					
42					
43					
44					
45					

© 2013 Cengage Learning. All Rights Reserved. May not be scanned, copied, duplicated, or posted to a publicly accessible website, in whole or in part.

SOLUTION (continued)

ADJUSTED TRIAL BALANCE		INCOME STATEMENT		BALANCE SHEET		
DEBIT	CREDIT	DEBIT	CREDIT	DEBIT	CREDIT	
2,560.00				2,560.00		7
7,428.00				7,428.00		8
430.00				430.00		9
192.00				192.00		10
4,270.00				4,270.00		11
	2,084.00				2,084.00	12
21,550.00				21,550.00		13
	8,620.00				8,620.00	14
	426.00				426.00	15
	31,314.00				31,314.00	16
60,000.00				60,000.00		17
	89,845.00		89,845.00			18
21,948.00		21,948.00				19
4,800.00		4,800.00				20
1,216.00		1,216.00				21
1,344.00		1,344.00				22
279.00		279.00				23
						24
	448.00				448.00	25
768.00		768.00				26
854.00		854.00				27
4,310.00		4,310.00				28
788.00		788.00				29
132,737.00	132,737.00	36,307.00	89,845.00	96,430.00	42,892.00	30
		53,538.00			53,538.00	31
		89,845.00	89,845.00	96,430.00	96,430.00	32

© 2013 Cengage Learning. All Rights Reserved. May not be scanned, copied, duplicated, or posted to a publicly accessible website, in whole or in part.

SOLUTION (continued)

GENERAL JOURNAL   PAGE _____

	DATE		DESCRIPTION	POST. REF.	DEBIT	CREDIT	
1	20—		*Adjusting Entries*				1
2	Dec.	31	Wages Expense		448.00		2
3			Wages Payable			448.00	3
4							4
5		31	Insurance Expense		768.00		5
6			Prepaid Insurance			768.00	6
7							7
8		31	Depreciation Expense, Equipment		854.00		8
9			Accum. Depr., Equipment			854.00	9
10							10
11		31	Depreciation Expense, Truck		4,310.00		11
12			Accumulated Depreciation, Truck			4,310.00	12
13							13
14		31	Supplies Expense		788.00		14
15			Supplies			788.00	15
16							16
17							17
18							18
19							19
20							20
21							21
22							22
23							23
24							24
25							25
26							26
27							27
28							28
29							29
30							30
31							31
32							32

© 2013 Cengage Learning. All Rights Reserved. May not be scanned, copied, duplicated, or posted to a publicly accessible website, in whole or in part.

SOLUTION (continued)

Rose Carpenters
Income Statement
For Month Ended December 31, 20—

Revenue:		
Income from Services	$89,845	
Total Revenue		$89,845
Expenses:		
Wages Expense	$21,948	
Rent Expense	4,800	
Advertising Expense	1,216	
Utilities Expense	1,344	
Insurance Expense	768	
Depreciation Expense, Equipment	854	
Depreciation Expense, Truck	4,310	
Supplies Expense	788	
Miscellaneous Expense	279	
Total Expenses		36,307
Net Income		$53,538

Rose Carpenters
Statement of Owner's Equity
For Month Ended December 31, 20—

H. Rose, Capital, January 1, 20—		$31,314
Investment during the year	$ 0	
Net Income for the year	53,538	
Subtotal	$53,538	
Less Withdrawals for the year	60,000	
Decrease in Capital		(6,462)
H. Rose, Capital, December 31, 20—		$24,852

© 2013 Cengage Learning. All Rights Reserved. May not be scanned, copied, duplicated, or posted to a publicly accessible website, in whole or in part.

SOLUTION (continued)

Rose Carpenters
Balance Sheet
December 31, 20—

Assets			
Cash		$ 2,560	
Accounts Receivable		7,428	
Supplies		430	
Prepaid Insurance		192	
Equipment	$ 4,270		
Less Accumulated Depreciation	2,084	2,186	
Equipment	$21,550		
Less Accumulated Depreciation	8,620	12,930	
Total Assets		$25,726	
Liabilities			
Accounts Payable	$ 426		
Wages Payable	448		
Total Liabilities		$ 874	
Owner's Equity			
H. Rose, Capital		24,852	
Total Liabilities and Owner's Equity		$25,726	

© 2013 Cengage Learning. All Rights Reserved. May not be scanned, copied, duplicated, or posted to a publicly accessible website, in whole or in part.

EXERCISES AND PROBLEMS

Exercise 4-1

TRIAL BALANCE		ADJUSTED TRIAL BALANCE		INCOME STATEMENT		BALANCE SHEET	
DEBIT	CREDIT	DEBIT	CREDIT	DEBIT	CREDIT	DEBIT	CREDIT
Assets		*Assets*				*Assets*	

Exercise 4-2

ACCOUNT	CLASSIFICATION	NORMAL BALANCE	INCOME STATEMENT (IS) OR BALANCE SHEET (BS) COLUMNS
0. Example: Wages Expense	E	Debit	IS
a. Prepaid Insurance			
b. Accounts Payable			
c. Wages Payable			
d. T. Bristol, Capital			
e. Accumulated Depreciation, Building			
f. T. Bristol, Drawing			
g. Rental Income			
h. Equipment			
i. Depreciation Expense, Equipment			
j. Supplies Expense			

© 2013 Cengage Learning. All Rights Reserved. May not be scanned, copied, duplicated, or posted to a publicly accessible website, in whole or in part.

Exercise 4-3

	Account Name (in trial balance order)	Reason for Adjusting This Account
a.	_____	_____
b.	_____	_____
c.	_____	_____
d.	_____	_____
e.	_____	_____
f.	_____	_____
g.	_____	_____
h.	_____	_____

Exercise 4-4

	ACCOUNT NAME	TRIAL BALANCE DEBIT	TRIAL BALANCE CREDIT	ADJUSTMENTS DEBIT	ADJUSTMENTS CREDIT
1					
2					
3					
4					
7	Cash	4,370.00			
8	Supplies	250.00			
9	Prepaid Insurance	1,800.00			
10	Equipment	4,880.00			
11	Accum. Depr., Equipment		1,350.00		
12	Accounts Payable		2,539.00		
13	M. Benson, Capital		4,544.00		
14	M. Benson, Drawing	2,000.00			
15	Income from Services		6,937.00		
16	Rent Expense	1,086.00			
17	Supplies Expense	256.00			
18	Wages Expense	660.00			
19	Miscellaneous Expense	68.00			
20		15,370.00	15,370.00		

© 2013 Cengage Learning. All Rights Reserved. May not be scanned, copied, duplicated, or posted to a publicly accessible website, in whole or in part.

Exercise 4-5

	ACCOUNT NAME	TRIAL BALANCE		ADJUSTMENTS		ADJUSTED TRIAL BALANCE	
		DEBIT	CREDIT	DEBIT	CREDIT	DEBIT	CREDIT
1							
2							
3							
4							
7	Cash	5,190.00					
8	Supplies	430.00					
9	Prepaid Insurance	1,200.00					
10	Equipment	4,678.00					
11	Accum. Depr., Equipment		1,556.00				
12	Accounts Payable		1,875.00				
13	S. Ramey, Capital		6,026.00				
14	S. Ramey, Drawing	1,700.00					
15	Service Fees		5,836.00				
16	Rent Expense	965.00					
17	Supplies Expense	267.00					
18	Wages Expense	765.00					
19	Miscellaneous Expense	98.00					
20		15,293.00	15,293.00				
21							
22							
23							
24							
25							
26							
27							
28							
29							
30							
31							
32							
33							
34							
35							
36							
37							
38							
39							
40							
41							

© 2013 Cengage Learning. All Rights Reserved. May not be scanned, copied, duplicated, or posted to a publicly accessible website, in whole or in part.

Exercise 4-6

	DATE		DESCRIPTION	POST. REF.	DEBIT	CREDIT	
1							1
2							2
3							3
4							4
5							5
6							6
7							7
8							8
9							9
10							10
11							11
12							12
13							13
14							14
15							15
16							16
17							17

Exercise 4-7

	DATE		DESCRIPTION	POST. REF.	DEBIT	CREDIT	
1							1
2							2
3							3
4							4
5							5
6							6
7							7
8							8
9							9
10							10
11							11
12							12
13							13
14							14
15							15
16							16
17							17

© 2013 Cengage Learning. All Rights Reserved. May not be scanned, copied, duplicated, or posted to a publicly accessible website, in whole or in part.

Exercise 4-8

	DATE		DESCRIPTION	POST. REF.	DEBIT	CREDIT	
1							1
2							2
3							3
4							4
5							5
6							6
7							7
8							8
9							9
10							10
11							11
12							12
13							13
14							14
15							15
16							16
17							17

Exercise 4-9

	Account	Financial Statement		Account	Financial Statement
a.			g.		
b.			h.		
c.			i.		
d.			j.		
e.			k.		
f.			l.		

© 2013 Cengage Learning. All Rights Reserved. May not be scanned, copied, duplicated, or posted to a publicly accessible website, in whole or in part.

Problem 4-1A or 4-1B

	ACCOUNT NAME	TRIAL BALANCE		ADJUSTMENTS	
		DEBIT	CREDIT	DEBIT	CREDIT
1					
2					
3					
4					
5					
6					
7	Cash				
8	Accounts Receivable				
9	Supplies				
10	Prepaid Insurance				
11	Office Equipment				
12	Accounts Payable				
13	, Capital				
14	, Drawing				
15	Commissions Earned				
16	Rent Expense				
17	Travel Expense				
18	Utilities Expense				
19	Miscellaneous Expense				
20					
21					
22					
23					
24					
25					
26					
27					
28					
29					
30					
31					
32					
33					
34					
35					
36					
37					
38					
39					
40					
41					
42					

© 2013 Cengage Learning. All Rights Reserved. May not be scanned, copied, duplicated, or posted to a publicly accessible website, in whole or in part.

Problem 4-1A or 4-1B (concluded)

		ADJUSTED TRIAL BALANCE		INCOME STATEMENT		BALANCE SHEET	
		DEBIT	CREDIT	DEBIT	CREDIT	DEBIT	CREDIT
1							
2							
3							
4							
5							
6							
7							
8							
9							
10							
11							
12							
13							
14							
15							
16							
17							
18							
19							
20							
21							
22							
23							
24							
25							
26							
27							
28							
29							
30							
31							
32							
33							
34							
35							
36							
37							
38							
39							
40							
41							
42							

© 2013 Cengage Learning. All Rights Reserved. May not be scanned, copied, duplicated, or posted to a publicly accessible website, in whole or in part.

Problem 4-2A or 4-2B

	ACCOUNT NAME	TRIAL BALANCE		ADJUSTMENTS	
		DEBIT	CREDIT	DEBIT	CREDIT
1					
2					
3					
4					
7	Cash				
8	Supplies				
9	Prepaid Insurance				
10	Equipment				
11	Accum. Depr., Equipment				
12	Accounts Payable				
13	, Capital				
14	, Drawing				
15	Income from Services				
16	Wages Expense				
17	Rent Expense				
18	Utilities Expense				
19	Telephone Expense				
20	Miscellaneous Expense				
21					
22					
23					
24					
25					
26					
27					
28					
29					
30					
31					
32					
33					
34					
35					
36					
37					
38					
39					
40					
41					
42					

© 2013 Cengage Learning. All Rights Reserved. May not be scanned, copied, duplicated, or posted to a publicly accessible website, in whole or in part.

Problem 4-2A or 4-2B (continued)

	ADJUSTED TRIAL BALANCE		INCOME STATEMENT		BALANCE SHEET	
	DEBIT	CREDIT	DEBIT	CREDIT	DEBIT	CREDIT

Problem 4-2A or 4-2B (concluded)

GENERAL JOURNAL   PAGE _____

	DATE		DESCRIPTION	POST. REF.	DEBIT	CREDIT	
1							1
2							2
3							3
4							4
5							5
6							6
7							7
8							8
9							9
10							10
11							11
12							12
13							13
14							14
15							15
16							16
17							17
18							18
19							19
20							20
21							21
22							22
23							23
24							24
25							25
26							26
27							27
28							28
29							29
30							30
31							31
32							32
33							33
34							34
35							35
36							36
37							37
38							38

© 2013 Cengage Learning. All Rights Reserved. May not be scanned, copied, duplicated, or posted to a publicly accessible website, in whole or in part.

Extra Form

GENERAL JOURNAL

PAGE _____

	DATE		DESCRIPTION	POST. REF.	DEBIT	CREDIT	
1							1
2							2
3							3
4							4
5							5
6							6
7							7
8							8
9							9
10							10
11							11
12							12
13							13
14							14
15							15
16							16
17							17
18							18
19							19
20							20
21							21
22							22
23							23
24							24
25							25
26							26
27							27
28							28
29							29
30							30
31							31
32							32
33							33
34							34
35							35
36							36
37							37
38							38

© 2013 Cengage Learning. All Rights Reserved. May not be scanned, copied, duplicated, or posted to a publicly accessible website, in whole or in part.

Problem 4-3A

	ACCOUNT NAME	TRIAL BALANCE DEBIT	TRIAL BALANCE CREDIT	ADJUSTMENTS DEBIT	ADJUSTMENTS CREDIT
1					*Chelsey Decorators*
2					*Work Sheet*
3					*For Month Ended March 31, 20—*
4					
5		TRIAL BALANCE		ADJUSTMENTS	
6	ACCOUNT NAME	DEBIT	CREDIT	DEBIT	CREDIT
7	Cash	6,230.00			
8	Supplies	532.00			(f) 180.00
9	Prepaid Insurance	1,248.00			(a) 260.00
10	Equipment	6,285.00			
11	Accum. Depr., Equipment		3,520.00		(b) 600.00
12	Office Furniture	3,680.00			
13	Accum. Depr., Office Furniture		2,816.00		(c) 470.00
14	Truck	23,799.00			
15	Accum. Depr., Truck		18,163.00		(d) 762.00
16	Accounts Payable		2,623.00		
17	D. Chelsey, Capital		10,672.00		
18	D. Chelsey, Drawing	3,500.00			
19	Professional Fees		12,589.00		
20	Salary Expense	2,455.00		(e) 480.00	
21	Rent Expense	1,325.00			
22	Travel Expense	398.00			
23	Utilities Expense	196.00			
24	Advertising Expense	590.00			
25	Miscellaneous Expense	145.00			
26		50,383.00	50,383.00		
27	Insurance Expense			(a) 260.00	
28	Depr. Exp., Equipment			(b) 600.00	
29	Depr. Exp., Office Furniture			(c) 470.00	
30	Depr. Exp., Truck			(d) 762.00	
31	Salaries Payable				(e) 480.00
32	Supplies Expense			(f) 180.00	
33				2,752.00	2,752.00
34	Net Income				
35					
36					
37					
38					
39					
40					
41					

© 2013 Cengage Learning. All Rights Reserved. May not be scanned, copied, duplicated, or posted to a publicly accessible website, in whole or in part.

Problem 4-3A (continued)

		ADJUSTED TRIAL BALANCE		INCOME STATEMENT		BALANCE SHEET		
		DEBIT	CREDIT	DEBIT	CREDIT	DEBIT	CREDIT	
		6,230.00				6,230.00		7
		352.00				352.00		8
		988.00				988.00		9
		6,285.00				6,285.00		10
			4,120.00				4,120.00	11
		3,680.00				3,680.00		12
			3,286.00				3,286.00	13
		23,799.00				23,799.00		14
			18,925.00				18,925.00	15
			2,623.00				2,623.00	16
			10,672.00				10,672.00	17
		3,500.00				3,500.00		18
			12,589.00		12,589.00			19
		2,935.00		2,935.00				20
		1,325.00		1,325.00				21
		398.00		398.00				22
		196.00		196.00				23
		590.00		590.00				24
		145.00		145.00				25
								26
		260.00		260.00				27
		600.00		600.00				28
		470.00		470.00				29
		762.00		762.00				30
			480.00				480.00	31
		180.00		180.00				32
		52,695.00	52,695.00	7,861.00	12,589.00	44,834.00	40,106.00	33
				4,728.00			4,728.00	34
				12,589.00	12,589.00	44,834.00	44,834.00	35
								36
								37
								38
								39
								40
								41

© 2013 Cengage Learning. All Rights Reserved. May not be scanned, copied, duplicated, or posted to a publicly accessible website, in whole or in part.

Problem 4-3A (continued)

GENERAL JOURNAL   PAGE _____

	DATE	DESCRIPTION	POST. REF.	DEBIT	CREDIT	
1						1
2						2
3						3
4						4
5						5
6						6
7						7
8						8
9						9
10						10
11						11
12						12
13						13
14						14
15						15
16						16
17						17
18						18
19						19
20						20
21						21
22						22
23						23
24						24
25						25
26						26
27						27
28						28
29						29
30						30
31						31
32						32
33						33
34						34
35						35
36						36
37						37

© 2013 Cengage Learning. All Rights Reserved. May not be scanned, copied, duplicated, or posted to a publicly accessible website, in whole or in part.

Problem 4-3A (continued)

© 2013 Cengage Learning. All Rights Reserved. May not be scanned, copied, duplicated, or posted to a publicly accessible website, in whole or in part.

Problem 4-3A (continued)

© 2013 Cengage Learning. All Rights Reserved. May not be scanned, copied, duplicated, or posted to a publicly accessible website, in whole or in part.

Problem 4-3A (concluded)

© 2013 Cengage Learning. All Rights Reserved. May not be scanned, copied, duplicated, or posted to a publicly accessible website, in whole or in part.

Problem 4-3B

	ACCOUNT NAME	TRIAL BALANCE DEBIT	TRIAL BALANCE CREDIT	ADJUSTMENTS DEBIT		ADJUSTMENTS CREDIT	
1					*Juarez Design*		
2					*Work Sheet*		
3					*For Month Ended March 31, 20—*		
7	Cash	4,587.00					
8	Supplies	480.00				(f)	300.00
9	Prepaid Insurance	1,860.00				(a)	155.00
10	Design Furnishings	13,824.00					
11	Accum. Depr., Design Furnishings		12,782.00			(b)	510.00
12	Office Furniture	5,673.00					
13	Accum. Depr., Office Furniture		1,684.00			(c)	370.00
14	Truck	24,394.00					
15	Accum. Depr., Truck		12,375.00			(d)	645.00
16	Accounts Payable		2,264.00				
17	T. Juarez, Capital		14,300.00				
18	T. Juarez, Drawing	2,400.00					
19	Professional Fees		16,282.00				
20	Salary Expense	2,267.00		(e)	450.00		
21	Rent Expense	1,864.00					
22	Utilities Expense	434.00					
23	Advertising Expense	942.00					
24	Travel Expense	840.00					
25	Miscellaneous Expense	122.00					
26		59,687.00	59,687.00				
27	Insurance Expense			(a)	155.00		
28	Depr. Exp., Design Furnishings			(b)	510.00		
29	Depr. Exp., Office Furniture			(c)	370.00		
30	Depr. Exp., Truck			(d)	645.00		
31	Salaries Payable					(e)	450.00
32	Supplies Expense			(f)	300.00		
33					2,430.00		2,430.00
34	Net Income						

© 2013 Cengage Learning. All Rights Reserved. May not be scanned, copied, duplicated, or posted to a publicly accessible website, in whole or in part.

Problem 4-3B (continued)

	ADJUSTED TRIAL BALANCE		INCOME STATEMENT		BALANCE SHEET	
	DEBIT	CREDIT	DEBIT	CREDIT	DEBIT	CREDIT
7	4,587.00				4,587.00	
8	180.00				180.00	
9	1,705.00				1,705.00	
10	13,824.00				13,824.00	
11		13,292.00				13,292.00
12	5,673.00				5,673.00	
13		2,054.00				2,054.00
14	24,394.00				24,394.00	
15		13,020.00				13,020.00
16		2,264.00				2,264.00
17		14,300.00				14,300.00
18	2,400.00				2,400.00	
19		16,282.00		16,282.00		
20	2,717.00		2,717.00			
21	1,864.00		1,864.00			
22	434.00		434.00			
23	942.00		942.00			
24	840.00		840.00			
25	122.00		122.00			
26						
27	155.00		155.00			
28	510.00		510.00			
29	370.00		370.00			
30	645.00		645.00			
31		450.00				450.00
32	300.00		300.00			
33	61,662.00	61,662.00	8,899.00	16,282.00	52,763.00	45,380.00
34			7,383.00			7,383.00
35			16,282.00	16,282.00	52,763.00	52,763.00
36						
37						
38						
39						
40						
41						

© 2013 Cengage Learning. All Rights Reserved. May not be scanned, copied, duplicated, or posted to a publicly accessible website, in whole or in part.

Problem 4-3B (continued)

GENERAL JOURNAL   PAGE _____

	DATE		DESCRIPTION	POST. REF.	DEBIT	CREDIT	
1							1
2							2
3							3
4							4
5							5
6							6
7							7
8							8
9							9
10							10
11							11
12							12
13							13
14							14
15							15
16							16
17							17
18							18
19							19
20							20
21							21
22							22
23							23
24							24
25							25
26							26
27							27
28							28
29							29
30							30
31							31
32							32
33							33
34							34
35							35
36							36
37							37
38							38

© 2013 Cengage Learning. All Rights Reserved. May not be scanned, copied, duplicated, or posted to a publicly accessible website, in whole or in part.

Problem 4-3B (continued)

© 2013 Cengage Learning. All Rights Reserved. May not be scanned, copied, duplicated, or posted to a publicly accessible website, in whole or in part.

Problem 4-3B (continued)

© 2013 Cengage Learning. All Rights Reserved. May not be scanned, copied, duplicated, or posted to a publicly accessible website, in whole or in part.

Problem 4-3B (concluded)

© 2013 Cengage Learning. All Rights Reserved. May not be scanned, copied, duplicated, or posted to a publicly accessible website, in whole or in part.

Problem 4-4A or 4-4B

#	ACCOUNT NAME	TRIAL BALANCE DEBIT	TRIAL BALANCE CREDIT	ADJUSTMENTS DEBIT	ADJUSTMENTS CREDIT
1					
2					
3					
4					
5		TRIAL BALANCE		ADJUSTMENTS	
6	ACCOUNT NAME	DEBIT	CREDIT	DEBIT	CREDIT
7	Cash				
8	Supplies				
9	Prepaid Insurance				
10	Equipment				
11	Accum. Depr., Equipment				
12	Repair Equipment				
13	Accum. Depr., Repair Equipment				
14	Accounts Payable				
15	, Capital				
16	, Drawing				
17	Fees				
18	Concession Fees				
19	Wages Expense				
20	Rent Expense				
21	Utilities Expense				
22	Repair Expense				
23	Miscellaneous Expense				
24					
25					
26					
27					
28					
29					
30					
31					
32					
33					
34					
35					
36					
37					
38					
39					
40					
41					

© 2013 Cengage Learning. All Rights Reserved. May not be scanned, copied, duplicated, or posted to a publicly accessible website, in whole or in part.

Problem 4-4A or 4-4B (continued)

						1
						2
						3
						4

ADJUSTED TRIAL BALANCE		INCOME STATEMENT		BALANCE SHEET		
DEBIT	CREDIT	DEBIT	CREDIT	DEBIT	CREDIT	
						7
						8
						9
						10
						11
						12
						13
						14
						15
						16
						17
						18
						19
						20
						21
						22
						23
						24
						25
						26
						27
						28
						29
						30
						31
						32
						33
						34
						35
						36
						37
						38
						39
						40
						41

© 2013 Cengage Learning. All Rights Reserved. May not be scanned, copied, duplicated, or posted to a publicly accessible website, in whole or in part.

Problem 4-4A or 4-4B (continued)

GENERAL JOURNAL   PAGE _____

	DATE		DESCRIPTION	POST. REF.	DEBIT	CREDIT	
1							1
2							2
3							3
4							4
5							5
6							6
7							7
8							8
9							9
10							10
11							11
12							12
13							13
14							14
15							15
16							16
17							17
18							18
19							19
20							20
21							21
22							22
23							23
24							24
25							25
26							26
27							27
28							28
29							29
30							30
31							31
32							32
33							33
34							34
35							35
36							36
37							37
38							38

© 2013 Cengage Learning. All Rights Reserved. May not be scanned, copied, duplicated, or posted to a publicly accessible website, in whole or in part.

Problem 4-4A or 4-4B (continued)

© 2013 Cengage Learning. All Rights Reserved. May not be scanned, copied, duplicated, or posted to a publicly accessible website, in whole or in part.

Problem 4-4A or 4-4B (continued)

© 2013 Cengage Learning. All Rights Reserved. May not be scanned, copied, duplicated, or posted to a publicly accessible website, in whole or in part.

Problem 4-4A or 4-4B (concluded)

© 2013 Cengage Learning. All Rights Reserved. May not be scanned, copied, duplicated, or posted to a publicly accessible website, in whole or in part.

Problem 4-5A or 4-5B

	ACCOUNT NAME	TRIAL BALANCE		ADJUSTMENTS	
		DEBIT	CREDIT	DEBIT	CREDIT
1					
2					
3					
4					
5					
6					
7	Cash				
8	Supplies				
9	Prepaid Insurance				
10	Equipment				
11	Accum. Depr., Equipment				
12	Accounts Payable				
13	, Capital				
14	, Drawing				
15	Fees				
16	Wages Expense				
17	Rent Expense				
18	Utilities Expense				
19	Repair Expense				
20	Miscellaneous Expense				
21					
22					
23					
24					
25					
26					
27					
28					
29					
30					
31					
32					
33					
34					
35					
36					
37					
38					
39					
40					
41					

© 2013 Cengage Learning. All Rights Reserved. May not be scanned, copied, duplicated, or posted to a publicly accessible website, in whole or in part.

Problem 4-5A or 4-5B (continued)

						1
						2
						3
						4

ADJUSTED TRIAL BALANCE		INCOME STATEMENT		BALANCE SHEET		
DEBIT	CREDIT	DEBIT	CREDIT	DEBIT	CREDIT	
						7
						8
						9
						10
						11
						12
						13
						14
						15
						16
						17
						18
						19
						20
						21
						22
						23
						24
						25
						26
						27
						28
						29
						30
						31
						32
						33
						34
						35
						36
						37
						38
						39
						40
						41

© 2013 Cengage Learning. All Rights Reserved. May not be scanned, copied, duplicated, or posted to a publicly accessible website, in whole or in part.

Problem 4-5A or 4-5B (continued)

GENERAL JOURNAL   PAGE _____

	DATE		DESCRIPTION	POST. REF.	DEBIT	CREDIT	
1							1
2							2
3							3
4							4
5							5
6							6
7							7
8							8
9							9
10							10
11							11
12							12
13							13
14							14
15							15
16							16
17							17

© 2013 Cengage Learning. All Rights Reserved. May not be scanned, copied, duplicated, or posted to a publicly accessible website, in whole or in part.

Problem 4-5A or 4-5B (concluded)

© 2013 Cengage Learning. All Rights Reserved. May not be scanned, copied, duplicated, or posted to a publicly accessible website, in whole or in part.

Answers to Study Guide Questions

CHAPTER 4

PART 1   True/False

1.	T	6.	T
2.	T	7.	T
3.	F	8.	T
4.	T	9.	F
5.	T	10.	T

PART 2   Completion—Accounting Language

1.	book value	6.	accounting cycle
2.	fiscal period	7.	mixed account
3.	contra	8.	matching principle
4.	adjustments	9.	depreciation
5.	accrued wages	10.	straight-line depreciation

PART 3   Adjusting Entries

Wages Expense			*Wages Payable*	
Bal.	8,100			Adj.	550
Adj.	550			

Accumulated Depreciation, Equipment			*Depreciation Expense, Equipment*	
		Bal.	6,750	Adj.	1,500
		Adj.	1,500	

Prepaid Insurance			*Insurance Expense*	
Bal.	950	Adj.	310	Adj.	310

Supplies			*Supplies Expense*	
Bal.	3,000	Adj.	900	Adj.	900

© 2013 Cengage Learning. All Rights Reserved. May not be scanned, copied, duplicated, or posted to a publicly accessible website, in whole or in part.

Answers to Study Guide Questions (continued)

PART 4   Analyzing the Work Sheet

ACCOUNT NAME	TRIAL BALANCE		ADJUSTMENTS		ADJUSTED TRIAL BALANCE		INCOME STATEMENT		BALANCE SHEET	
	DEBIT	CREDIT	DEBIT	CREDIT	DEBIT	CREDIT	DEBIT	CREDIT	DEBIT	CREDIT
0. Equipment	X				X				X	
1. Cash	X				X				X	
2. C. Tumi, Capital		X				X				X
3. Advertising Expense	X				X		X			
4. Accounts Receivable	X				X				X	
5. Wages Expense	X		X		X		X			
6. Accumulated Depreciation, Equipment		X		X		X				X
7. Wages Payable				X		X				X
8. C. Tumi, Drawing	X				X				X	
9. Service Revenue		X				X		X		
10. Supplies	X			X	X				X	
11. Depreciation Expense, Equipment			X		X		X			

© 2013 Cengage Learning. All Rights Reserved. May not be scanned, copied, duplicated, or posted to a publicly accessible website, in whole or in part.

5 | Closing Entries and the Post-Closing Trial Balance

LEARNING OBJECTIVES

1. List the steps in the accounting cycle.
2. Journalize and post closing entries for a service enterprise.
3. Prepare a post-closing trial balance.
4. Define cash basis and accrual basis accounting.
5. Prepare interim statements.

ACCOUNTING LANGUAGE

Accrual basis of accounting
Cash basis of accounting
Closing entries
Income Summary account

Interim statements
Nominal (temporary-equity) accounts
Post-closing trial balance
Real (permanent) accounts

STUDY GUIDE QUESTIONS

PART 1   True/False

For each of the following statements, circle T if the statement is true and F if the statement is false.

T   F   1. The post-closing trial balance includes only the balances of real or permanent accounts.

T   F   2. The purpose of the closing entries is to close the asset and liability accounts because their balances apply to only one fiscal period.

T   F   3. After the closing entries have been posted, the final balance of the Capital account is the same as the amount recorded on the last line of the statement of owner's equity.

T   F   4. If you have to debit Income Summary to close it, this indicates a net loss.

T   F   5. The post-closing trial balance is final proof that the total of the debit balances equals the total of the credit balances.

T   F   6. The total of the expense accounts is recorded in Income Summary as a credit.

T   F   7. The last step in the closing procedure is to close the Drawing account into the Capital account.

T   F   8. Generally, the closing procedure is completed by making three entries.

T   F   9. Income Summary is an example of a nominal or temporary-equity account.

T   F   10. The first step in the closing procedure is to close the expense accounts into the Income Summary account.

© 2013 Cengage Learning. All Rights Reserved. May not be scanned, copied, duplicated, or posted to a publicly accessible website, in whole or in part.

PART 2   Completion—Accounting Language

Complete each of the following statements by writing the appropriate words in the spaces provided.

1. After the closing entries have been journalized and posted, the _____
    _____ is prepared as final proof that
    the accounts are in balance.

2. Financial statements that are prepared during the fiscal period and cover a period of time less
    than the fiscal period are called _____ statements.

3. The accounts that have balances carried over to the next fiscal period are called
    _____ accounts.

4. The _____ account is used only during the closing procedure.

5. A journal entry that is made to clear an account or make the balance of that account equal
    to zero is called a(n) _____ entry.

6. The _____ accounts apply to only
    one fiscal period and are closed at the end of the fiscal period.

7. An accounting basis under which revenue is recorded only when it is earned and expenses are
    recorded only when they are incurred is called the _____.

PART 3   Closing Entries

Using the following list of account titles, determine the account titles to be debited and
credited for the closing entries below. Enter the letter for the account in the space provided.

a.	Rent Expense	**c.**	B. Austin, Drawing	**e.**	B. Austin, Capital
b.	Wages Expense	**d.**	Income Summary	**f.**	Service Income

		Debit	Credit
1.	Close out the balance of the revenue account.	_____	_____
2.	Close out the balances of the expense accounts.	_____	_____
3.	Close out the amount of the net income for the period.	_____	_____
4.	Close out the balance of the Drawing account.	_____	_____

© 2013 Cengage Learning. All Rights Reserved. May not be scanned, copied, duplicated, or posted to a publicly accessible website, in whole or in part.

PART 4   Posting Closing Entries

After the first closing entries have been journalized and posted, the remaining accounts are shown below in T account form. Based on the T accounts, answer the following questions.

Income Summary		F. Landry, Capital		F. Landry, Drawing	
Debit	Credit	Debit	Credit	Debit	Credit
55,000	51,000		Bal. 135,000	Bal. 12,000	

1. The amount of the total revenue is $_____.

2. The amount of the total expenses is $_____.

3. The amount of the net income or net loss is $_____.

4. The amount of the total withdrawals is $_____.

5. The entry to close Income Summary is a debit to _____

    and a credit to _____ .

6. The entry to close F. Landry, Drawing, is a debit to _____

    and a credit to _____ .

7. The amount of the increase or decrease in capital for the period is $_____.

8. The ending balance of F. Landry, Capital, is $_____.

DEMONSTRATION PROBLEM

After the adjusting entries have been posted, the ledger of L. Thompson, a financial planner, contains the following account balances as of December 31:

Cash	$ 3,064
Accounts Receivable	8,000
Supplies	450
Equipment	10,500
Accumulated Depreciation, Equipment	4,200
Accounts Payable	756
L. Thompson, Capital	18,378
L. Thompson, Drawing	80,000
Income Summary	—
Commissions Earned	92,824
Income from Services	23,050
Salary Expense	21,600
Rent Expense	11,200
Supplies Expense	1,635
Depreciation Expense, Equipment	2,100
Miscellaneous Expense	659

Instructions

Record the closing entries in general journal form.

© 2013 Cengage Learning. All Rights Reserved. May not be scanned, copied, duplicated, or posted to a publicly accessible website, in whole or in part.

SOLUTION

GENERAL JOURNAL   PAGE _____

	DATE		DESCRIPTION	POST. REF.	DEBIT	CREDIT	
1	20—		*Closing Entries*				1
2	Dec.	31	Commissions Earned		92,824.00		2
3			Income from Services		23,050.00		3
4			Income Summary			115,874.00	4
5							5
6		31	Income Summary		37,194.00		6
7			Salary Expense			21,600.00	7
8			Rent Expense			11,200.00	8
9			Supplies Expense			1,635.00	9
10			Depreciation Expense, Equipment			2,100.00	10
11			Miscellaneous Expense			659.00	11
12							12
13		31	Income Summary		78,680.00		13
14			L. Thompson, Capital			78,680.00	14
15							15
16		31	L. Thompson, Capital		80,000.00		16
17			L. Thompson, Drawing			80,000.00	17
18							18

166

© 2013 Cengage Learning. All Rights Reserved. May not be scanned, copied, duplicated, or posted to a publicly accessible website, in whole or in part.

EXERCISES AND PROBLEMS

Exercise 5-1

ACCOUNT TITLE	REAL	NOMINAL	CLOSED YES	CLOSED NO	INCOME STATEMENT	BALANCE SHEET
0. Example: Building	X			X		X
a. Prepaid Insurance						
b. Accounts Payable						
c. Wages Payable						
d. Service Revenue						
e. Rent Expense						
f. Supplies Expense						
g. Accum. Depr., Equipment						

Exercise 5-2

a.

GENERAL JOURNAL   PAGE _____

	DATE	DESCRIPTION	POST. REF.	DEBIT	CREDIT	
1						1
2						2
3						3
4						4
5						5
6						6
7						7
8						8
9						9
10						10
11						11
12						12
13						13
14						14
15						15
16						16

b. _____

© 2013 Cengage Learning. All Rights Reserved. May not be scanned, copied, duplicated, or posted to a publicly accessible website, in whole or in part.

Exercise 5-3

GENERAL JOURNAL

PAGE _____

	DATE		DESCRIPTION	POST. REF.	DEBIT	CREDIT	
1							1
2							2
3							3
4							4
5							5
6							6
7							7
8							8
9							9
10							10
11							11
12							12
13							13
14							14
15							15
16							16
17							17
18							18

Exercise 5-4

GENERAL JOURNAL

PAGE _____

	DATE		DESCRIPTION	POST. REF.	DEBIT	CREDIT	
1							1
2							2
3							3
4							4
5							5
6							6
7							7
8							8
9							9
10							10
11							11
12							12
13							13
14							14
15							15
16							16
17							17
18							18

© 2013 Cengage Learning. All Rights Reserved. May not be scanned, copied, duplicated, or posted to a publicly accessible website, in whole or in part.

Exercise 5-5

GENERAL JOURNAL   PAGE _____

	DATE		DESCRIPTION	POST. REF.	DEBIT	CREDIT	
1							1
2							2
3							3
4							4
5							5
6							6
7							7
8							8
9							9
10							10
11							11
12							12
13							13
14							14
15							15
16							16
17							17
18							18

Exercise 5-6

a.

12						12
13						13
14						14
15						15
16						16
17						17
18						18

b. _____

© 2013 Cengage Learning. All Rights Reserved. May not be scanned, copied, duplicated, or posted to a publicly accessible website, in whole or in part.

Exercise 5-7

	ACCOUNT TITLE	POST-CLOSING TRIAL BALANCE	
		YES	NO
0.	Example: Cash	X	
a.	Income from Services		
b.	Prepaid Insurance		
c.	Supplies Expense		
d.	Accounts Payable		
e.	F. Oz, Drawing		
f.	Depreciation Expense, Equipment		
g.	Wages Payable		
h.	Accounts Receivable		
i.	Wages Expense		
j.	Accumulated Depreciation, Equipment		
k.	F. Oz, Capital		

Exercise 5-8

a. _____

b. _____

c. _____

d. _____

© 2013 Cengage Learning. All Rights Reserved. May not be scanned, copied, duplicated, or posted to a publicly accessible website, in whole or in part.

Exercise 5-9

	ITEM	INCOME STATEMENT	STATEMENT OF OWNER'S EQUITY	BALANCE SHEET
0.	*Example: The total liabilities of the business at the end of the year.*			X
a.	The amount of the owner's Capital balance at the end of the year.			
b.	The amount of depreciation expense on equipment during the year.			
c.	The amount of the company's net income for the year.			
d.	The book value of the equipment.			
e.	Total insurance expired during the year.			
f.	Total accounts receivable at the end of the year.			
g.	Total withdrawals by the owner.			
h.	The cost of utilities used during the year.			
i.	The amount of the owner's Capital balance at the beginning of the year.			

Exercise 5-10

© 2013 Cengage Learning. All Rights Reserved. May not be scanned, copied, duplicated, or posted to a publicly accessible website, in whole or in part.

Problem 5-1A or 5-1B

Owner's Equity

Assets	=	Liabilities	+	Capital	−	Drawing	+	Revenue	−	Expenses
Dr. | Cr.		Dr. | Cr.		Dr. | Cr.		Dr. | Cr.		Dr. | Cr.		Dr. | Cr.
+ | −		− | +		− | +		+ | −		− | +		+ | −

, Capital

Income Summary

, Drawing

Commissions Earned

Rent Expense

Supplies Expense

Depreciation Expense, Office Equipment

Utilities Expense

Miscellaneous Expense

© 2013 Cengage Learning. All Rights Reserved. May not be scanned, copied, duplicated, or posted to a publicly accessible website, in whole or in part.

Problem 5-1A or 5-1B (concluded)

GENERAL JOURNAL   PAGE _____

	DATE		DESCRIPTION	POST. REF.	DEBIT	CREDIT	
1							1
2							2
3							3
4							4
5							5
6							6
7							7
8							8
9							9
10							10
11							11
12							12
13							13
14							14
15							15
16							16
17							17
18							18
19							19
20							20

© 2013 Cengage Learning. All Rights Reserved. May not be scanned, copied, duplicated, or posted to a publicly accessible website, in whole or in part.

Problem 5-2A or 5-2B

Owner's Equity

Assets	=	Liabilities	+	Capital	−	Drawing	+	Revenue	−	Expenses
Dr. | Cr.		Dr. | Cr.		Dr. | Cr.		Dr. | Cr.		Dr. | Cr.		Dr. | Cr.
+ | −		− | +		− | +		+ | −		− | +		+ | −

, Capital

Income Summary

, Drawing

Rent Expense

Wages Expense

Supplies Expense

Insurance Expense

Depreciation Expense, Equipment

Miscellaneous Expense

© 2013 Cengage Learning. All Rights Reserved. May not be scanned, copied, duplicated, or posted to a publicly accessible website, in whole or in part.

Problem 5-2A or 5-2B (concluded)

GENERAL JOURNAL   PAGE _____

	DATE		DESCRIPTION	POST. REF.	DEBIT	CREDIT	
1							1
2							2
3							3
4							4
5							5
6							6
7							7
8							8
9							9
10							10
11							11
12							12
13							13
14							14
15							15
16							16
17							17
18							18
19							19
20							20

© 2013 Cengage Learning. All Rights Reserved. May not be scanned, copied, duplicated, or posted to a publicly accessible website, in whole or in part.

Problem 5-3A

1							*Valerie Insurance Agency*	
2							*Work Sheet*	
3							*For Year Ended December 31, 20—*	
4								
5			TRIAL BALANCE			ADJUSTMENTS		
6	ACCOUNT NAME	DEBIT	CREDIT		DEBIT		CREDIT	
7	Cash	7,532.00						
8	Office Supplies	315.00				(c)		75.00
9	Office Equipment	2,398.00						
10	Accum. Depr., Office Equipment		420.00			(a)		420.00
11	M. Valerie, Capital		18,614.00					
12	M. Valerie, Drawing	18,000.00						
13	Premiums Earned		33,400.00					
14	Wages Expense	20,500.00		(b)	428.00			
15	Rent Expense	2,200.00						
16	Telephone Expense	736.00						
17	Advertising Expense	645.00						
18	Miscellaneous Expense	108.00						
19		52,434.00	52,434.00					
20	Office Supplies Expense			(c)	75.00			
21	Depr. Exp., Office Equipment			(a)	420.00			
22	Wages Payable					(b)		428.00
23					923.00			923.00
24	Net Income							
25								
26								
27								
28								
29								
30								
31								
32								
33								
34								
35								
36								
37								

© 2013 Cengage Learning. All Rights Reserved. May not be scanned, copied, duplicated, or posted to a publicly accessible website, in whole or in part.

Problem 5-3A (continued)

ADJUSTED TRIAL BALANCE		INCOME STATEMENT		BALANCE SHEET		
DEBIT	CREDIT	DEBIT	CREDIT	DEBIT	CREDIT	
7,532.00				7,532.00		7
240.00				240.00		8
2,398.00				2,398.00		9
	840.00				840.00	10
	18,614.00				18,614.00	11
18,000.00				18,000.00		12
	33,400.00		33,400.00			13
20,928.00		20,928.00				14
2,200.00		2,200.00				15
736.00		736.00				16
645.00		645.00				17
108.00		108.00				18
						19
75.00		75.00				20
420.00		420.00				21
	428.00				428.00	22
53,282.00	53,282.00	25,112.00	33,400.00	28,170.00	19,882.00	23
		8,288.00			8,288.00	24
		33,400.00	33,400.00	28,170.00	28,170.00	25

© 2013 Cengage Learning. All Rights Reserved. May not be scanned, copied, duplicated, or posted to a publicly accessible website, in whole or in part.

Problem 5-3A (continued)

GENERAL JOURNAL   PAGE ____17____

	DATE		DESCRIPTION	POST. REF.	DEBIT	CREDIT	
1							1
2							2
3							3
4							4
5							5
6							6
7							7
8							8
9							9
10							10
11							11
12							12
13							13
14							14
15							15
16							16
17							17
18							18
19							19
20							20
21							21
22							22
23							23
24							24
25							25
26							26
27							27
28							28
29							29
30							30
31							31
32							32

© 2013 Cengage Learning. All Rights Reserved. May not be scanned, copied, duplicated, or posted to a publicly accessible website, in whole or in part.

Problem 5-3A (continued)

GENERAL LEDGER

ACCOUNT *Cash*   ACCOUNT NO. *111*

DATE	ITEM	POST. REF.	DEBIT	CREDIT	BALANCE	
					DEBIT	CREDIT

ACCOUNT *Office Supplies*   ACCOUNT NO. *115*

DATE	ITEM	POST. REF.	DEBIT	CREDIT	BALANCE	
					DEBIT	CREDIT

ACCOUNT *Office Equipment*   ACCOUNT NO. *124*

DATE	ITEM	POST. REF.	DEBIT	CREDIT	BALANCE	
					DEBIT	CREDIT

ACCOUNT *Accumulated Depreciation, Office Equipment*   ACCOUNT NO. *125*

DATE	ITEM	POST. REF.	DEBIT	CREDIT	BALANCE	
					DEBIT	CREDIT

ACCOUNT *Wages Payable*   ACCOUNT NO. *222*

DATE	ITEM	POST. REF.	DEBIT	CREDIT	BALANCE	
					DEBIT	CREDIT

ACCOUNT *M. Valerie, Capital*   ACCOUNT NO. *311*

DATE	ITEM	POST. REF.	DEBIT	CREDIT	BALANCE	
					DEBIT	CREDIT

© 2013 Cengage Learning. All Rights Reserved. May not be scanned, copied, duplicated, or posted to a publicly accessible website, in whole or in part.

Problem 5-3A (continued)

ACCOUNT   *M. Valerie, Drawing*   ACCOUNT NO.   *312*

DATE		ITEM	POST. REF.	DEBIT	CREDIT	BALANCE	
						DEBIT	CREDIT

ACCOUNT   *Income Summary*   ACCOUNT NO.   *313*

DATE		ITEM	POST. REF.	DEBIT	CREDIT	BALANCE	
						DEBIT	CREDIT

ACCOUNT   *Premiums Earned*   ACCOUNT NO.   *411*

DATE		ITEM	POST. REF.	DEBIT	CREDIT	BALANCE	
						DEBIT	CREDIT

ACCOUNT   *Wages Expense*   ACCOUNT NO.   *511*

DATE		ITEM	POST. REF.	DEBIT	CREDIT	BALANCE	
						DEBIT	CREDIT

ACCOUNT   *Rent Expense*   ACCOUNT NO.   *512*

DATE		ITEM	POST. REF.	DEBIT	CREDIT	BALANCE	
						DEBIT	CREDIT

© 2013 Cengage Learning. All Rights Reserved. May not be scanned, copied, duplicated, or posted to a publicly accessible website, in whole or in part.

Problem 5-3A (continued)

ACCOUNT   *Office Supplies Expense*   ACCOUNT NO.   *513*

DATE	ITEM	POST. REF.	DEBIT	CREDIT	BALANCE DEBIT	BALANCE CREDIT

ACCOUNT   *Depreciation Expense, Office Equipment*   ACCOUNT NO.   *514*

DATE	ITEM	POST. REF.	DEBIT	CREDIT	BALANCE DEBIT	BALANCE CREDIT

ACCOUNT   *Telephone Expense*   ACCOUNT NO.   *515*

DATE	ITEM	POST. REF.	DEBIT	CREDIT	BALANCE DEBIT	BALANCE CREDIT

ACCOUNT   *Advertising Expense*   ACCOUNT NO.   *516*

DATE	ITEM	POST. REF.	DEBIT	CREDIT	BALANCE DEBIT	BALANCE CREDIT

ACCOUNT   *Miscellaneous Expense*   ACCOUNT NO.   *519*

DATE	ITEM	POST. REF.	DEBIT	CREDIT	BALANCE DEBIT	BALANCE CREDIT

© 2013 Cengage Learning. All Rights Reserved. May not be scanned, copied, duplicated, or posted to a publicly accessible website, in whole or in part.

Problem 5-3A (concluded)

ACCOUNT NAME	DEBIT	CREDIT	

© 2013 Cengage Learning. All Rights Reserved. May not be scanned, copied, duplicated, or posted to a publicly accessible website, in whole or in part.

Extra Form

GENERAL JOURNAL   PAGE _____

	DATE	DESCRIPTION	POST. REF.	DEBIT	CREDIT	
1						1
2						2
3						3
4						4
5						5
6						6
7						7
8						8
9						9
10						10
11						11
12						12
13						13
14						14
15						15
16						16
17						17
18						18
19						19
20						20
21						21
22						22
23						23
24						24
25						25
26						26
27						27
28						28
29						29
30						30
31						31
32						32
33						33
34						34
35						35
36						36
37						37
38						38
39						39
40						40

© 2013 Cengage Learning. All Rights Reserved. May not be scanned, copied, duplicated, or posted to a publicly accessible website, in whole or in part.

Problem 5-3B

	ACCOUNT NAME	TRIAL BALANCE DEBIT	TRIAL BALANCE CREDIT	ADJUSTMENTS DEBIT		ADJUSTMENTS CREDIT	
1						*Oliver Tour Company*	
2						*Work Sheet*	
3						*For Year Ended December 31, 20—*	
4							
5		TRIAL BALANCE		ADJUSTMENTS			
6	ACCOUNT NAME	DEBIT	CREDIT	DEBIT		CREDIT	
7	Cash	4,827.00					
8	Office Supplies	360.00				(c)	82.00
9	Office Equipment	4,042.00					
10	Accum. Depr., Office Equipment		546.00			(a)	386.00
11	S. Oliver, Capital		26,756.00				
12	S. Oliver, Drawing	24,000.00					
13	Tour Revenue		34,057.00				
14	Wages Expense	22,820.00		(b)	528.00		
15	Rent Expense	2,930.00					
16	Telephone Expense	941.00					
17	Advertising Expense	1,237.00					
18	Miscellaneous Expense	202.00					
19		61,359.00	61,359.00				
20	Depr. Exp., Office Equipment			(a)	386.00		
21	Wages Payable					(b)	528.00
22	Office Supplies Expense			(c)	82.00		
23					996.00		996.00
24	Net Income						
25							
26							
27							
28							
29							
30							
31							
32							
33							
34							
35							
36							
37							
38							

© 2013 Cengage Learning. All Rights Reserved. May not be scanned, copied, duplicated, or posted to a publicly accessible website, in whole or in part.

Problem 5-3B (continued)

	ADJUSTED TRIAL BALANCE		INCOME STATEMENT		BALANCE SHEET		
	DEBIT	CREDIT	DEBIT	CREDIT	DEBIT	CREDIT	
	4,827.00				4,827.00		7
	278.00				278.00		8
	4,042.00				4,042.00		9
		932.00				932.00	10
		26,756.00				26,756.00	11
	24,000.00				24,000.00		12
		34,057.00		34,057.00			13
	23,348.00		23,348.00				14
	2,930.00		2,930.00				15
	941.00		941.00				16
	1,237.00		1,237.00				17
	202.00		202.00				18
							19
	386.00		386.00				20
		528.00				528.00	21
	82.00		82.00				22
	62,273.00	62,273.00	29,126.00	34,057.00	33,147.00	28,216.00	23
			4,931.00			4,931.00	24
			34,057.00	34,057.00	33,147.00	33,147.00	25

185

© 2013 Cengage Learning. All Rights Reserved. May not be scanned, copied, duplicated, or posted to a publicly accessible website, in whole or in part.

Problem 5-3B (continued)

GENERAL JOURNAL   PAGE _____ *17* _____

	DATE		DESCRIPTION	POST. REF.	DEBIT	CREDIT	
1							1
2							2
3							3
4							4
5							5
6							6
7							7
8							8
9							9
10							10
11							11
12							12
13							13
14							14
15							15
16							16
17							17
18							18
19							19
20							20
21							21
22							22
23							23
24							24
25							25
26							26
27							27
28							28
29							29
30							30

© 2013 Cengage Learning. All Rights Reserved. May not be scanned, copied, duplicated, or posted to a publicly accessible website, in whole or in part.

Problem 5-3B (continued)

GENERAL LEDGER

ACCOUNT   *Cash*   ACCOUNT NO. _____ *111*_____

DATE	ITEM	POST. REF.	DEBIT	CREDIT	BALANCE	
					DEBIT	CREDIT

ACCOUNT   *Office Supplies*   ACCOUNT NO. _____ *115*_____

DATE	ITEM	POST. REF.	DEBIT	CREDIT	BALANCE	
					DEBIT	CREDIT

ACCOUNT   *Office Equipment*   ACCOUNT NO. _____ *124*_____

DATE	ITEM	POST. REF.	DEBIT	CREDIT	BALANCE	
					DEBIT	CREDIT

ACCOUNT   *Accumulated Depreciation, Office Equipment*   ACCOUNT NO. _____ *125*_____

DATE	ITEM	POST. REF.	DEBIT	CREDIT	BALANCE	
					DEBIT	CREDIT

ACCOUNT   *Wages Payable*   ACCOUNT NO. _____ *222*_____

DATE	ITEM	POST. REF.	DEBIT	CREDIT	BALANCE	
					DEBIT	CREDIT

© 2013 Cengage Learning. All Rights Reserved. May not be scanned, copied, duplicated, or posted to a publicly accessible website, in whole or in part.

Problem 5-3B (continued)

ACCOUNT   *S. Oliver, Capital*   ACCOUNT NO.   *311*

DATE		ITEM	POST. REF.	DEBIT	CREDIT	BALANCE	
						DEBIT	CREDIT

ACCOUNT   *S. Oliver, Drawing*   ACCOUNT NO.   *312*

DATE		ITEM	POST. REF.	DEBIT	CREDIT	BALANCE	
						DEBIT	CREDIT

ACCOUNT   *Income Summary*   ACCOUNT NO.   *313*

DATE		ITEM	POST. REF.	DEBIT	CREDIT	BALANCE	
						DEBIT	CREDIT

ACCOUNT   *Tour Revenue*   ACCOUNT NO.   *411*

DATE		ITEM	POST. REF.	DEBIT	CREDIT	BALANCE	
						DEBIT	CREDIT

ACCOUNT   *Wages Expense*   ACCOUNT NO.   *511*

DATE		ITEM	POST. REF.	DEBIT	CREDIT	BALANCE	
						DEBIT	CREDIT

© 2013 Cengage Learning. All Rights Reserved. May not be scanned, copied, duplicated, or posted to a publicly accessible website, in whole or in part.

Problem 5-3B (concluded)

ACCOUNT   *Rent Expense*   ACCOUNT NO.   *512*

DATE	ITEM	POST. REF.	DEBIT	CREDIT	BALANCE	
					DEBIT	CREDIT

ACCOUNT   *Office Supplies Expense*   ACCOUNT NO.   *513*

DATE	ITEM	POST. REF.	DEBIT	CREDIT	BALANCE	
					DEBIT	CREDIT

ACCOUNT   *Depreciation Expense, Office Equipment*   ACCOUNT NO.   *514*

DATE	ITEM	POST. REF.	DEBIT	CREDIT	BALANCE	
					DEBIT	CREDIT

ACCOUNT   *Telephone Expense*   ACCOUNT NO.   *515*

DATE	ITEM	POST. REF.	DEBIT	CREDIT	BALANCE	
					DEBIT	CREDIT

ACCOUNT   *Advertising Expense*   ACCOUNT NO.   *516*

DATE	ITEM	POST. REF.	DEBIT	CREDIT	BALANCE	
					DEBIT	CREDIT

ACCOUNT   *Miscellaneous Expense*   ACCOUNT NO.   *519*

DATE	ITEM	POST. REF.	DEBIT	CREDIT	BALANCE	
					DEBIT	CREDIT

© 2013 Cengage Learning. All Rights Reserved. May not be scanned, copied, duplicated, or posted to a publicly accessible website, in whole or in part.

Problem 5-3B (concluded)

ACCOUNT NAME	DEBIT	CREDIT	

© 2013 Cengage Learning. All Rights Reserved. May not be scanned, copied, duplicated, or posted to a publicly accessible website, in whole or in part.

Extra Form

GENERAL JOURNAL   PAGE _____

	DATE		DESCRIPTION	POST. REF.	DEBIT	CREDIT	
1							1
2							2
3							3
4							4
5							5
6							6
7							7
8							8
9							9
10							10
11							11
12							12
13							13
14							14
15							15
16							16
17							17
18							18
19							19
20							20
21							21
22							22
23							23
24							24
25							25
26							26
27							27
28							28
29							29
30							30
31							31
32							32
33							33
34							34
35							35
36							36
37							37
38							38
39							39
40							40

© 2013 Cengage Learning. All Rights Reserved. May not be scanned, copied, duplicated, or posted to a publicly accessible website, in whole or in part.

Problem 5-4A or 5-4B

	ACCOUNT NAME	TRIAL BALANCE		ADJUSTMENTS	
		DEBIT	CREDIT	DEBIT	CREDIT
1					
2					
3					
4					
5					
6					
7					
8					
9					
10					
11					
12					
13					
14					
15					
16					
17					
18					
19					
20					
21					
22					
23					
24					
25					
26					
27					
28					
29					
30					
31					
32					
33					
34					
35					
36					
37					
38					

© 2013 Cengage Learning. All Rights Reserved. May not be scanned, copied, duplicated, or posted to a publicly accessible website, in whole or in part.

Problem 5-4A or 5-4B (continued)

ADJUSTED TRIAL BALANCE		INCOME STATEMENT		BALANCE SHEET	
DEBIT	CREDIT	DEBIT	CREDIT	DEBIT	CREDIT

© 2013 Cengage Learning. All Rights Reserved. May not be scanned, copied, duplicated, or posted to a publicly accessible website, in whole or in part.

Problem 5-4A or 5-4B (continued)

GENERAL JOURNAL   PAGE _____

	DATE	DESCRIPTION	POST. REF.	DEBIT	CREDIT	
1						1
2						2
3						3
4						4
5						5
6						6
7						7
8						8
9						9
10						10
11						11
12						12
13						13
14						14
15						15
16						16
17						17

© 2013 Cengage Learning. All Rights Reserved. May not be scanned, copied, duplicated, or posted to a publicly accessible website, in whole or in part.

Problem 5-4A or 5-4B (continued)

© 2013 Cengage Learning. All Rights Reserved. May not be scanned, copied, duplicated, or posted to a publicly accessible website, in whole or in part.

Problem 5-4A or 5-4B (continued)

© 2013 Cengage Learning. All Rights Reserved. May not be scanned, copied, duplicated, or posted to a publicly accessible website, in whole or in part.

Problem 5-4A or 5-4B (concluded)

GENERAL JOURNAL   PAGE _____

	DATE		DESCRIPTION	POST. REF.	DEBIT	CREDIT	
1							1
2							2
3							3
4							4
5							5
6							6
7							7
8							8
9							9
10							10
11							11
12							12
13							13
14							14
15							15
16							16
17							17
18							18
19							19
20							20
21							21
22							22

© 2013 Cengage Learning. All Rights Reserved. May not be scanned, copied, duplicated, or posted to a publicly accessible website, in whole or in part.

Problem 5-5A

	ACCOUNT NAME	TRIAL BALANCE DEBIT	TRIAL BALANCE CREDIT	ADJUSTMENTS DEBIT		ADJUSTMENTS CREDIT	
1							
2							
3							
4							
7	Cash	6,500.00					
8	Accounts Receivable	1,250.00					
9	Supplies	415.00				(e)	200.00
10	Prepaid Insurance	2,175.00				(a)	175.00
11	Equipment	3,500.00					
12	Accum. Depr., Equipment		1,200.00			(b)	75.00
13	Truck	18,300.00					
14	Accumulated Depreciation, Truck		4,000.00			(c)	300.00
15	Accounts Payable		800.00				
16	J. Williams, Capital		16,940.00				
17	J. Williams, Drawing	3,000.00					
18	Fees Earned		15,000.00				
19	Salary Expense	1,200.00		(d)	125.00		
20	Advertising Expense	600.00					
21	Truck Operating Expense	250.00					
22	Utilities Expense	600.00					
23	Miscellaneous Expense	150.00					
24		37,940.00	37,940.00				
25	Insurance Expense			(a)	175.00		
26	Depr. Exp., Equipment			(b)	75.00		
27	Depreciation Expense, Truck			(c)	300.00		
28	Salaries Payable					(d)	125.00
29	Supplies Expense			(e)	200.00		
30					875.00		875.00
31	Net Income						

© 2013 Cengage Learning. All Rights Reserved. May not be scanned, copied, duplicated, or posted to a publicly accessible website, in whole or in part.

Problem 5-5A (continued)

ADJUSTED TRIAL BALANCE		INCOME STATEMENT		BALANCE SHEET		
DEBIT	CREDIT	DEBIT	CREDIT	DEBIT	CREDIT	
6,500.00						7
1,250.00						8
215.00						9
2,000.00						10
3,500.00						11
	1,275.00					12
18,300.00						13
	4,300.00					14
	800.00					15
	16,940.00					16
3,000.00						17
	15,000.00					18
1,325.00						19
600.00						20
250.00						21
600.00						22
150.00						23
						24
175.00						25
75.00						26
300.00						27
	125.00					28
200.00						29
38,440.00	38,440.00					30
						31
						32
						33
						34
						35
						36
						37
						38

© 2013 Cengage Learning. All Rights Reserved. May not be scanned, copied, duplicated, or posted to a publicly accessible website, in whole or in part.

Problem 5-5A (continued)

© 2013 Cengage Learning. All Rights Reserved. May not be scanned, copied, duplicated, or posted to a publicly accessible website, in whole or in part.

Problem 5-5A (continued)

© 2013 Cengage Learning. All Rights Reserved. May not be scanned, copied, duplicated, or posted to a publicly accessible website, in whole or in part.

Problem 5-5A (continued)

GENERAL JOURNAL   PAGE _____

	DATE		DESCRIPTION	POST. REF.	DEBIT	CREDIT	
1							1
2							2
3							3
4							4
5							5
6							6
7							7
8							8
9							9
10							10
11							11
12							12
13							13
14							14
15							15
16							16
17							17
18							18
19							19
20							20
21							21
22							22

© 2013 Cengage Learning. All Rights Reserved. May not be scanned, copied, duplicated, or posted to a publicly accessible website, in whole or in part.

Problem 5-5A (concluded)

© 2013 Cengage Learning. All Rights Reserved. May not be scanned, copied, duplicated, or posted to a publicly accessible website, in whole or in part.

Problem 5-5B

	ACCOUNT NAME	TRIAL BALANCE DEBIT	TRIAL BALANCE CREDIT	ADJUSTMENTS DEBIT		ADJUSTMENTS CREDIT	
1							
2							
3							
4							
5							
6							
7	Cash	2,400.00					
8	Accounts Receivable	800.00					
9	Supplies	225.00				(e)	80.00
10	Prepaid Insurance	1,200.00				(a)	100.00
11	Equipment	2,220.00					
12	Accum. Depr., Equipment		370.00			(b)	185.00
13	Truck	25,000.00					
14	Accumulated Depreciation, Truck		5,000.00			(c)	1,000.00
15	Accounts Payable		250.00				
16	Y. Tom, Capital		26,500.00				
17	Y. Tom, Drawing	1,500.00					
18	Fees Earned		2,400.00				
19	Salary Expense	640.00		(d)	80.00		
20	Advertising Expense	130.00					
21	Truck Operating Expense	125.00					
22	Utilities Expense	200.00					
23	Miscellaneous Expense	80.00					
24		34,520.00	34,520.00				
25	Insurance Expense			(a)	100.00		
26	Depr. Exp., Equipment			(b)	185.00		
27	Depreciation Expense, Truck			(c)	1,000.00		
28	Salaries Payable					(d)	80.00
29	Supplies Expense			(e)	80.00		
30					1,445.00		1,445.00
31	Net Loss						
32							
33							
34							
35							
36							
37							
38							

© 2013 Cengage Learning. All Rights Reserved. May not be scanned, copied, duplicated, or posted to a publicly accessible website, in whole or in part.

Problem 5-5B (continued)

						1
						2
						3
						4
ADJUSTED TRIAL BALANCE		INCOME STATEMENT		BALANCE SHEET		5
DEBIT	CREDIT	DEBIT	CREDIT	DEBIT	CREDIT	6
2,400.00						7
800.00						8
145.00						9
1,100.00						10
2,220.00						11
	555.00					12
25,000.00						13
	6,000.00					14
	250.00					15
	26,500.00					16
1,500.00						17
	2,400.00					18
720.00						19
130.00						20
125.00						21
200.00						22
80.00						23
						24
100.00						25
185.00						26
1,000.00						27
	80.00					28
80.00						29
35,785.00	35,785.00					30
						31
						32
						33
						34
						35
						36
						37
						38

© 2013 Cengage Learning. All Rights Reserved. May not be scanned, copied, duplicated, or posted to a publicly accessible website, in whole or in part.

Problem 5-5B (continued)

© 2013 Cengage Learning. All Rights Reserved. May not be scanned, copied, duplicated, or posted to a publicly accessible website, in whole or in part.

Problem 5-5B (continued)

© 2013 Cengage Learning. All Rights Reserved. May not be scanned, copied, duplicated, or posted to a publicly accessible website, in whole or in part.

Problem 5-5B (concluded)

GENERAL JOURNAL   PAGE _____

	DATE		DESCRIPTION	POST. REF.	DEBIT	CREDIT	
1							1
2							2
3							3
4							4
5							5
6							6
7							7
8							8
9							9
10							10
11							11
12							12
13							13
14							14
15							15
16							16
17							17
18							18
19							19
20							20
21							21
22							22

© 2013 Cengage Learning. All Rights Reserved. May not be scanned, copied, duplicated, or posted to a publicly accessible website, in whole or in part.

ACCOUNTING CYCLE REVIEW PROBLEM A—BLAST OFF!

Suggested Audit Questions

1. What was the amount incurred for advertising on July 5?
2. How much of the concessions income was received in cash?
3. What was the amount of the principal paid on the mortgage?
4. How much did Judar withdraw from the business?
5. What is the amount of accrued wages?
6. How much insurance expired during the month?
7. What is the amount of depreciation of the pool/slide facility?
8. What is the ending balance of Judar's Capital account?
9. As of the end of the month, what is the amount of the book value of the pool/slide facility?
10. How much cash did Judar pay as a down payment on the purchase of Blast Off!?

Answers

1. _____
2. _____
3. _____
4. _____
5. _____
6. _____
7. _____
8. _____
9. _____
10. _____

© 2013 Cengage Learning. All Rights Reserved. May not be scanned, copied, duplicated, or posted to a publicly accessible website, in whole or in part.

ACCOUNTING CYCLE REVIEW PROBLEM A (continued)

GENERAL JOURNAL   PAGE ____1____

	DATE		DESCRIPTION	POST. REF.	DEBIT	CREDIT	
1							1
2							2
3							3
4							4
5							5
6							6
7							7
8							8
9							9
10							10
11							11
12							12
13							13
14							14
15							15
16							16
17							17
18							18
19							19
20							20
21							21
22							22
23							23
24							24
25							25
26							26
27							27
28							28
29							29
30							30
31							31
32							32
33							33
34							34
35							35
36							36
37							37
38							38
39							39
40							40
41							41
42							42
43							43

© 2013 Cengage Learning. All Rights Reserved. May not be scanned, copied, duplicated, or posted to a publicly accessible website, in whole or in part.

ACCOUNTING CYCLE REVIEW PROBLEM A (continued)

GENERAL JOURNAL   PAGE _____2_____

	DATE		DESCRIPTION	POST. REF.	DEBIT	CREDIT	
1							1
2							2
3							3
4							4
5							5
6							6
7							7
8							8
9							9
10							10
11							11
12							12
13							13
14							14
15							15
16							16
17							17
18							18
19							19
20							20
21							21
22							22
23							23
24							24
25							25
26							26
27							27
28							28
29							29
30							30
31							31
32							32
33							33
34							34
35							35
36							36
37							37
38							38
39							39
40							40
41							41
42							42
43							43

© 2013 Cengage Learning. All Rights Reserved. May not be scanned, copied, duplicated, or posted to a publicly accessible website, in whole or in part.

ACCOUNTING CYCLE REVIEW PROBLEM A (continued)

GENERAL JOURNAL   PAGE _____3_____

	DATE		DESCRIPTION	POST. REF.	DEBIT	CREDIT	
1							1
2							2
3							3
4							4
5							5
6							6
7							7
8							8
9							9
10							10
11							11
12							12
13							13
14							14
15							15
16							16
17							17
18							18
19							19
20							20
21							21
22							22
23							23
24							24
25							25
26							26
27							27
28							28
29							29
30							30
31							31
32							32
33							33
34							34
35							35
36							36
37							37
38							38
39							39
40							40
41							41
42							42
43							43

© 2013 Cengage Learning. All Rights Reserved. May not be scanned, copied, duplicated, or posted to a publicly accessible website, in whole or in part.

ACCOUNTING CYCLE REVIEW PROBLEM A (continued)

GENERAL JOURNAL   PAGE _____ 4 _____

	DATE		DESCRIPTION	POST. REF.	DEBIT	CREDIT	
1							1
2							2
3							3
4							4
5							5
6							6
7							7
8							8
9							9
10							10
11							11
12							12
13							13
14							14
15							15
16							16
17							17
18							18
19							19
20							20
21							21
22							22
23							23
24							24
25							25
26							26
27							27
28							28
29							29
30							30
31							31
32							32
33							33
34							34
35							35
36							36
37							37
38							38
39							39
40							40
41							41
42							42
43							43

© 2013 Cengage Learning. All Rights Reserved. May not be scanned, copied, duplicated, or posted to a publicly accessible website, in whole or in part.

ACCOUNTING CYCLE REVIEW PROBLEM A (continued)

GENERAL JOURNAL   PAGE ____5____

	DATE		DESCRIPTION	POST. REF.	DEBIT	CREDIT	
1							1
2							2
3							3
4							4
5							5
6							6
7							7
8							8
9							9
10							10
11							11
12							12
13							13
14							14
15							15
16							16
17							17
18							18
19							19
20							20
21							21
22							22
23							23
24							24
25							25
26							26
27							27
28							28
29							29
30							30
31							31
32							32
33							33
34							34
35							35
36							36
37							37
38							38
39							39
40							40
41							41
42							42
43							43

© 2013 Cengage Learning. All Rights Reserved. May not be scanned, copied, duplicated, or posted to a publicly accessible website, in whole or in part.

ACCOUNTING CYCLE REVIEW PROBLEM A (continued)
GENERAL LEDGER

ACCOUNT   *Cash*   ACCOUNT NO.   *111*

DATE	ITEM	POST. REF.	DEBIT	CREDIT	BALANCE DEBIT	BALANCE CREDIT

ACCOUNT   *Accounts Receivable*   ACCOUNT NO.   *112*

DATE	ITEM	POST. REF.	DEBIT	CREDIT	BALANCE DEBIT	BALANCE CREDIT

ACCOUNT   *Prepaid Insurance*   ACCOUNT NO.   *114*

DATE	ITEM	POST. REF.	DEBIT	CREDIT	BALANCE DEBIT	BALANCE CREDIT

© 2013 Cengage Learning. All Rights Reserved. May not be scanned, copied, duplicated, or posted to a publicly accessible website, in whole or in part.

ACCOUNTING CYCLE REVIEW PROBLEM A (continued)

ACCOUNT _Land_   ACCOUNT NO. _121_

DATE	ITEM	POST. REF.	DEBIT	CREDIT	BALANCE	
					DEBIT	CREDIT

ACCOUNT _Building_   ACCOUNT NO. _122_

DATE	ITEM	POST. REF.	DEBIT	CREDIT	BALANCE	
					DEBIT	CREDIT

ACCOUNT _Accumulated Depreciation, Building_   ACCOUNT NO. _123_

DATE	ITEM	POST. REF.	DEBIT	CREDIT	BALANCE	
					DEBIT	CREDIT

ACCOUNT _Pool/Slide Facility_   ACCOUNT NO. _124_

DATE	ITEM	POST. REF.	DEBIT	CREDIT	BALANCE	
					DEBIT	CREDIT

ACCOUNT _Accumulated Depreciation, Pool/Slide Facility_   ACCOUNT NO. _125_

DATE	ITEM	POST. REF.	DEBIT	CREDIT	BALANCE	
					DEBIT	CREDIT

© 2013 Cengage Learning. All Rights Reserved. May not be scanned, copied, duplicated, or posted to a publicly accessible website, in whole or in part.

ACCOUNTING CYCLE REVIEW PROBLEM A (continued)

ACCOUNT *Pool Furniture*   ACCOUNT NO. 126

DATE	ITEM	POST. REF.	DEBIT	CREDIT	BALANCE DEBIT	BALANCE CREDIT

ACCOUNT *Accumulated Depreciation, Pool Furniture*   ACCOUNT NO. 127

DATE	ITEM	POST. REF.	DEBIT	CREDIT	BALANCE DEBIT	BALANCE CREDIT

ACCOUNT *Accounts Payable*   ACCOUNT NO. 221

DATE	ITEM	POST. REF.	DEBIT	CREDIT	BALANCE DEBIT	BALANCE CREDIT

ACCOUNT *Wages Payable*   ACCOUNT NO. 222

DATE	ITEM	POST. REF.	DEBIT	CREDIT	BALANCE DEBIT	BALANCE CREDIT

© 2013 Cengage Learning. All Rights Reserved. May not be scanned, copied, duplicated, or posted to a publicly accessible website, in whole or in part.

ACCOUNTING CYCLE REVIEW PROBLEM A (continued)

ACCOUNT   *Mortgage Payable*   ACCOUNT NO. _____ *223*

DATE		ITEM	POST. REF.	DEBIT	CREDIT	BALANCE	
						DEBIT	CREDIT

ACCOUNT   *L. Judar, Capital*   ACCOUNT NO. _____ *311*

DATE		ITEM	POST. REF.	DEBIT	CREDIT	BALANCE	
						DEBIT	CREDIT

ACCOUNT   *L. Judar, Drawing*   ACCOUNT NO. _____ *312*

DATE		ITEM	POST. REF.	DEBIT	CREDIT	BALANCE	
						DEBIT	CREDIT

ACCOUNT   *Income Summary*   ACCOUNT NO. _____ *313*

DATE		ITEM	POST. REF.	DEBIT	CREDIT	BALANCE	
						DEBIT	CREDIT

ACCOUNT   *Income from Services*   ACCOUNT NO. _____ *411*

DATE		ITEM	POST. REF.	DEBIT	CREDIT	BALANCE	
						DEBIT	CREDIT

© 2013 Cengage Learning. All Rights Reserved. May not be scanned, copied, duplicated, or posted to a publicly accessible website, in whole or in part.

ACCOUNTING CYCLE REVIEW PROBLEM A (continued)

ACCOUNT   *Concessions Income*   ACCOUNT NO.   *412*

DATE		ITEM	POST. REF.	DEBIT	CREDIT	BALANCE	
						DEBIT	CREDIT

ACCOUNT   *Pool Maintenance Expense*   ACCOUNT NO.   *511*

DATE		ITEM	POST. REF.	DEBIT	CREDIT	BALANCE	
						DEBIT	CREDIT

ACCOUNT   *Wages Expense*   ACCOUNT NO.   *512*

DATE		ITEM	POST. REF.	DEBIT	CREDIT	BALANCE	
						DEBIT	CREDIT

ACCOUNT   *Advertising Expense*   ACCOUNT NO.   *513*

DATE		ITEM	POST. REF.	DEBIT	CREDIT	BALANCE	
						DEBIT	CREDIT

© 2013 Cengage Learning. All Rights Reserved. May not be scanned, copied, duplicated, or posted to a publicly accessible website, in whole or in part.

ACCOUNTING CYCLE REVIEW PROBLEM A (continued)

ACCOUNT **Utilities Expense**   ACCOUNT NO. *514*

DATE	ITEM	POST. REF.	DEBIT	CREDIT	BALANCE DEBIT	BALANCE CREDIT

ACCOUNT **Interest Expense**   ACCOUNT NO. *515*

DATE	ITEM	POST. REF.	DEBIT	CREDIT	BALANCE DEBIT	BALANCE CREDIT

ACCOUNT **Insurance Expense**   ACCOUNT NO. *517*

DATE	ITEM	POST. REF.	DEBIT	CREDIT	BALANCE DEBIT	BALANCE CREDIT

ACCOUNT **Depreciation Expense, Building**   ACCOUNT NO. *518*

DATE	ITEM	POST. REF.	DEBIT	CREDIT	BALANCE DEBIT	BALANCE CREDIT

ACCOUNT **Depreciation Expense, Pool/Slide Facility**   ACCOUNT NO. *519*

DATE	ITEM	POST. REF.	DEBIT	CREDIT	BALANCE DEBIT	BALANCE CREDIT

© 2013 Cengage Learning. All Rights Reserved. May not be scanned, copied, duplicated, or posted to a publicly accessible website, in whole or in part.

ACCOUNTING CYCLE REVIEW PROBLEM A (continued)

ACCOUNT   *Depreciation Expense, Pool Furniture*   ACCOUNT NO.   *520*

DATE	ITEM	POST. REF.	DEBIT	CREDIT	BALANCE DEBIT	CREDIT

ACCOUNT   *Miscellaneous Expense*   ACCOUNT NO.   *522*

DATE	ITEM	POST. REF.	DEBIT	CREDIT	BALANCE DEBIT	CREDIT

© 2013 Cengage Learning. All Rights Reserved. May not be scanned, copied, duplicated, or posted to a publicly accessible website, in whole or in part.

ACCOUNTING CYCLE REVIEW PROBLEM A (continued)

	ACCOUNT NAME	TRIAL BALANCE		ADJUSTMENTS	
		DEBIT	CREDIT	DEBIT	CREDIT
1					
2					
3					
4					
5					
6					
7					
8					
9					
10					
11					
12					
13					
14					
15					
16					
17					
18					
19					
20					
21					
22					
23					
24					
25					
26					
27					
28					
29					
30					
31					
32					
33					
34					
35					
36					
37					
38					
39					
40					
41					

© 2013 Cengage Learning. All Rights Reserved. May not be scanned, copied, duplicated, or posted to a publicly accessible website, in whole or in part.

ACCOUNTING CYCLE REVIEW PROBLEM A (continued)

ADJUSTED TRIAL BALANCE		INCOME STATEMENT		BALANCE SHEET	
DEBIT	CREDIT	DEBIT	CREDIT	DEBIT	CREDIT

© 2013 Cengage Learning. All Rights Reserved. May not be scanned, copied, duplicated, or posted to a publicly accessible website, in whole or in part.

ACCOUNTING CYCLE REVIEW PROBLEM A (continued)

© 2013 Cengage Learning. All Rights Reserved. May not be scanned, copied, duplicated, or posted to a publicly accessible website, in whole or in part.

ACCOUNTING CYCLE REVIEW PROBLEM A (continued)

© 2013 Cengage Learning. All Rights Reserved. May not be scanned, copied, duplicated, or posted to a publicly accessible website, in whole or in part.

ACCOUNTING CYCLE REVIEW PROBLEM A (concluded)

© 2013 Cengage Learning. All Rights Reserved. May not be scanned, copied, duplicated, or posted to a publicly accessible website, in whole or in part.

ACCOUNTING CYCLE REVIEW PROBLEM B—WIND IN YOUR SAILS

Suggested Audit Questions

1.   What was the amount of cash paid for advertising on June 3?
2.   How much of the concession income was received in cash?
3.   What was the amount of the principal paid on the mortgage?
4.   How much did Cury withdraw from the business?
5.   What is the amount of accrued wages?
6.   How much insurance expired during the month?
7.   What is the amount of depreciation of the fan system in June?
8.   What is the ending balance of Cury's Capital account?
9.   As of the end of the month, what is the amount of the book value of the pool structure?
10. How much cash did Cury pay as a down payment on the purchase of Wind In Your Sails?

Answers

1. _____
2. _____
3. _____
4. _____
5. _____
6. _____
7. _____
8. _____
9. _____
10. _____

© 2013 Cengage Learning. All Rights Reserved. May not be scanned, copied, duplicated, or posted to a publicly accessible website, in whole or in part.

ACCOUNTING CYCLE REVIEW PROBLEM B (continued)

GENERAL JOURNAL   PAGE _____1_____

	DATE		DESCRIPTION	POST. REF.	DEBIT	CREDIT	
1							1
2							2
3							3
4							4
5							5
6							6
7							7
8							8
9							9
10							10
11							11
12							12
13							13
14							14
15							15
16							16
17							17
18							18
19							19
20							20
21							21
22							22
23							23
24							24
25							25
26							26
27							27
28							28
29							29
30							30
31							31
32							32
33							33
34							34
35							35
36							36
37							37
38							38
39							39
40							40
41							41
42							42
43							43

© 2013 Cengage Learning. All Rights Reserved. May not be scanned, copied, duplicated, or posted to a publicly accessible website, in whole or in part.

ACCOUNTING CYCLE REVIEW PROBLEM B (continued)

GENERAL JOURNAL   PAGE ___2___

	DATE		DESCRIPTION	POST. REF.	DEBIT	CREDIT	
1							1
2							2
3							3
4							4
5							5
6							6
7							7
8							8
9							9
10							10
11							11
12							12
13							13
14							14
15							15
16							16
17							17
18							18
19							19
20							20
21							21
22							22
23							23
24							24
25							25
26							26
27							27
28							28
29							29
30							30
31							31
32							32
33							33
34							34
35							35
36							36
37							37
38							38
39							39
40							40
41							41
42							42
43							43

© 2013 Cengage Learning. All Rights Reserved. May not be scanned, copied, duplicated, or posted to a publicly accessible website, in whole or in part.

ACCOUNTING CYCLE REVIEW PROBLEM B (continued)

GENERAL JOURNAL   PAGE _____ *3* _____

	DATE		DESCRIPTION	POST. REF.	DEBIT	CREDIT	
1							1
2							2
3							3
4							4
5							5
6							6
7							7
8							8
9							9
10							10
11							11
12							12
13							13
14							14
15							15
16							16
17							17
18							18
19							19
20							20
21							21
22							22
23							23
24							24
25							25
26							26
27							27
28							28
29							29
30							30
31							31
32							32
33							33
34							34
35							35
36							36
37							37
38							38
39							39
40							40
41							41
42							42
43							43

© 2013 Cengage Learning. All Rights Reserved. May not be scanned, copied, duplicated, or posted to a publicly accessible website, in whole or in part.

ACCOUNTING CYCLE REVIEW PROBLEM B (continued)

GENERAL JOURNAL   PAGE ___4___

	DATE	DESCRIPTION	POST. REF.	DEBIT	CREDIT	
1						1
2						2
3						3
4						4
5						5
6						6
7						7
8						8
9						9
10						10
11						11
12						12
13						13
14						14
15						15
16						16
17						17
18						18
19						19
20						20
21						21
22						22
23						23
24						24
25						25
26						26
27						27
28						28
29						29
30						30
31						31
32						32
33						33
34						34
35						35
36						36
37						37
38						38
39						39
40						40
41						41
42						42
43						43

© 2013 Cengage Learning. All Rights Reserved. May not be scanned, copied, duplicated, or posted to a publicly accessible website, in whole or in part.

ACCOUNTING CYCLE REVIEW PROBLEM B (continued)

GENERAL JOURNAL   PAGE _____ 5 _____

	DATE		DESCRIPTION	POST. REF.	DEBIT	CREDIT	
1							1
2							2
3							3
4							4
5							5
6							6
7							7
8							8
9							9
10							10
11							11
12							12
13							13
14							14
15							15
16							16
17							17
18							18
19							19
20							20
21							21
22							22
23							23
24							24
25							25
26							26
27							27
28							28
29							29
30							30
31							31
32							32
33							33
34							34
35							35
36							36
37							37
38							38
39							39
40							40
41							41
42							42
43							43

© 2013 Cengage Learning. All Rights Reserved. May not be scanned, copied, duplicated, or posted to a publicly accessible website, in whole or in part.

ACCOUNTING CYCLE REVIEW PROBLEM B (continued)

GENERAL LEDGER

ACCOUNT   *Cash*   ACCOUNT NO.   *111*

DATE	ITEM	POST. REF.	DEBIT	CREDIT	BALANCE	
					DEBIT	CREDIT

ACCOUNT   *Accounts Receivable*   ACCOUNT NO.   *112*

DATE	ITEM	POST. REF.	DEBIT	CREDIT	BALANCE	
					DEBIT	CREDIT

ACCOUNT   *Prepaid Insurance*   ACCOUNT NO.   *114*

DATE	ITEM	POST. REF.	DEBIT	CREDIT	BALANCE	
					DEBIT	CREDIT

© 2013 Cengage Learning. All Rights Reserved. May not be scanned, copied, duplicated, or posted to a publicly accessible website, in whole or in part.

ACCOUNTING CYCLE REVIEW PROBLEM B (continued)

ACCOUNT *Land*   ACCOUNT NO. *121*

DATE	ITEM	POST. REF.	DEBIT	CREDIT	BALANCE	
					DEBIT	CREDIT

ACCOUNT *Pool Structure*   ACCOUNT NO. *125*

DATE	ITEM	POST. REF.	DEBIT	CREDIT	BALANCE	
					DEBIT	CREDIT

ACCOUNT *Accumulated Depreciation, Pool Structure*   ACCOUNT NO. *126*

DATE	ITEM	POST. REF.	DEBIT	CREDIT	BALANCE	
					DEBIT	CREDIT

ACCOUNT *Fan System*   ACCOUNT NO. *127*

DATE	ITEM	POST. REF.	DEBIT	CREDIT	BALANCE	
					DEBIT	CREDIT

ACCOUNT *Accumulated Depreciation, Fan System*   ACCOUNT NO. *128*

DATE	ITEM	POST. REF.	DEBIT	CREDIT	BALANCE	
					DEBIT	CREDIT

© 2013 Cengage Learning. All Rights Reserved. May not be scanned, copied, duplicated, or posted to a publicly accessible website, in whole or in part.

ACCOUNTING CYCLE REVIEW PROBLEM B (continued)

ACCOUNT *Sailboats*   ACCOUNT NO. *129*

DATE	ITEM	POST. REF.	DEBIT	CREDIT	BALANCE	
					DEBIT	CREDIT

ACCOUNT *Accumulated Depreciation, Sailboats*   ACCOUNT NO. *130*

DATE	ITEM	POST. REF.	DEBIT	CREDIT	BALANCE	
					DEBIT	CREDIT

ACCOUNT *Accounts Payable*   ACCOUNT NO. *221*

DATE	ITEM	POST. REF.	DEBIT	CREDIT	BALANCE	
					DEBIT	CREDIT

ACCOUNT *Wages Payable*   ACCOUNT NO. *222*

DATE	ITEM	POST. REF.	DEBIT	CREDIT	BALANCE	
					DEBIT	CREDIT

© 2013 Cengage Learning. All Rights Reserved. May not be scanned, copied, duplicated, or posted to a publicly accessible website, in whole or in part.

ACCOUNTING CYCLE REVIEW PROBLEM B (continued)

ACCOUNT *Mortgage Payable* ACCOUNT NO. *223*

DATE	ITEM	POST. REF.	DEBIT	CREDIT	BALANCE DEBIT	BALANCE CREDIT

ACCOUNT *R. Cury, Capital* ACCOUNT NO. *311*

DATE	ITEM	POST. REF.	DEBIT	CREDIT	BALANCE DEBIT	BALANCE CREDIT

ACCOUNT *R. Cury, Drawing* ACCOUNT NO. *312*

DATE	ITEM	POST. REF.	DEBIT	CREDIT	BALANCE DEBIT	BALANCE CREDIT

ACCOUNT *Income Summary* ACCOUNT NO. *313*

DATE	ITEM	POST. REF.	DEBIT	CREDIT	BALANCE DEBIT	BALANCE CREDIT

ACCOUNT *Income from Services* ACCOUNT NO. *411*

DATE	ITEM	POST. REF.	DEBIT	CREDIT	BALANCE DEBIT	BALANCE CREDIT

© 2013 Cengage Learning. All Rights Reserved. May not be scanned, copied, duplicated, or posted to a publicly accessible website, in whole or in part.

ACCOUNTING CYCLE REVIEW PROBLEM B (continued)

ACCOUNT *Concessions Income*   ACCOUNT NO. *412*

DATE	ITEM	POST. REF.	DEBIT	CREDIT	BALANCE DEBIT	BALANCE CREDIT

ACCOUNT *Sailboat Rental Expense*   ACCOUNT NO. *511*

DATE	ITEM	POST. REF.	DEBIT	CREDIT	BALANCE DEBIT	BALANCE CREDIT

ACCOUNT *Wages Expense*   ACCOUNT NO. *512*

DATE	ITEM	POST. REF.	DEBIT	CREDIT	BALANCE DEBIT	BALANCE CREDIT

ACCOUNT *Advertising Expense*   ACCOUNT NO. *513*

DATE	ITEM	POST. REF.	DEBIT	CREDIT	BALANCE DEBIT	BALANCE CREDIT

© 2013 Cengage Learning. All Rights Reserved. May not be scanned, copied, duplicated, or posted to a publicly accessible website, in whole or in part.

ACCOUNTING CYCLE REVIEW PROBLEM B (continued)

ACCOUNT   *Utilities Expense*   ACCOUNT NO.   *514*

DATE	ITEM	POST. REF.	DEBIT	CREDIT	BALANCE DEBIT	BALANCE CREDIT

ACCOUNT   *Interest Expense*   ACCOUNT NO.   *515*

DATE	ITEM	POST. REF.	DEBIT	CREDIT	BALANCE DEBIT	BALANCE CREDIT

ACCOUNT   *Insurance Expense*   ACCOUNT NO.   *516*

DATE	ITEM	POST. REF.	DEBIT	CREDIT	BALANCE DEBIT	BALANCE CREDIT

ACCOUNT   *Depreciation Expense, Pool Structure*   ACCOUNT NO.   *517*

DATE	ITEM	POST. REF.	DEBIT	CREDIT	BALANCE DEBIT	BALANCE CREDIT

ACCOUNT   *Depreciation Expense, Fan System*   ACCOUNT NO.   *518*

DATE	ITEM	POST. REF.	DEBIT	CREDIT	BALANCE DEBIT	BALANCE CREDIT

© 2013 Cengage Learning. All Rights Reserved. May not be scanned, copied, duplicated, or posted to a publicly accessible website, in whole or in part.

ACCOUNTING CYCLE REVIEW PROBLEM B (continued)

ACCOUNT   *Depreciation Expense, Sailboats*   ACCOUNT NO.   *519*

DATE		ITEM	POST. REF.	DEBIT	CREDIT	BALANCE	
						DEBIT	CREDIT

ACCOUNT   *Miscellaneous Expense*   ACCOUNT NO.   *522*

DATE		ITEM	POST. REF.	DEBIT	CREDIT	BALANCE	
						DEBIT	CREDIT

© 2013 Cengage Learning. All Rights Reserved. May not be scanned, copied, duplicated, or posted to a publicly accessible website, in whole or in part.

ACCOUNTING CYCLE REVIEW PROBLEM B (continued)

	ACCOUNT NAME	TRIAL BALANCE		ADJUSTMENTS	
		DEBIT	CREDIT	DEBIT	CREDIT
7					
8					
9					
10					
11					
12					
13					
14					
15					
16					
17					
18					
19					
20					
21					
22					
23					
24					
25					
26					
27					
28					
29					
30					
31					
32					
33					
34					
35					
36					
37					
38					
39					
40					
41					

© 2013 Cengage Learning. All Rights Reserved. May not be scanned, copied, duplicated, or posted to a publicly accessible website, in whole or in part.

ACCOUNTING CYCLE REVIEW PROBLEM B (continued)

ADJUSTED TRIAL BALANCE		INCOME STATEMENT		BALANCE SHEET	
DEBIT	CREDIT	DEBIT	CREDIT	DEBIT	CREDIT

© 2013 Cengage Learning. All Rights Reserved. May not be scanned, copied, duplicated, or posted to a publicly accessible website, in whole or in part.

ACCOUNTING CYCLE REVIEW PROBLEM B (continued)

© 2013 Cengage Learning. All Rights Reserved. May not be scanned, copied, duplicated, or posted to a publicly accessible website, in whole or in part.

ACCOUNTING CYCLE REVIEW PROBLEM B (continued)

© 2013 Cengage Learning. All Rights Reserved. May not be scanned, copied, duplicated, or posted to a publicly accessible website, in whole or in part.

ACCOUNTING CYCLE REVIEW PROBLEM B (concluded)

ACCOUNT NAME	DEBIT	CREDIT	

© 2013 Cengage Learning. All Rights Reserved. May not be scanned, copied, duplicated, or posted to a publicly accessible website, in whole or in part.

Answers to Study Guide Questions

CHAPTER 5

PART 1   True/False

1.	T	6.	F
2.	F	7.	T
3.	T	8.	F
4.	F	9.	T
5.	T	10.	F

PART 2   Completion—Accounting Language

1. post-closing trial balance
2. interim
3. real or permanent
4. Income Summary
5. closing
6. nominal or temporary-equity
7. accrual basis

PART 3   Closing Entries

	Debit	Credit
1.	f	d
2.	d	a, b
3.	d	e
4.	e	c

PART 4   Posting Closing Entries

1. $51,000
2. $55,000
3. $4,000 net loss ($55,000 − $51,000)
4. $12,000
5. F. Landry, Capital; Income Summary
6. F. Landry, Capital; F. Landry, Drawing
7. $16,000 decrease ($12,000 + $4,000 net loss)
8. $119,000 ($135,000 − $16,000)

© 2013 Cengage Learning. All Rights Reserved. May not be scanned, copied, duplicated, or posted to a publicly accessible website, in whole or in part.

6 Bank Accounts, Cash Funds, and Internal Controls

LEARNING OBJECTIVES

1. List internal controls for cash receipts and cash payments.
2. Describe the procedures for recording deposits and withdrawals.
3. Reconcile a bank statement.
4. Record the required journal entries from the bank reconciliation.
5. Record journal entries to establish a Petty Cash Fund.
6. Complete petty cash vouchers, petty cash payments record and reimburse the petty cash fund.
7. Record the journal entries to establish a Change Fund.
8. Record journal entries for transactions involving Cash Short and Over.

ACCOUNTING LANGUAGE

ATMs (automated teller machines)	Internal Control
Bank reconciliation	Ledger balance of cash
Bank Routing Number	NSF (not sufficient funds) checks
Bank statement	Online banking
Canceled checks	Outstanding checks
Cash funds	Payee
Change Fund	Petty Cash Fund
Collections	Petty cash payments record
Denominations	Petty cash voucher
Deposit in transit	Personal identification number (PIN)
Deposit slips	Positive Pay
Drawer	Promissory Note
Electronic Funds Transfer (EFT)	Remote Deposit
Endorsement	Service Charge
Errors	Signature Card
Interest Income	Substitute Check

STUDY GUIDE QUESTIONS
PART 1   True/False

For each of the following statements, circle T if the statement is true and F if the statement is false.

T   F   1.   The amount set aside for change will vary by the type and size of the business.

T   F   2.   Each petty cash payment is entered separately in the petty cash payments record, not the general journal.

T   F   3.   Cash receipts, deposits, and bank reconciliations should always be handled by the same person.

T   F   4.   Before recording an amount in the Cash Short and Over account, one must deduct the amount of the change fund and then compare the actual cash and the amount sold for cash.

© 2013 Cengage Learning. All Rights Reserved. May not be scanned, copied, duplicated, or posted to a publicly accessible website, in whole or in part.

T   F   5.   The entry for an NSF check involves a debit to Accounts Receivable and a credit to Cash.

T   F   6.   Payments made from the Petty Cash Fund are journalized by account when the Petty Cash Fund is reimbursed.

T   F   7.   A credit memo increases the depositor's bank balance.

T   F   8.   The entry to reimburse the Petty Cash Fund involves a debit to Petty Cash Fund and a credit to Cash.

T   F   9.   On a bank reconciliation, outstanding checks are deducted from the bank statement balance.

T   F   10.   A credit balance in the Cash Short and Over account is listed on the income statement under Miscellaneous Expense.

PART 2   Completion—Accounting Language

Complete each of the following statements by writing the appropriate words in the spaces provided.

1.   The party who receives the check is called the _____.

2.   The amount that the bank charges a depositor for handling checks and collections is called a(n) _____ .

3.   The handling of assets in a manner that will prevent employees from stealing cash funds is known as _____.

4.   The method used to transfer title of a check is known as a(n) _____.

5.   Checks issued by the depositor that have been paid by the bank and included with the bank statement are called _____.

6.   _____ is the interest earned for keeping cash in the bank account.

7.   The party that writes a check is called the _____ .

8.   On a bank reconciliation, the balance of the Cash account in the general ledger is called the _____.

9.   A deposit not recorded on the bank statement because the deposit was made between the bank's cut-off date and the time the statement is received is called a(n) _____ _____.

10.   The _____ is a cash fund used to handle transactions where customers pay cash for goods and services.

11.   _____ are checks that have been written by the depositor and deducted on the depositor's records but have not yet reached the bank for payment.

12.   The procedure used to determine why there is a difference between the balance of Cash in the company's general ledger and in the company's bank records is called a(n) _____ _____.

13.   A(n) _____ must be used to account for every payment from the petty cash fund.

© 2013 Cengage Learning. All Rights Reserved. May not be scanned, copied, duplicated, or posted to a publicly accessible website, in whole or in part.

PART 3　Reimbursing the Petty Cash Fund

Sprinkles Bakery has the petty cash payments record shown below.

The amount of the debit balance of the Petty Cash Fund account is $_____.

Record the entry in general journal form to reimburse the Petty Cash Fund.

PETTY CASH PAYMENTS RECORD

PERIOD OF TIME　*June 20—*　　　　　　　　　PAGE ____37____

	DATE		VOU. NO.	EXPLANATION	PAYMENTS	REPAIR EXPENSE	DELIVERY EXPENSE	MISC. EXPENSE	OTHER ACCOUNTS ACCOUNT	AMOUNT	
1	20—										1
2	June	3	1	T. Walker	8.00				T. Walker,		2
3									Drawing	8.00	3
4		7	2	Marking pens	3.75			3.75			4
5		9	3	Ben's Delivery	5.85		5.85				5
6		12	4	Lightbulbs	6.32			6.32			6
7		17	5	Postage stamps	5.35			5.35			7
8		21	6	Repair fuses	8.15	8.15					8
9		29	7	T. Walker	9.45				T. Walker,		9
10									Drawing	9.45	10
11		30		Totals	46.87	8.15	5.85	15.42		17.45	11
12											12
13											13
14				Balance in Fund	$13.13						14
15				Reimbursed Ck.							15
16				No. 711	46.87						16
17				Total	$60.00						17
18											18

GENERAL JOURNAL　　　　PAGE _____

	DATE		DESCRIPTION	POST. REF.	DEBIT	CREDIT	
1							1
2							2
3							3
4							4
5							5
6							6
7							7
8							8
9							9
10							10
11							11
12							12
13							13
14							14

© 2013 Cengage Learning. All Rights Reserved. May not be scanned, copied, duplicated, or posted to a publicly accessible website, in whole or in part.

DEMONSTRATION PROBLEM

Barton Company made the following transactions during June of this year involving its Petty Cash Fund, Change Fund, Cash Short and Over, and Income from Services accounts:

June 1   Established a Change Fund, $200.

3   Established a Petty Cash Fund, $100.

14   Recorded cash revenue for period June 1 through 14: cash register tape, $4,980.21; cash count, $5,175.39.

30   Reimbursed the Petty Cash Fund, $94. The petty cash payments record indicated the following expenditures: Supplies, $32; Delivery Expense, $16; Advertising Expense, $35; Miscellaneous Expense, $11.

30   Recorded cash revenue for period June 15 through 30: cash register tape, $5,239.16; cash count, $5,441.09.

30   Recorded an NSF check received from J. Blakely listed on the bank reconciliation, $157.

Instructions

Record the transactions in general journal form.

© 2013 Cengage Learning. All Rights Reserved. May not be scanned, copied, duplicated, or posted to a publicly accessible website, in whole or in part.

SOLUTION

GENERAL JOURNAL   PAGE _____

	DATE		DESCRIPTION	POST. REF.	DEBIT	CREDIT	
1	20—						1
2	June	1	Change Fund		200.00		2
3			Cash			200.00	3
4			Established a Change Fund.				4
5							5
6		3	Petty Cash Fund		100.00		6
7			Cash			100.00	7
8			Established a Petty Cash Fund.				8
9							9
10		14	Cash		4,975.39		10
11			Cash Short and Over		4.82		11
12			Income from Services			4,980.21	12
13			To record cash revenue for period				13
14			June 1 through 14 involving a				14
15			cash shortage of $4.82.				15
16							16
17		30	Supplies		32.00		17
18			Delivery Expense		16.00		18
19			Advertising Expense		35.00		19
20			Miscellaneous Expense		11.00		20
21			Cash			94.00	21
22			Reimbursed the Petty Cash Fund.				22
23							23
24		30	Cash		5,241.09		24
25			Income from Services			5,239.16	25
26			Cash Short and Over			1.93	26
27			To record cash revenue for period				27
28			June 15 through 30 involving a				28
29			cash overage of $1.93.				29
30							30
31		30	Accounts Receivable		157.00		31
32			Cash			157.00	32
33			To record an NSF check received				33
34			from J. Blakely.				34
35							35

© 2013 Cengage Learning. All Rights Reserved. May not be scanned, copied, duplicated, or posted to a publicly accessible website, in whole or in part.

EXERCISES AND PROBLEMS

Exercise 6-1

Bank Statement Balance				$3,764.00
Add:	Deposit in transit		(a)	_____
				$4,031.00
Deduct:	Outstanding checks			
	No. 211	$212.00		
	No. 225		(b)	
	No. 228	318.00		850.00
Adjusted Bank Statement Balance			(c)	
Ledger Balance of Cash				$2,837.00
Add:	Note collected by bank			430.00
			(d)	
Deduct:	Bank service and collection charges		(e)	
	NSF check from customer	74.00		86.00
Adjusted Ledger Balance of Cash			(f)	

Exercise 6-2

GENERAL JOURNAL   PAGE _____

	DATE	DESCRIPTION	POST. REF.	DEBIT	CREDIT	
1						1
2						2
3						3
4						4
5						5
6						6
7						7
8						8
9						9
10						10
11						11
12						12
13						13
14						14
15						15
16						16
17						17
18						18
19						19
20						20
21						21
22						22
23						23

© 2013 Cengage Learning. All Rights Reserved. May not be scanned, copied, duplicated, or posted to a publicly accessible website, in whole or in part.

Exercise 6-3

Bank Statement Balance $ _____

Add: _____ _____

         $ _____

Deduct: _____ _____ (_____ – _____)

Adjusted Bank Statement Balance $ _____

Exercise 6-4

ITEM	ADD TO BANK STATEMENT BALANCE	SUBTRACT FROM BANK STATEMENT BALANCE	ADD TO LEDGER BALANCE OF CASH	SUBTRACT FROM LEDGER BALANCE OF CASH
a. A check-printing charge				
b. An outstanding check				
c. A deposit for $197 listed incorrectly on the bank statement as $179				
d. A collection charge the bank made for a note it collected for its depositor				
e. A check written for $41.73 and recorded incorrectly in the checkbook as $41.37				
f. A deposit in transit				
g. An NSF check received from a customer				
h. A check written for $82.40 and recorded incorrectly in the checkbook as $820.40				

© 2013 Cengage Learning. All Rights Reserved. May not be scanned, copied, duplicated, or posted to a publicly accessible website, in whole or in part.

Exercise 6-5

Hosung Company
Bank Reconciliation
August 31, 20—

Bank Statement Balance .... $ _____

Add: _____ $ _____

_____

_____ $ _____

Deduct: _____ $ _____

_____

_____

Adjusted Bank Statement Balance .... $ _____

Ledger Balance of Cash .... $ _____

Add: _____ $ _____

Deduct: _____ $ _____

_____

Adjusted Ledger Balance of Cash .... $ _____

© 2013 Cengage Learning. All Rights Reserved. May not be scanned, copied, duplicated, or posted to a publicly accessible website, in whole or in part.

Exercise 6-6

GENERAL JOURNAL   PAGE _____

	DATE		DESCRIPTION	POST. REF.	DEBIT	CREDIT	
1							1
2							2
3							3
4							4
5							5
6							6
7							7
8							8
9							9
10							10
11							11
12							12
13							13
14							14
15							15
16							16
17							17
18							18
19							19
20							20
21							21
22							22
23							23
24							24

© 2013 Cengage Learning. All Rights Reserved. May not be scanned, copied, duplicated, or posted to a publicly accessible website, in whole or in part.

Exercise 6-7

GENERAL JOURNAL   PAGE _____

	DATE		DESCRIPTION	POST. REF.	DEBIT	CREDIT	
1							1
2							2
3							3
4							4
5							5
6							6
7							7

Exercise 6-8

a. _____

_____

_____

_____

_____

_____

_____

_____

b. _____

_____

_____

_____

_____

_____

_____

© 2013 Cengage Learning. All Rights Reserved. May not be scanned, copied, duplicated, or posted to a publicly accessible website, in whole or in part.

Problem 6-1A or 6-1B

Bank Reconciliation

Bank Statement Balance $

Add: _____ $ _____ _____

     _____

     _____

     _____

     _____ $

Deduct: _____ $

     _____

     _____

     _____

     _____

Adjusted Bank Statement Balance $

Ledger Balance of Cash $

Add: _____ $

     _____

     _____

     _____ $

Deduct: _____ $

     _____

     _____

     _____

Adjusted Ledger Balance of Cash $

GENERAL JOURNAL   PAGE _____

	DATE	DESCRIPTION	POST. REF.	DEBIT	CREDIT	
1						1
2						2
3						3
4						4
5						5
6						6
7						7
8						8
9						9
10						10
11						11
12						12
13						13
14						14
15						15
16						16

257

© 2013 Cengage Learning. All Rights Reserved. May not be scanned, copied, duplicated, or posted to a publicly accessible website, in whole or in part.

Problem 6-2A or 6-2B

GENERAL JOURNAL   PAGE _____

	DATE		DESCRIPTION	POST. REF.	DEBIT	CREDIT	
1							1
2							2
3							3
4							4
5							5
6							6
7							7
8							8
9							9
10							10
11							11
12							12
13							13
14							14
15							15
16							16
17							17
18							18
19							19
20							20
21							21
22							22
23							23
24							24
25							25
26							26
27							27
28							28
29							29
30							30
31							31
32							32
33							33
34							34
35							35
36							36
37							37

© 2013 Cengage Learning. All Rights Reserved. May not be scanned, copied, duplicated, or posted to a publicly accessible website, in whole or in part.

Problem 6-2A or 6-2B (concluded)

	DATE	VOUCHER	EXPLANATION	PAYMENTS	OFFICE SUPPLIES	DELIVERY EXPENSE	MISC. EXPENSE	ACCOUNT	AMOUNT	
1	PETTY CASH PAYMENTS RECORD									1
2					DISTRIBUTION OF PAYMENTS					2
3					OFFICE	DELIVERY	MISC.	OTHER ACCOUNTS		3
4					SUPPLIES	EXPENSE	EXPENSE	ACCOUNT	AMOUNT	4
5										5
6										6
7										7
8										8
9										9
10										10
11										11
12										12
13										13
14										14
15										15
16										16
17										17
18										18
19										19
20										20
21										21
22										22
23										23
24										24
25										25
26										26

© 2013 Cengage Learning. All Rights Reserved. May not be scanned, copied, duplicated, or posted to a publicly accessible website, in whole or in part.

Problem 6-3A or 6-3B

GENERAL JOURNAL   PAGE _____

	DATE		DESCRIPTION	POST. REF.	DEBIT	CREDIT	
1							1
2							2
3							3
4							4
5							5
6							6
7							7
8							8
9							9
10							10
11							11
12							12
13							13
14							14
15							15
16							16
17							17
18							18
19							19
20							20
21							21
22							22
23							23
24							24
25							25
26							26
27							27
28							28
29							29
30							30
31							31
32							32
33							33
34							34
35							35
36							36
37							37

© 2013 Cengage Learning. All Rights Reserved. May not be scanned, copied, duplicated, or posted to a publicly accessible website, in whole or in part.

Problem 6-4A or 6-4B

Bank Reconciliation

Bank Statement Balance — $ _____

Add: $ _____ _____
_____
_____
_____
$ _____

Deduct: $ _____
_____
_____
_____

Adjusted Bank Statement Balance — $ _____

Ledger Balance of Cash — $ _____

Add: $ _____
_____
_____
$ _____

Deduct: $ _____
_____
_____

Adjusted Ledger Balance of Cash — $ _____

GENERAL JOURNAL   PAGE _____

	DATE	DESCRIPTION	POST. REF.	DEBIT	CREDIT	
1						1
2						2
3						3
4						4
5						5
6						6
7						7
8						8
9						9
10						10
11						11
12						12
13						13
14						14
15						15
16						16

© 2013 Cengage Learning. All Rights Reserved. May not be scanned, copied, duplicated, or posted to a publicly accessible website, in whole or in part.

Problem 6-4A or 6-4B (concluded)

THIS FORM IS PROVIDED TO HELP YOU BALANCE
YOUR BANK STATEMENT

CHECKS OUTSTANDING—NOT
CHARGED TO ACCOUNT

No.	$
TOTAL	**$**

BEFORE YOU START

PLEASE BE SURE YOU HAVE ENTERED IN YOUR CHECK-
BOOK ALL AUTOMATIC TRANSACTIONS SHOWN ON
THE FRONT OF YOUR STATEMENT.

YOU SHOULD HAVE ADDED
IF ANY OCCURRED:

1. Loan advances.
2. Credit memos.
3. Other automatic deposits.

YOU SHOULD HAVE SUB-
TRACTED IF ANY OCCURRED:

1. Automatic loan payments.
2. Automatic savings transfers.
3. Service charges.
4. Debit memos.
5. Other automatic deductions
   and payments.

BANK BALANCE SHOWN
ON THIS STATEMENT $ _____

ADD

DEPOSITS NOT SHOWN
ON THIS STATEMENT
(*IF ANY*) $ _____

_____

_____

TOTAL $ _____

SUBTRACT

CHECKS OUTSTANDING $ _____

BALANCE $ _____

SHOULD AGREE WITH YOUR CHECKBOOK BALANCE
AFTER DEDUCTING SERVICE CHARGE (IF ANY)
SHOWN ON THIS STATEMENT.

Please examine immediately and report if incorrect. If no reply is received within 10 days, the account will be considered correct.

IN CASE OF ERRORS OR INQUIRIES ABOUT YOUR BILL

Send your inquiry in writing on a separate sheet so that the creditor receives it within 60 days after the bill was mailed to you. Your written inquiry must include:

1. Your name and account number;
2. A description of the error and why (to the extent you can explain) you believe it is an error; and
3. The dollar amount of the suspected error.

If you have authorized your creditor to automatically pay your bill from your checking or savings account, you can stop or reverse payment on any amount you think is wrong by mailing your notice so that the creditor receives it within 11 days after the bill was sent to you.

You remain obligated to pay the parts of your bill not in dispute, but you do not have to pay any amount in dispute during the time the creditor is resolving the dispute. During that same time, the creditor may not take any action to collect disputed amounts or report disputed amounts as delinquent.

This is a summary of your rights; a full statement of your rights and the creditor's responsibilities under the Federal Fair Credit Billing Act will be sent to you both upon request and in response to a billing error notice.

© 2013 Cengage Learning. All Rights Reserved. May not be scanned, copied, duplicated, or posted to a publicly accessible website, in whole or in part.

Problem 6-5A or 6-5B

Bank Reconciliation

Bank Statement Balance $ _____

Add: _____ $ _____   _____

_____

_____

_____

_____   _____

$ _____

Deduct: _____ $ _____

_____

_____

_____

_____

_____   _____

Adjusted Bank Statement Balance $ _____

Ledger Balance of Cash $ _____

Add: _____ $ _____

_____

_____

_____   _____

$ _____

Deduct: _____ $ _____

_____

_____

_____   _____

Adjusted Ledger Balance of Cash $ _____

© 2013 Cengage Learning. All Rights Reserved. May not be scanned, copied, duplicated, or posted to a publicly accessible website, in whole or in part.

Problem 6-5A or 6-5B (concluded)

GENERAL JOURNAL   PAGE _____

	DATE		DESCRIPTION	POST. REF.	DEBIT	CREDIT	
1							1
2							2
3							3
4							4
5							5
6							6
7							7
8							8
9							9
10							10
11							11
12							12
13							13
14							14
15							15
16							16
17							17
18							18
19							19
20							20
21							21
22							22
23							23
24							24
25							25
26							26
27							27
28							28
29							29
30							30
31							31
32							32
33							33
34							34
35							35
36							36
37							37
38							38

© 2013 Cengage Learning. All Rights Reserved. May not be scanned, copied, duplicated, or posted to a publicly accessible website, in whole or in part.

Answers to Study Guide Questions

CHAPTER 6

PART 1   True/False

1.	T	6.	T
2.	T	7.	T
3.	F	8.	F
4.	T	9.	T
5.	T	10.	F

PART 2   Completion—Accounting Language

1. payee
2. service charge
3. internal control
4. endorsement
5. canceled checks
6. interest income
7. drawer
8. ledger balance of cash
9. deposit in transit
10. Change Fund
11. Outstanding checks
12. bank reconciliation
13. petty cash voucher

PART 3   Reimbursing the Petty Cash Fund

The amount of the debit balance of the Petty Cash Fund account is $60.00.

GENERAL JOURNAL   PAGE _____

	DATE		DESCRIPTION	POST. REF.	DEBIT	CREDIT	
1	20—						1
2	June	30	Repair Expense		8.15		2
3			Delivery Expense		5.85		3
4			Miscellaenous Expense		15.42		4
5			T. Walker, Drawing		17.45		5
6			Cash			46.87	6
7			Issued Ck. No. 711 to reimburse				7
8			the Petty Cash Fund.				8
9							9

© 2013 Cengage Learning. All Rights Reserved. May not be scanned, copied, duplicated, or posted to a publicly accessible website, in whole or in part.

Employee Earnings and Deductions

LEARNING OBJECTIVES

1. Recognize the role of income tax laws that affect payroll deductions and contributions.
2. Calculate total earnings based on an hourly, salary, piece-rate, or commission basis.
3. Determine deductions from gross pay, such as federal income tax withheld, Social Security tax, and Medicare tax, to calculate net pay.
4. Complete a payroll register.
5. Journalize the payroll entry from a payroll register.
6. Maintain employees' individual earnings records.

ACCOUNTING LANGUAGE

Calendar year	Medicare taxes
Current Tax Payment Act	Net pay
Employee	Payroll bank account
Employee's individual earnings record	Payroll register
Employee's Withholding Allowance Certificate (Form W-4)	Pre-tax deductions
	Social Security Act of 1935
Exemption	Social Security taxes
Fair Labor Standards Act	Taxable earnings
FICA taxes	Wage-bracket tax tables
Gross pay	Withholding allowance
Independent contractor	Workers' compensation laws

STUDY GUIDE QUESTIONS

PART 1   True/False

For each of the following statements, circle T if the statement is true and F if the statement is false.

T   F   1. On a payroll register, an employee's net amount paid equals total earnings minus total individual deductions.

T   F   2. There is a tax ceiling or limit to the amount of earnings taxable under both Social Security and Medicare.

T   F   3. Information for an employee's individual earnings record is taken directly from the general journal.

T   F   4. The Current Tax Payment Act provides for minimum standards for both wages and overtime.

T   F   5. Social Security and Medicare taxes are paid by both the employer and the employee.

T   F   6. The basis for the payroll register is the payroll journal entry.

T   F   7. Individual earnings records need not be kept for salaried employees.

© 2013 Cengage Learning. All Rights Reserved. May not be scanned, copied, duplicated, or posted to a publicly accessible website, in whole or in part.

T	F	8.	Some businesses use a special payroll bank account.
T	F	9.	Employees (with a few exceptions) are required by law to participate in the Social Security program provided by the Federal Insurance Contributions Act.
T	F	10.	The difference between an employee's net pay and take-home pay is the amount of personal deductions.

PART 2   Completion—Accounting Language

Complete each of the following statements by writing the appropriate words in the spaces provided.

1. Total earnings for an employee are called the employee's _____.

2. Another term having the same meaning as take-home pay is _____.

3. Each employee's personal payroll information for the year is listed in the employee's

    _____ .

4. A(n) _____ is one who works for compensation under the direction or control of an employer.

5. Someone who is engaged for a definite job and who chooses his or her own means of doing the work is a(n) _____.

6. Another term having the same meaning as withholding allowance is _____.

7. If a deduction is _____, the employee does not have to pay income tax on the amount withheld.

PART 3   Calculation of Earnings

Meza Company pays its employees time-and-a-half for all hours worked in excess of 40 per week. For the first week of October, determine the total earnings for each of the following employees.

Employee's Name	Hours Worked	Regular Hourly Rate	Total Earnings
J. R. Matthews	42	$ 7.60	
T. J. Rasmussen	45	9.40	
F. P. Conway	46	11.20	

PART 4   Payroll Entry

Using the column totals for the week ended March 14 as listed in the payroll register, give the entry in general journal form to record the payroll. Number the page 79.

Total Earnings	$95,540.00
Federal Income Tax Deduction	9,500.00
Social Security Tax Deduction	5,923.48
Medicare Tax Deduction	1,385.33
Charitable Contributions Deduction	900.00
Union Dues Deduction	1,200.00
Medical Insurance Deduction	2,000.00
Net Amount	74,631.19
Sales Salary Expense	74,000.00
Office Salary Expense	21,540.00

© 2013 Cengage Learning. All Rights Reserved. May not be scanned, copied, duplicated, or posted to a publicly accessible website, in whole or in part.

DEMONSTRATION PROBLEM

Northwest Sales Company's payroll register reveals the following information concerning its two employees for the month ended July 31 of this year:

D. C. Garcia		**T. C. Bennett**	
Total earnings	$ 4,000.00	Total earnings	$ 3,600.00
Federal income tax withheld	(321.17)	Federal income tax withheld	(261.17)
Social Security tax withheld	(168.00)	Social Security tax withheld	(151.20)
Medicare tax withheld	(58.00)	Medicare tax withheld	(52.20)
United Way withheld	(258.00)	United Way withheld	(125.00)
Net amount (Ck. No. 6701)	$ 3,194.83	Net amount (Ck. No. 6702)	$ 3,010.43

The employees are paid by checks issued on the firm's regular bank account.

Instructions

Prepare the entry to record the payroll in a general journal.

SOLUTION

GENERAL JOURNAL   PAGE _____

	DATE		DESCRIPTION	POST. REF.	DEBIT	CREDIT	
1	20—						1
2	July	31	Salary Expense		7,600.00		2
3			Employees' Federal Income Tax Payable			582.34	3
4			FICA Taxes Payable			429.40	4
5			($168.00 + $151.20 + $58.00 + $52.20)				5
6			United Way Payable			383.00	6
7			Cash			6,205.26	7
8			Paid salaries for the month				8
9			(D. C. Garcia, $3,194.83, Ck. No. 6701;				9
10			T. C. Bennett, $3,010.43, Ck. No. 6702).				10
11							11
12							12

© 2013 Cengage Learning. All Rights Reserved. May not be scanned, copied, duplicated, or posted to a publicly accessible website, in whole or in part.

EXERCISES AND PROBLEMS

Exercise 7-1

a. _____ hours at straight time × _____ per hour $ _____

_____ hours overtime × _____ per hour

Total gross pay $ _____

b. _____ hours at straight time × _____ per hour $ _____

_____ hours overtime × _____ per hour

Total gross pay $ _____

c. _____ × _____ $ _____

d. _____

_____

_____ $ _____

_____ $ _____

Exercise 7-2

a. _____ hours at straight time × _____ per hour $ _____

b. _____ hours overtime × _____ per hour

c. Total gross pay $ _____

d. Federal income tax withholding $ 256.81

e. Social Security tax withholding at 4.2 percent

f. Medicare tax withholding at 1.45 percent   _____

g. Total withholding   _____

h. Net pay $ _____

© 2013 Cengage Learning. All Rights Reserved. May not be scanned, copied, duplicated, or posted to a publicly accessible website, in whole or in part.

Exercise 7-3

EMPLOYEE	ALLOWANCES	TOTAL EARNINGS	FEDERAL INCOME TAX WITHHELD	SOCIAL SECURITY TAX WITHHELD	MEDICARE TAX WITHHELD	UNION DUES WITHHELD	UNITED WAY WITHHELD	NET PAY
a. Aston, F. B.	1	$ 900.00				$ 25.00	$ 35.00	
b. Dwyer, S. J.	2	920.00				25.00	35.00	
c. Flynn, K. A.	3	1,110.00				25.00	40.00	
d. Harden, J. L.	0	1,025.00				25.00	40.00	
e. Nguyen, H.	2	925.00				25.00	35.00	
Totals		$4,880.00				$125.00	$185.00	

Exercise 7-4

1. _____
2. _____
3. _____
4. _____
5. _____
6. _____

Exercise 7-5

	A	B	C	D	E	F	G
						TAXABLE EARNINGS	
1							
2		BEGINNING CUMULATIVE EARNINGS	TOTAL EARNINGS	ENDING CUMULATIVE EARNINGS			
3	EMPLOYEE				UNEMPLOYMENT	SOCIAL SECURITY	MEDICARE
4	Axton, C.	106,000.00	7,691.00	113,691.00			
5	Edgar, E.	145,465.00	10,900.00	156,365.00			
6	Gorman, L.	36,879.00	3,064.00	39,943.00			
7	Jolson, R.	24,634.00	2,325.00	26,959.00			
8	Nixel, P.	6,850.00	2,463.00	9,313.00			
9							

© 2013 Cengage Learning. All Rights Reserved. May not be scanned, copied, duplicated, or posted to a publicly accessible website, in whole or in part.

Exercise 7-6

GENERAL JOURNAL   PAGE _____

	DATE		DESCRIPTION	POST. REF.	DEBIT	CREDIT	
1							1
2							2
3							3
4							4
5							5
6							6
7							7
8							8
9							9
10							10
11							11
12							12

Exercise 7-7

	Brown	Ringness	Total
Regular earnings	$ 3,500.00	$	$
Overtime earnings		120.00	
Total earnings	$ 3,646.00	$	
Federal income tax withheld	$ 268.07	$	$
State income tax withheld		26.37	
Social Security tax withheld	153.13	115.00	
Medicare tax withheld	52.87	39.70	
Charity withheld	35.00	97.00	
Total deductions	$ 562.68	$ 409.94	$
Net pay		$ 2,328.06	$

© 2013 Cengage Learning. All Rights Reserved. May not be scanned, copied, duplicated, or posted to a publicly accessible website, in whole or in part.

Exercise 7-8

GENERAL JOURNAL

PAGE _____

	DATE		DESCRIPTION	POST. REF.	DEBIT	CREDIT	
1							1
2							2
3							3
4							4
5							5
6							6
7							7
8							8
9							9
10							10
11							11
12							12
13							13
14							14

© 2013 Cengage Learning. All Rights Reserved. May not be scanned, copied, duplicated, or posted to a publicly accessible website, in whole or in part.

Problem 7-1A or 7-1B

REGULAR PAY	OVERTIME PAY	GROSS PAY	NET PAY
hours	hours		
× $ _____ per hour	× $ _____ per hour	**Regular pay**	**Gross pay** $
$ _____	$ _____	**Overtime pay** $	**Less:**
		Gross pay $	**Federal income tax** $
			_____
			_____
			Total deductions _____
			Net pay $

© 2013 Cengage Learning. All Rights Reserved. May not be scanned, copied, duplicated, or posted to a publicly accessible website, in whole or in part.

Problem 7-2A or 7-2B

	A	B	C	D	E	F	G	H	I	J	K	L	M	N	O	P
															PAYMENTS	
1																
2			PAYROLL REGISTER FOR WEEK ENDED						TAXABLE EARNINGS			DEDUCTIONS				
3				EARNINGS												
4	NAME	TOTAL HOURS	BEGINNING CUMULATIVE EARNINGS	REGULAR	OVERTIME	TOTAL	ENDING CUMULATIVE EARNINGS	UNEMPLOY-MENT	SOCIAL SECURITY	MEDICARE	FEDERAL INCOME TAX	SOCIAL SECURITY TAX	MEDICARE TAX	TOTAL	NET AMOUNT	CK. NO.
5																
6																
7																
8																
9																
10																
11																
12																
13																
14																

© 2013 Cengage Learning. All Rights Reserved. May not be scanned, copied, duplicated, or posted to a publicly accessible website, in whole or in part.

Problem 7-2A or 7-2B (concluded)

GENERAL JOURNAL   PAGE _____

	DATE		DESCRIPTION	POST. REF.	DEBIT	CREDIT	
1							1
2							2
3							3
4							4
5							5
6							6
7							7
8							8
9							9
10							10
11							11
12							12
13							13
14							14
15							15

© 2013 Cengage Learning. All Rights Reserved. May not be scanned, copied, duplicated, or posted to a publicly accessible website, in whole or in part.

Problem 7-3A or 7-3B

	A	B	C	D	E	F	G	H	I	J	K	L	M	N	O	P
				PAYROLL REGISTER FOR WEEK ENDED _____										PAYMENTS	
				EARNINGS			TAXABLE EARNINGS			DEDUCTIONS					
1															
2															
4	NAME	TOTAL HOURS	BEGINNING CUMULATIVE EARNINGS	REGULAR	OVERTIME	TOTAL	ENDING CUMULATIVE EARNINGS	UNEMPLOY-MENT	SOCIAL SECURITY	MEDICARE	FEDERAL INCOME TAX	SOCIAL SECURITY TAX	MEDICARE TAX	TOTAL	NET AMOUNT	CK. NO.
5																
6																
7																
8																
9																
10																
11																
12																
13																
14																
15																
16																
17																

© 2013 Cengage Learning. All Rights Reserved. May not be scanned, copied, duplicated, or posted to a publicly accessible website, in whole or in part.

Problem 7-3A or 7-3B (concluded)

GENERAL JOURNAL

PAGE _____

	DATE		DESCRIPTION	POST. REF.	DEBIT	CREDIT	
1							1
2							2
3							3
4							4
5							5
6							6
7							7
8							8
9							9
10							10
11							11
12							12
13							13
14							14
15							15

© 2013 Cengage Learning. All Rights Reserved. May not be scanned, copied, duplicated, or posted to a publicly accessible website, in whole or in part.

Problem 7-4A or 7-4B

PAYROLL REGISTER FOR WEEK ENDED _____

	A	B	C	D	E	F	G	H	I	J	K	L	M	N	O	P	Q
						TAXABLE EARNINGS			DEDUCTIONS					PAYMENTS		EXPENSE ACCOUNT DEBITED	
	NAME	TOTAL HOURS	BEGINNING CUMULATIVE EARNINGS	TOTAL EARNINGS	ENDING CUMULATIVE EARNINGS	UNEMPLOY-MENT	SOCIAL SECURITY	MEDICARE	FEDERAL INCOME TAX	SOCIAL SECURITY TAX	MEDI-CARE TAX	AMOUNT	TOTAL	NET AMOUNT	CK. NO.	SALES SALARY	OFFICE SALARY
1																	
2																	
3																	
4																	
5																	
6																	
7																	
8																	
9																	
10																	
11																	
12																	
13																	
14																	
15																	
16																	
17																	
18																	

© 2013 Cengage Learning. All Rights Reserved. May not be scanned, copied, duplicated, or posted to a publicly accessible website, in whole or in part.

Problem 7-4A or 7-4B (concluded)

GENERAL JOURNAL   PAGE _____

	DATE		DESCRIPTION	POST. REF.	DEBIT	CREDIT	
1							1
2							2
3							3
4							4
5							5
6							6
7							7
8							8
9							9
10							10
11							11
12							12
13							13
14							14
15							15
16							16
17							17
18							18

© 2013 Cengage Learning. All Rights Reserved. May not be scanned, copied, duplicated, or posted to a publicly accessible website, in whole or in part.

Problem 7-5A or 7-5B

REGULAR PAY	OVERTIME PAY	GROSS PAY	NET PAY
hours	hours	Regular pay	Gross pay $
× $ per hour	× $ per hour	Overtime pay $	Less:
$	$	Gross pay $	Federal income tax $
			Total deductions
			Net pay $

© 2013 Cengage Learning. All Rights Reserved. May not be scanned, copied, duplicated, or posted to a publicly accessible website, in whole or in part.

Answers to Study Guide Questions

CHAPTER 7

PART 1   True/False

1.	T	6.	F
2.	F	7.	F
3.	F	8.	T
4.	F	9.	T
5.	T	10.	F

PART 2   Completion—Accounting Language

1. gross pay
2. net pay
3. individual earnings record
4. employee
5. independent contractor
6. exemption
7. pre-tax

PART 3   Calculation of Earnings

Employee's Name	Hours Worked	Regular Hourly Rate	Total Earnings
J. R. Matthews	42	$ 7.60	$326.80
T. J. Rasmussen	45	9.40	446.50
F. P. Conway	46	11.20	548.80

J. R. Matthews (40 × $7.60) + (2 × $7.60 × 1.5) = $326.80
T. J. Rasmussen (40 × $9.40) + (5 × $9.40 × 1.5) = $446.50
F. P. Conway (40 × $11.20) + (6 × $11.20 × 1.5) = $548.80

PART 4   Payroll Entry

GENERAL JOURNAL   PAGE _____79_____

	DATE		DESCRIPTION	POST. REF.	DEBIT	CREDIT	
1	20—						1
2	Mar.	14	Sales Salary Expense		74,000.00		2
3			Office Salary Expense		21,540.00		3
4			Employees' Federal Income Tax Payable			9,500.00	4
5			FICA Taxes Payable ($5,923.48 + $1,385.33)			7,308.81	5
6			Employees' Charitable Contributions				6
7			Deductions Payable			900.00	7
8			Employees' Union Dues Payable			1,200.00	8
9			Employees' Medical Insurance Payable			2,000.00	9
10			Salaries Payable			74,631.19	10
11			To record payroll for the week ended				11
12			March 14.				12
13							13

© 2013 Cengage Learning. All Rights Reserved. May not be scanned, copied, duplicated, or posted to a publicly accessible website, in whole or in part.

Employer Taxes, Payments, and Reports

LEARNING OBJECTIVES

1.   Calculate the amount of payroll tax expense and journalize the entry.

2.   Journalize the entry for the deposit of employees' federal income taxes withheld and FICA tax (both employees' withheld and employer's share) and prepare the deposit.

3.   Journalize the entries for the payment of employer's state and federal unemployment taxes.

4.   Journalize the entry for the deposit of employees' state income taxes withheld.

5.   Complete Employer's Quarterly Federal Tax Return, Form 941.

6.   Prepare W-2 and W-3 forms and Form 940.

7.   Calculate the premium for workers' compensation insurance, and prepare the entry for payment in advance.

8.   Determine the amount of the end-of-the-year adjustments for (a) workers' compensation insurance and (b) accrued salaries and wages and record the adjustments.

ACCOUNTING LANGUAGE

Electronic Federal Tax Payment System (EFTPS)   Form W-2
Employer Identification Number (EIN)   Form W-3
Federal unemployment tax (FUTA)   Payroll Tax Expense
Form 940   Quarter
Form 941   State unemployment tax (SUTA)
Form 941-V   Workers' compensation insurance

STUDY GUIDE QUESTIONS
PART 1   True/False

For each of the following statements, circle T if the statement is true and F if the statement is false.

T   F   1.   Form 940 is an annual tax return that relates to federal unemployment tax.

T   F   2.   The Payroll Tax Expense account handles the unemployment taxes as well as the employer's and employee's FICA taxes and employee income taxes.

T   F   3.   A premium for workers' compensation insurance is paid at the beginning of the year.

T   F   4.   The times for making deposits of FICA taxes and employees' income taxes withheld depend strictly on the number of employees involved.

T   F   5.   Companies must furnish their employees with W-2 forms by April 15.

T   F   6.   The purpose of Form 941 is to report employee income taxes and employer and employee Social Security and Medicare taxes.

© 2013 Cengage Learning. All Rights Reserved. May not be scanned, copied, duplicated, or posted to a publicly accessible website, in whole or in part.

T   F   7.   Form W-4 is submitted to the Internal Revenue Service along with copies of the employees' W-2 forms.

T   F   8.   The federal unemployment tax is usually paid by the employer only.

T   F   9.   If the Unemployment Taxable Earnings column of the payroll register is blank, this indicates that the employee has cumulative earnings for the calendar year of more than the maximum unemployment taxable income.

T   F   10. The state unemployment tax is determined by multiplying the net amount as shown in the payroll register by the state unemployment tax rate.

PART 2   Completion—Accounting Language

Complete each of the following statements by writing the appropriate word in the spaces provided.

1.   Employers' reports submitted to the Internal Revenue Service all must contain the

_____ .

2.   _____ provides an employee with his or her total earnings and tax deductions for the year.

3.   The second _____ of the year consists of the months of April, May, and June.

4.   The _____ account is used to record the employees' and employer's matching portion of FICA taxes, the federal unemployment tax, and the state unemployment tax.

5.   _____ is the Employer's Quarterly Federal Tax Return.

6.   Form _____ is submitted to the Social Security Administration accompanied by copies of W-2 forms.

7.   _____ is used to provide benefits for employees injured on the job.

8.   For any balance due on the 941 report, a _____ form accompanies the report and payment.

© 2013 Cengage Learning. All Rights Reserved. May not be scanned, copied, duplicated, or posted to a publicly accessible website, in whole or in part.

PART 3   Completing Form W-2

Complete the Form W-2 provided for Lisa A. Keller. Keller is employed by Barr Company, 1620 Hampton Place, Boston, Massachusetts 02116. Barr Company's federal employer identification number is 72-1162127, and its state identification number is 42-6916. The following information is taken from Keller's Individual Earnings Record. Her address is 2219 Henderson Street, Boston, Massachusetts 02121. Her Social Security number is 562-25-6329. During the year, Keller earned $34,218.42. Her withholdings were as follows: federal income tax, $3,716.22; state income tax, $1,780.04; Social Security tax withheld, $2,121.54; Medicare tax withheld, $496.17.

a Employee's social security number OMB No. 1545-0008 Safe, accurate, FAST! Use **IRS e·file** Visit the IRS website at www.irs.gov/efile		
b Employer identification number (EIN)	**1** Wages, tips, other compensation	**2** Federal income tax withheld
c Employer's name, address, and ZIP code	**3** Social security wages	**4** Social security tax withheld
	5 Medicare wages and tips	**6** Medicare tax withheld
	7 Social security tips	**8** Allocated tips
d Control number	**9** Advance EIC payment	**10** Dependent care benefits
e Employee's first name and initial Last name Suff.	**11** Nonqualified plans	**12a** See instructions for box 12
	13 Statutory employee Retirement plan Third-party sick pay	**12b**
	14 Other	**12c**
		12d
f Employee's address and ZIP code		

15 State Employer's state ID number	**16** State wages, tips, etc.	**17** State income tax	**18** Local wages, tips, etc.	**19** Local income tax	**20** Locality name

Form **W-2** Wage and Tax Statement   **20—**   Department of the Treasury—Internal Revenue Service

Copy B—To Be Filed With Employee's FEDERAL Tax Return.
This information is being furnished to the Internal Revenue Service.

© 2013 Cengage Learning. All Rights Reserved. May not be scanned, copied, duplicated, or posted to a publicly accessible website, in whole or in part.

DEMONSTRATION PROBLEM

The totals of the payroll register for Precision Moving are given below. Assume the employment taxes are as follows:

Social Security, 6.2 percent (Employer)
Social Security, 4.2 percent (Employee)
Medicare, 1.45 percent (Employer and Employee)
State Unemployment, 5.4 percent
Federal Unemployment, 0.6 percent

Total Earnings..	$96,345
State Unemployment Taxable Earnings.............................	21,200
Federal Unemployment Taxable Earnings.........................	21,200
Social Security Taxable Earnings....................................	84,500
Medicare Taxable Earnings...	96,345
Federal Income Tax Deduction......................................	26,964
Social Security Tax Deduction.......................................	3,549
Medicare Tax Deduction..	1,397
Charitable Contribution Deduction.................................	1,560

Instructions

Journalize the following entries:

a. To record the payroll, assuming the use of a payroll bank account.

b. To record the payroll tax expense.

c. To pay the payroll.

d. To record the deposit of federal taxes that will be reported on the Employer's Quarterly Federal Tax Return (Form 941): employees' income taxes withheld, employees' FICA taxes withheld, and employer's share of FICA taxes.

e. To record payment of state unemployment insurance that will be reported on the state unemployment insurance tax form.

f. To record the deposit of federal unemployment insurance that will be reported on the Employer's Annual Federal Unemployment (FUTA) Tax Return (Form 940).

g. To record payment of employees' charitable contributions withheld.

© 2013 Cengage Learning. All Rights Reserved. May not be scanned, copied, duplicated, or posted to a publicly accessible website, in whole or in part.

SOLUTION

GENERAL JOURNAL   PAGE _____

	DATE		DESCRIPTION	POST. REF.	DEBIT	CREDIT	
1		a.	Wages Expense		96,345.00		1
2			Employees' Federal Income Tax Payable			26,964.00	2
3			FICA Taxes Payable			4,946.00	3
4			($84,500 × 0.042) + ($96,345 × 0.0145)				4
5			Employees' Charitable Contributions Payable			1,560.00	5
6			Wages Payable			62,875.00	6
7			To record wages as listed in the payroll				7
8			register.				8
9							9
10		b.	Payroll Tax Expense		7,908.00		10
11			FICA Taxes Payable			6,636.00	11
12			($84,500 × 0.062) + ($96,345 × 0.0145)				12
13			State Unemployment Tax Payable			1,144.80	13
14			($21,200 × 0.054)				14
15			Federal Unemployment Tax Payable			127.20	15
16			($21,200 × 0.006)				16
17			To record employer's share of FICA taxes				17
18			and federal and state unemployment taxes.				18
19							19
20		c.	Wages Payable		62,875.00		20
21			Cash—Payroll Bank Account			62,875.00	21
22			Paid wages.				22
23							23
24		d.	Employees' Federal Income Tax Payable		26,964.00		24
25			FICA Taxes Payable ($4,946 + $6,636)		11,582.00		25
26			Cash			38,546.00	26
27			Issued check to record deposit of federal				27
28			taxes.				28
29							29
30		e.	State Unemployment Tax Payable		1,144.80		30
31			Cash			1,144.80	31
32			Issued check for payment of state				32
33			unemployment tax.				33
34							34
35		f.	Federal Unemployment Tax Payable		127.20		35
36			Cash			127.20	36
37			Issued check for payment of federal				37
38			unemployment tax.				38
39							39
40		g.	Employees' Charitable Contributions Payable		1,560.00		40
41			Cash			1,560.00	41
42			To record payment of employees' charitable				42
43			contributions withheld.				43
44							44

© 2013 Cengage Learning. All Rights Reserved. May not be scanned, copied, duplicated, or posted to a publicly accessible website, in whole or in part.

EXERCISES AND PROBLEMS

Exercise 8-1

GENERAL JOURNAL

PAGE _____

	DATE	DESCRIPTION	POST. REF.	DEBIT	CREDIT	
1						1
2						2
3						3
4						4
5						5
6						6
7						7
8						8
9						9
10						10
11						11

© 2013 Cengage Learning. All Rights Reserved. May not be scanned, copied, duplicated, or posted to a publicly accessible website, in whole or in part.

Exercise 8-2

a. _____

_____

_____

_____

_____

GENERAL JOURNAL   PAGE _____

	DATE	DESCRIPTION	POST. REF.	DEBIT	CREDIT	
1						1
2						2
3						3
4						4
5						5
6						6
7						7
8						8
9						9
10						10
11						11
12						12

b. _____

_____

_____

_____

GENERAL JOURNAL   PAGE _____

	DATE	DESCRIPTION	POST. REF.	DEBIT	CREDIT	
1						1
2						2
3						3
4						4
5						5
6						6
7						7
8						8
9						9

© 2013 Cengage Learning. All Rights Reserved. May not be scanned, copied, duplicated, or posted to a publicly accessible website, in whole or in part.

Exercise 8-3

GENERAL JOURNAL   PAGE _____

a.

	DATE		DESCRIPTION	POST. REF.	DEBIT	CREDIT	
1							1
2							2
3							3
4							4
5							5
6							6
7							7
8							8
9							9
10							10
11							11
12							12
13							13

GENERAL JOURNAL   PAGE _____

b.

	DATE		DESCRIPTION	POST. REF.	DEBIT	CREDIT	
1							1
2							2
3							3
4							4
5							5
6							6
7							7
8							8
9							9
10							10
11							11
12							12
13							13
14							14

© 2013 Cengage Learning. All Rights Reserved. May not be scanned, copied, duplicated, or posted to a publicly accessible website, in whole or in part.

Exercise 8-4

	A	C	F	G	H	I	J	
		BEGINNING CUMULATIVE EARNINGS	TOTAL EARNINGS	ENDING CUMULATIVE EARNINGS	TAXABLE EARNINGS			
	NAME				UNEMPLOY-MENT	SOCIAL SECURITY	MEDICARE	
4								4
5								5
6								6
7								7
8								8
9								9
10								10
11								11

GENERAL JOURNAL   PAGE _____

	DATE	DESCRIPTION	POST. REF.	DEBIT	CREDIT	
1						1
2						2
3						3
4						4
5						5
6						6
7						7
8						8
9						9
10						10
11						11
12						12

Exercise 8-5

GENERAL JOURNAL   PAGE _____

	DATE	DESCRIPTION	POST. REF.	DEBIT	CREDIT	
1						1
2						2
3						3
4						4
5						5
6						6
7						7
8						8

© 2013 Cengage Learning. All Rights Reserved. May not be scanned, copied, duplicated, or posted to a publicly accessible website, in whole or in part.

Exercise 8-6

GENERAL JOURNAL   PAGE _____

	DATE		DESCRIPTION	POST. REF.	DEBIT	CREDIT	
1							1
2							2
3							3
4							4
5							5
6							6
7							7
8							8
9							9
10							10
11							11
12							12
13							13
14							14
15							15
16							16
17							17
18							18

Exercise 8-7

GENERAL JOURNAL   PAGE _____

	DATE		DESCRIPTION	POST. REF.	DEBIT	CREDIT	
1							1
2							2
3							3
4							4
5							5
6							6
7							7
8							8
9							9
10							10
11							11
12							12
13							13
14							14
15							15
16							16
17							17
18							18

© 2013 Cengage Learning. All Rights Reserved. May not be scanned, copied, duplicated, or posted to a publicly accessible website, in whole or in part.

Exercise 8-8

GENERAL JOURNAL   PAGE _____

a.

	DATE		DESCRIPTION	POST. REF.	DEBIT	CREDIT	
1							1
2							2
3							3
4							4
5							5
6							6
7							7
8							8

GENERAL JOURNAL   PAGE _____

b.

	DATE		DESCRIPTION	POST. REF.	DEBIT	CREDIT	
1							1
2							2
3							3
4							4
5							5
6							6
7							7
8							8
9							9
10							10
11							11

© 2013 Cengage Learning. All Rights Reserved. May not be scanned, copied, duplicated, or posted to a publicly accessible website, in whole or in part.

Problem 8-1A or 8-1B

GENERAL JOURNAL   PAGE _____

	DATE		DESCRIPTION	POST. REF.	DEBIT	CREDIT	
1							1
2							2
3							3
4							4
5							5
6							6
7							7
8							8
9							9
10							10
11							11
12							12
13							13
14							14
15							15
16							16
17							17
18							18
19							19
20							20
21							21
22							22
23							23
24							24
25							25
26							26
27							27
28							28
29							29

1. (rows 1–12)

2. (rows 13–24)

3. (rows 25–29)

© 2013 Cengage Learning. All Rights Reserved. May not be scanned, copied, duplicated, or posted to a publicly accessible website, in whole or in part.

Problem 8-2A or 8-2B

1.

NAME	BEGINNING CUMULATIVE EARNINGS	TOTAL EARNINGS	ENDING CUMULATIVE EARNINGS	TAXABLE EARNINGS			DEDUCTIONS					PAYMENTS		SALARY EXPENSE DEBIT
				UNEMPLOY-MENT	SOCIAL SECURITY	MEDICARE	FEDERAL INCOME TAX	STATE INCOME TAX	SOCIAL SECURITY TAX	MEDICARE TAX	TOTAL	NET AMOUNT	CK. NO.	

© 2013 Cengage Learning. All Rights Reserved. May not be scanned, copied, duplicated, or posted to a publicly accessible website, in whole or in part.

Problem 8-2A or 8-2B (concluded)

GENERAL JOURNAL   PAGE _____

	DATE	DESCRIPTION	POST. REF.	DEBIT	CREDIT	
1						1
2						2
3						3
4						4
5						5
6						6
7						7
8						8
9						9
10						10
11						11
12						12
13						13
14						14
15						15
16						16
17						17
18						18
19						19
20						20
21						21
22						22
23						23
24						24
25						25
26						26
27						27
28						28
29						29

2. (rows 2) 3. (row 13) 4. (row 25)

© 2013 Cengage Learning. All Rights Reserved. May not be scanned, copied, duplicated, or posted to a publicly accessible website, in whole or in part.

Problem 8-3A or 8-3B

Form **941 for 20—:** **Employer's QUARTERLY Federal Tax Return**
(Rev. January 20—)   Department of the Treasury — Internal Revenue Service

950111

OMB No. 1545-0029

(EIN)
Employer identification number ☐☐ – ☐☐☐☐☐☐☐

Name *(not your trade name)*

Trade name *(if any)*

Address

Number   Street   Suite or room number

City   State   ZIP code

Report for this Quarter of 20 —
(Check one.)

☐ 1: January, February, March

☐ 2: April, May, June

☐ 3: July, August, September

☐ 4: October, November, December

Prior-year forms are available at
www.irs.gov/form941.

Read the separate instructions before you complete Form 941. Type or print within the boxes.

Part 1:   Answer these questions for this quarter.

1	Number of employees who received wages, tips, or other compensation for the pay period including: *Mar. 12* (Quarter 1), *June 12* (Quarter 2), *Sept. 12* (Quarter 3), or *Dec. 12* (Quarter 4)	1	
2	Wages, tips, and other compensation	2	.
3	Income tax withheld from wages, tips, and other compensation	3	.
4	If no wages, tips, and other compensation are subject to social security or Medicare tax		☐ Check and go to line 6e.

		Column 1		Column 2		
5a	Taxable social security wages .		.	x .104 =	.	For 20—, the employee social security tax rate is 4.2% and the Medicare tax rate is 1.45%. The employer social security tax rate is 6.2% and the Medicare tax rate is 1.45%.
5b	Taxable social security tips . .		.	x .104 =	.	
5c	Taxable Medicare wages & tips.		.	x .029 =	.	

5d	Add *Column 2* line 5a, *Column 2* line 5b, and *Column 2* line 5c	5d	.
5e	Section 3121(q) Notice and Demand—Tax due on unreported tips (see instructions) . .	5e	.
6a	Reserved for future use.		
6b	Reserved for future use.		
6c	Reserved for future use.		

Do Not Complete Lines 6a-6d

6e	Total taxes before adjustments (add lines 3, 5d, and 5e)	6e	.
7	Current quarter's adjustment for fractions of cents	7	.
8	Current quarter's adjustment for sick pay	8	.
9	Current quarter's adjustments for tips and group-term life insurance	9	.
10	Total taxes after adjustments. Combine lines 6e through 9	10	.
11	Total deposits, including prior quarter overpayments	11	.
12a	COBRA premium assistance payments (see instructions)	12a	.
12b	Number of individuals provided COBRA premium assistance . .		
13	Add lines 11 and 12a	13	.
14	Balance due. If line 10 is more than line 13, enter the difference and see instructions . . .	14	.
15	Overpayment. If line 13 is more than line 10, enter the difference	.	Check one: ☐ Apply to next return. ☐ Send a refund.

▶ You MUST complete both pages of Form 941 and SIGN it.

Next ▶

For Privacy Act and Paperwork Reduction Act Notice, see the back of the Payment Voucher.   Cat. No. 17001Z   Form **941** (Rev. 1-20—)

© 2013 Cengage Learning. All Rights Reserved. May not be scanned, copied, duplicated, or posted to a publicly accessible website, in whole or in part.

Problem 8-4A or 8-4B

GENERAL JOURNAL

PAGE ___77___

	DATE		DESCRIPTION	POST. REF.	DEBIT	CREDIT	
1							1
2							2
3							3
4							4
5							5
6							6
7							7
8							8
9							9
10							10
11							11
12							12
13							13
14							14
15							15
16							16
17							17
18							18
19							19
20							20
21							21
22							22
23							23
24							24
25							25
26							26
27							27
28							28
29							29
30							30
31							31
32							32

© 2013 Cengage Learning. All Rights Reserved. May not be scanned, copied, duplicated, or posted to a publicly accessible website, in whole or in part.

Problem 8-4A or 8-4B (concluded)

GENERAL JOURNAL   PAGE _____ *78* _____

	DATE		DESCRIPTION	POST. REF.	DEBIT	CREDIT	
1							1
2							2
3							3
4							4
5							5
6							6
7							7
8							8
9							9
10							10
11							11
12							12
13							13
14							14
15							15
16							16
17							17
18							18
19							19
20							20
21							21
22							22
23							23

© 2013 Cengage Learning. All Rights Reserved. May not be scanned, copied, duplicated, or posted to a publicly accessible website, in whole or in part.

Problem 8-5A or 8-5B

Form **940 for 20 — :** **Employer's Annual Federal Unemployment (FUTA) Tax Return**   850110

Department of the Treasury — Internal Revenue Service

OMB No. 1545-0028

(EIN)
Employer identification number ☐☐ – ☐☐☐☐☐☐☐

Name *(not your trade name)*

Trade name *(if any)*

Address

Number   Street

Suite or room number

City   State   ZIP code

Type of Return
(Check all that apply.)

☐ a. Amended

☐ b. Successor employer

☐ c. No payments to employees in 20 —

☐ d. Final: Business closed or stopped paying wages

Read the separate instructions before you fill out this form. Please type or print within the boxes.

Part 1: Tell us about your return. If any line does NOT apply, leave it blank.

1   If you were required to pay your state unemployment tax in ...

1a   **One state only,** write the state abbreviation . . . . .   **1a** ☐☐
     - OR -

1b   **More than one state** (You are a multi-state employer) . . . .   **1b** ☐ Check here. Fill out Schedule A.

2   If you paid wages in a state that is subject to **CREDIT REDUCTION** . . . .   **2** ☐ Check here. Fill out Schedule A (Form 940), Part 2.

Part 2: Determine your FUTA tax before adjustments for 20 —. If any line does NOT apply, leave it blank.

3   Total payments to all employees . . . .   **3** ⬚.

4   Payments exempt from FUTA tax . . . .   **4** ⬚.

     Check all that apply: **4a** ☐ Fringe benefits   **4c** ☐ Retirement/Pension **4e** ☐ Other
     4b ☐ Group-term life insurance **4d** ☐ Dependent care

5   Total of payments made to each employee in excess of $7,000 . . . . .   **5** ⬚.

6   Subtotal (line 4 + line 5 = line 6) . . . .   **6** ⬚.

7   Total taxable FUTA wages (line 3 – line 6 = line 7) . . . .   **7** ⬚.

8   FUTA tax before adjustments (line 7 × .006 = line 8) . . . .   **8** ⬚.

Part 3: Determine your adjustments. If any line does NOT apply, leave it blank.

9   If ALL of the taxable FUTA wages you paid were excluded from state unemployment tax, multiply line 7 by .054 (line 7 × .054 = line 9). Then go to line 12 . . . .   **9** ⬚.

10   If SOME of the taxable FUTA wages you paid were excluded from state unemployment tax, OR you paid ANY state unemployment tax late (after the due date for filing Form 940), fill out the worksheet in the instructions. Enter the amount from line 7 of the worksheet . . . . .   **10** ⬚.

11   If credit reduction applies, enter the amount from line 3 of Schedule A (Form 940) . . . .   **11** ⬚.

Part 4: Determine your FUTA tax and balance due or overpayment for 20 —. If any line does NOT apply, leave it blank.

12   Total FUTA tax after adjustments (lines 8 + 9 + 10 + 11 = line 12) . . . .   **12** ⬚.

13   FUTA tax deposited for the year, including any overpayment applied from a prior year .   **13** ⬚.

14   Balance due (If line 12 is more than line 13, enter the difference on line 14.)
     • If line 14 is more than $500, you must deposit your tax.
     • If line 14 is $500 or less, you may pay with this return. For more information on how to pay, see the separate instructions . . . .   **14** ⬚.

15   Overpayment (If line 13 is more than line 12, enter the difference on line 15 and check a box below.) . . . .   **15** ⬚.

Check one: ☐ Apply to next return.
            ☐ Send a refund.

► You **MUST** fill out both pages of this form and **SIGN** it.

Next ➡

For Privacy Act and Paperwork Reduction Act Notice, see the back of Form 940-V, Payment Voucher.   Cat. No. 112340   Form **940** (20 —)

© 2013 Cengage Learning. All Rights Reserved. May not be scanned, copied, duplicated, or posted to a publicly accessible website, in whole or in part.

Problem 8-5A or 8-5B (continued)

850210

Name *(not your trade name)*	Employer identification number (EIN)

Part 5: Report your FUTA tax liability by quarter only if line 12 is more than $500. If not, go to Part 6.

16   Report the amount of your FUTA tax liability for each quarter; do NOT enter the amount you deposited. If you had no liability for a quarter, leave the line blank.

    16a   1st quarter (January 1 – March 31) . . . .   **16a**   .

    16b   2nd quarter (April 1 – June 30) . . . .   **16b**   .

    16c   3rd quarter (July 1 – September 30) . . . .   **16c**   .

    16d   4th quarter (October 1 – December 31) . . . .   **16d**   .

17   Total tax liability for the year (lines 16a + 16b + 16c + 16d = line 17) **17**   .   **Total must equal line 12.**

Part 6: May we speak with your third-party designee?

Do you want to allow an employee, a paid tax preparer, or another person to discuss this return with the IRS? See the instructions for details.

☐ **Yes.**   Designee's name and phone number

                Select a 5-digit Personal Identification Number (PIN) to use when talking to IRS

☑ **No.**

Part 7: Sign here. You MUST fill out both pages of this form and SIGN it.

Under penalties of perjury, I declare that I have examined this return, including accompanying schedules and statements, and to the best of my knowledge and belief, it is true, correct, and complete, and that no part of any payment made to a state unemployment fund claimed as a credit was, or is to be, deducted from the payments made to employees. Declaration of preparer (other than taxpayer) is based on all information of which preparer has any knowledge.

✗ **Sign your name here**

Print your name here

Print your title here

Date   /   /

Best daytime phone

© 2013 Cengage Learning. All Rights Reserved. May not be scanned, copied, duplicated, or posted to a publicly accessible website, in whole or in part.

Problem 8-5A or 8-5B (concluded)

▼   **Detach Here and Mail With Your Payment and Form 940.**   ▼   ✂

Form **940-V**	**Payment Voucher**	OMB No. 1545-0028
Department of the Treasury Internal Revenue Service	▶ Do not staple or attach this voucher to your payment.	20 —

1 Enter your employer identification number (EIN).	2 **Enter the amount of your payment.** ▶	Dollars	Cents
	3 Enter your business name (individual name if sole proprietor).		
	Enter your address.		
	Enter your city, state, and ZIP code.		

GENERAL JOURNAL   PAGE _____

	DATE	DESCRIPTION	POST. REF.	DEBIT	CREDIT	
1						1
2						2
3						3
4						4
5						5
6						6
7						7

© 2013 Cengage Learning. All Rights Reserved. May not be scanned, copied, duplicated, or posted to a publicly accessible website, in whole or in part.

Answers to Study Guide Questions

CHAPTER 8

PART 1   True/False

1.	T	6.	T
2.	F	7.	F
3.	T	8.	T
4.	F	9.	T
5.	F	10.	F

PART 2   Completion—Accounting Language

1. employer identification number
2. Form W-2
3. quarter
4. Payroll Tax Expense
5. Form 941
6. W-3
7. Workers' compensation insurance
8. 941-V

PART 3   Completing Form W-2

Form W-2 Wage and Tax Statement

a Employee's social security number: 562-25-6329
OMB No. 1545-0008

b Employer identification number (EIN): 72-1162127

c Employer's name, address, and ZIP code:
Barr Company
1620 Hampton Place
Boston, MA 02116

e Employee's first name and initial / Last name:
Lisa A. Keller
2219 Henderson Street
Boston, MA 02121

1 Wages, tips, other compensation: 34,218.42
2 Federal income tax withheld: 3,716.22
3 Social security wages: 34,218.42
4 Social security tax withheld: 2,121.54
5 Medicare wages and tips: 34,218.42
6 Medicare tax withheld: 496.17
7 Social security tips: 0
8 Allocated tips: 0

15 State: MA
Employer's state ID number: 42-6916
16 State wages, tips, etc.: 34,218.42
17 State income tax: 1,780.04

Department of the Treasury—Internal Revenue Service

Copy B—To Be Filed With Employee's FEDERAL Tax Return.
This information is being furnished to the Internal Revenue Service.

© 2013 Cengage Learning. All Rights Reserved. May not be scanned, copied, duplicated, or posted to a publicly accessible website, in whole or in part.

9 | Sales and Purchases

LEARNING OBJECTIVES

1. Describe the nature of a merchandising business.

2. Using a general journal and the periodic inventory system, record sales and sale-related transactions; then post to the general ledger and accounts receivable ledger.

3. Prepare a schedule of accounts receivable.

4. Using a general journal and the periodic inventory system, record purchase and purchase-related transactions; then post to the general ledger and the accounts payable ledger.

5. Prepare a schedule of accounts payable.

6. Using a general journal and the perpetual inventory system, record sales and sale-related transactions.

7. Using a general journal and the perpetual inventory system, record purchase and purchase-related transactions.

8. Record transactions in a sales journal and post to the general ledger and accounts receivable ledger.

9. Record transactions in a three-column purchases journal and post to the general ledger and accounts payable ledger.

ACCOUNTING LANGUAGE

Accounts payable ledger
Accounts receivable ledger
Controlling account
Cost of Goods Sold account
Credit memorandum
FOB destination
FOB shipping point
Invoices
Merchandise inventory
Merchandising businesses
Periodic inventory system

Perpetual inventory system
Purchases account
Purchases journal
Purchases Returns and Allowances account
Sales account
Sales journal
Sales Returns and Allowances account
Sales Tax Payable account
Special journals
Subsidiary ledger

© 2013 Cengage Learning. All Rights Reserved. May not be scanned, copied, duplicated, or posted to a publicly accessible website, in whole or in part.

STUDY GUIDE QUESTIONS—GENERAL JOURNAL AND SALES

PART 1   True/False

For each of the following statements, circle T if the statement is true and F if the statement is false.

T   F   1.   Sales transactions can be recorded two ways—either by recording them directly into the general journal or by using a special journal.

T   F   2.   When using a general journal, the entry for merchandise sold on account includes a credit to Accounts Receivable.

T   F   3.   The schedule of accounts receivable lists the balances of all the credit customer accounts at the end of the month.

T   F   4.   A business can list customer accounts in alphabetical order in its accounts receivable ledger.

T   F   5.   Increases in Sales Returns and Allowances are recorded on the credit side.

T   F   6.   At the end of the month, after all posting is completed, the total of the schedule of accounts receivable should equal the balance of the Sales account in the general ledger.

T   F   7.   The Accounts Receivable account in the general ledger contains a separate account for each customer.

T   F   8.   When using a general journal, the entry for sales transactions that include sales tax involves a credit to Sales Tax Payable.

T   F   9.   Under a perpetual inventory system, the company maintains continuous records of inventories.

T   F   10.   Under a periodic inventory system, the company maintains continuous records of inventories.

PART 2   Completion—Accounting Language

Complete each of the following statements by writing the appropriate words in the spaces provided.

1.   A stock of ready-made goods that a company buys and intends to resell at a profit is called

_____.

2.   The Accounts Receivable account in the general ledger is called a(n) _____

_____.

3.   The accounts receivable ledger may be called a special ledger or a(n) _____

_____.

4.   A document issued by the seller to a customer allowing a reduction from the price at which the goods were originally sold is called a(n) _____

© 2013 Cengage Learning. All Rights Reserved. May not be scanned, copied, duplicated, or posted to a publicly accessible website, in whole or in part.

STUDY GUIDE QUESTIONS—GENERAL JOURNAL AND PURCHASES

PART 1   True/False

For each of the following statements, circle T if the statement is true and F if the statement is false.

T	F	1.	The purchase requisition is sent to the supplier.
T	F	2.	The Purchases account is used to record the buying of merchandise for resale only.
T	F	3.	Increases in the Purchases Returns and Allowances account are recorded on the debit side.
T	F	4.	If the freight charges are FOB shipping point, the buyer pays the transportation charges.
T	F	5.	Each purchase is posted daily to the accounts payable ledger.
T	F	6.	At the end of the month, the total of the schedule of accounts payable should equal the balance of the Purchases account.
T	F	7.	If the transportation terms are FOB destination, the cost of the freight charge is included in the selling price.
T	F	8.	A debit memorandum is a document sent by the seller to the buyer, indicating that the Accounts Receivable account is being reduced on the seller's books.
T	F	9.	Terms of 1/15, n/30 means that if the buyer pays the amount due within 15 days, the buyer will receive a 1 percent discount; otherwise, the entire amount is due in 30 days.
T	F	10.	The Purchases Returns and Allowances account has a normal credit balance.

PART 2   Completion—Accounting Language

Complete each of the following statements by writing the appropriate words in the spaces provided.

1. The form sent to the supplier of merchandise to indicate an order is called a(n) _____.

2. When the buyer pays the transportation charges on incoming merchandise, the shipping terms are called _____.

3. From the buyer's viewpoint, the form prepared by the seller listing the items shipped, their costs, and the mode of shipment is called a(n) _____.

4. A transportation arrangement in which the seller retains title to the goods in transit is called _____.

© 2013 Cengage Learning. All Rights Reserved. May not be scanned, copied, duplicated, or posted to a publicly accessible website, in whole or in part.

STUDY GUIDE QUESTIONS—SALES JOURNAL

PART 1   True/False

For each of the following statements, circle T if the statement is true and F if the statement is false.

T   F   1. Posting from the sales journal to the accounts receivable ledger accounts should take place after each entry.

T   F   2. When using special journals, the sales journal is used to record all sales.

T   F   3. Check marks in the Post. Ref. column of the sales journal indicate that the amounts are not to be posted.

T   F   4. When using a sales journal, you do not have to post to any accounts in the general ledger.

T   F   5. When using a sales journal, each sale is supposed to be posted monthly to the individual customer accounts.

PART 2   Completion—Accounting Language

Complete each of the following statements by writing the appropriate words in the spaces provided.

1. The book of original entry used to record sales of merchandise on account is called a(n)

    _____.

2. Books of original entry used to record specialized types of transactions are referred to as

    _____.

3. Transactions involving sales tax that are recorded in the sales journal will need three columns: Accounts Receivable Debit, Sales Tax Payable _____ ,

    and Sales _____.

© 2013 Cengage Learning. All Rights Reserved. May not be scanned, copied, duplicated, or posted to a publicly accessible website, in whole or in part.

STUDY GUIDE QUESTIONS—PURCHASES JOURNAL

PART 1   True/False

For each of the following statements, circle T if the statement is true and F if the statement is false.

T   F   1.   The purchases journal is used for the buying of merchandise for cash and on account.

T   F   2.   The purchases journal contains an Accounts Payable Debit column, a Freight In Debit column, and a Purchases Credit column.

T   F   3.   Check marks in the Post. Ref. column of the purchases journal indicate that the amounts in the Accounts Payable column have been posted to the accounts payable ledger.

T   F   4.   When using a purchases journal, the accountant posts the totals of each column into the appropriate general ledger account daily.

T   F   5.   Transactions involving the buying of fixed assets should be journalized in the three-column purchases journal.

PART 2   Completion—Accounting Language

Complete each of the following statements by writing the appropriate words in the spaces provided.

1.   When posting from the purchases journal to the general ledger, in the Post. Ref. column of the ledger accounts, _____ designates the purchases journal.

2.   _____ in the Post. Ref. column of the purchases jour indicate that the column totals have been posted for the month.

3.   After posting the column totals from the purchases journal to the general ledger, the accountant records the _____ in parentheses directly below the tot

© 2013 Cengage Learning. All Rights Reserved. May not be scanned, copied, duplicated, or posted to a publicly accessible website, in whole or in part.

DEMONSTRATION PROBLEM 1—GENERAL JOURNAL

In February, the Montgomery Company completed the following selected transactions:

Feb. 3 Bought merchandise on account from Wong Company, invoice no. 887, $2,486; terms 2/10, n/30; dated February 1; FOB shipping point, freight prepaid and added to the invoice, $224 (total $2,710).

   6 Sold merchandise on account to Holland Company, invoice no. 857, $4,786.

   10 Bought supplies on account from Banks Company, invoice no. 820, $483; terms net 30 days; dated February 10; FOB destination.

   12 Received credit memo no. 485 from Wong Company, $486, for merchandise returned.

   20 Sold merchandise on account to Santos Company, invoice no. 858, $5,331.

   27 Santos Company returned $488 worth of merchandise relating to sales invoice no. 858. Montgomery Company issued credit memo no. 47.

Instructions

1. Record the transactions in the general journal (page 28).

2. Post the entries from the general journal to the general ledger and the accounts receivable or accounts payable ledger, as appropriate.

3. Prepare a schedule of accounts receivable.

4. Prepare a schedule of accounts payable.

5. Compare the total of the schedule of accounts receivable with the February 28 balance of the Accounts Receivable (controlling) account.

6. Compare the total of the schedule of accounts payable with the February 28 balance of the Accounts Payable (controlling) account.

© 2013 Cengage Learning. All Rights Reserved. May not be scanned, copied, duplicated, or posted to a publicly accessible website, in whole or in part.

DEMONSTRATION SOLUTION 1

	DATE		DESCRIPTION	POST. REF.	DEBIT	CREDIT	
1	20—						1
2	Feb.	3	Purchases	511	2,486.00		2
3			Freight In	514	224.00		3
4			Accounts Payable, Wong Company	212/ ✓		2,710.00	4
5			Purchased merchandise on account,				5
6			invoice no. 887, invoice dated 2/1,				6
7			terms 2/10, n/30.				7
8							8
9		6	Accounts Receivable, Holland Company	113/ ✓	4,786.00		9
10			Sales	411		4,786.00	10
11			Sold merchandise on account,				11
12			invoice no. 857.				12
13							13
14		10	Supplies	114	483.00		14
15			Accounts Payable, Banks Company	212/ ✓		483.00	15
16			Purchased supplies on account,				16
17			invoice no. 820, invoice dated 2/10,				17
18			terms net 30.				18
19							19
20		12	Accounts Payable, Wong Company	212/ ✓	486.00		20
21			Purchases Returns and Allowances	512		486.00	21
22			Credit memo no. 485 for return of				22
23			merchandise.				23
24							24
25		20	Accounts Receivable, Santos Company	113/ ✓	5,331.00		25
26			Sales	411		5,331.00	26
27			Sold merchandise on account,				27
28			invoice no. 858.				28
29							29
30		27	Sales Returns and Allowances	412	488.00		30
31			Accounts Receivable, Santos Company	113/ ✓		488.00	31
32			Issued credit memo no. 47.				32
33							33
34							34

GENERAL JOURNAL   PAGE   **28**

© 2013 Cengage Learning. All Rights Reserved. May not be scanned, copied, duplicated, or posted to a publicly accessible website, in whole or in part.

DEMONSTRATION SOLUTION 1 (continued)

GENERAL LEDGER

ACCOUNT   *Accounts Receivable*   ACCOUNT NO.   *113*

DATE		ITEM	POST. REF.	DEBIT	CREDIT	BALANCE	
						DEBIT	CREDIT
20—							
Feb.	1	Balance	✓			4,815.24	
	6		J28	4,786.00		9,601.24	
	20		J28	5,331.00		14,932.24	
	27		J28		488.00	14,444.24	

ACCOUNT   *Supplies*   ACCOUNT NO.   *114*

DATE		ITEM	POST. REF.	DEBIT	CREDIT	BALANCE	
						DEBIT	CREDIT
20—							
Feb.	1	Balance	✓			432.33	
	10		J28	483.00		915.33	

ACCOUNT   *Accounts Payable*   ACCOUNT NO.   *212*

DATE		ITEM	POST. REF.	DEBIT	CREDIT	BALANCE	
						DEBIT	CREDIT
20—							
Feb.	1	Balance	✓				7,849.25
	3		J28		2,710.00		10,559.25
	10		J28		483.00		11,042.25
	12		J28	486.00			10,556.25

ACCOUNT   *Sales*   ACCOUNT NO.   *411*

DATE		ITEM	POST. REF.	DEBIT	CREDIT	BALANCE	
						DEBIT	CREDIT
20—							
Feb.	1	Balance	✓				15,486.15
	6		J28		4,786.00		20,272.15
	20		J28		5,331.00		25,603.15

312

© 2013 Cengage Learning. All Rights Reserved. May not be scanned, copied, duplicated, or posted to a publicly accessible website, in whole or in part.

DEMONSTRATION SOLUTION 1 (continued)

ACCOUNT Sales Returns and Allowances   ACCOUNT NO. __412__

DATE		ITEM	POST. REF.	DEBIT	CREDIT	BALANCE DEBIT	BALANCE CREDIT
20—							
Feb.	1	Balance	✓			2,458.75	
	27		J28	488.00		2,946.75	

ACCOUNT Purchases   ACCOUNT NO. __511__

DATE		ITEM	POST. REF.	DEBIT	CREDIT	BALANCE DEBIT	BALANCE CREDIT
20—							
Feb.	1	Balance	✓			8,941.54	
	3		J28	2,486.00		11,427.54	

ACCOUNT Purchases Returns and Allowances   ACCOUNT NO. __512__

DATE		ITEM	POST. REF.	DEBIT	CREDIT	BALANCE DEBIT	BALANCE CREDIT
20—							
Feb.	1	Balance	✓				1,458.10
	12		J28		486.00		1,944.10

ACCOUNT Freight In   ACCOUNT NO. __514__

DATE		ITEM	POST. REF.	DEBIT	CREDIT	BALANCE DEBIT	BALANCE CREDIT
20—							
Feb.	1	Balance	✓			587.40	
	3		J28	224.00		811.40	

© 2013 Cengage Learning. All Rights Reserved. May not be scanned, copied, duplicated, or posted to a publicly accessible website, in whole or in part.

DEMONSTRATION SOLUTION 1 (continued)

ACCOUNTS RECEIVABLE LEDGER

NAME   *Holland Company*

ADDRESS   *2340 Thunderbird Lane*

            Atlanta, GA 30305

DATE		ITEM	POST. REF.	DEBIT	CREDIT	BALANCE
20—						
Feb.	*1*	*Balance*	✓			*4,815.24*
	6		*J28*	*4,786.00*		*9,601.24*

NAME   *Santos Company*

ADDRESS   *8945 Williams Drive*

            Atlanta, GA 30307

DATE		ITEM	POST. REF.	DEBIT	CREDIT	BALANCE
20—						
Feb.	*1*	*Balance*	✓			*0.00*
	20		*J28*	*5,331.00*		*5,331.00*
	27		*J28*		*488.00*	*4,843.00*

Montgomery Company

Schedule of Accounts Receivable

February 28, 20—

Holland Company	*$ 9,601.24*
Santos Company	*4,843.00*
Total Accounts Receivable	*$14,444.24*

© 2013 Cengage Learning. All Rights Reserved. May not be scanned, copied, duplicated, or posted to a publicly accessible website, in whole or in part.

DEMONSTRATION SOLUTION 1 (concluded)

ACCOUNTS PAYABLE LEDGER

NAME   Banks Company
ADDRESS 3459 Main Street
         Des Moines, IA   50367

DATE		ITEM	POST. REF.	DEBIT	CREDIT	BALANCE
20—						
Feb.	1	Balance	✓			2,996.25
	10		J28		483.00	3,479.25

NAME   Wong Company
ADDRESS 3249 Raindance Road
         Des Moines, IA 50380

DATE		ITEM	POST. REF.	DEBIT	CREDIT	BALANCE
20—						
Feb.	1	Balance	✓			4,853.00
	3		J28		2,710.00	7,563.00
	12		J28	486.00		7,077.00

Montgomery Company

Schedule of Accounts Payable

February 28, 20—

Banks Company	$ 3,479.25
Wong Company	7,077.00
Total Accounts Payable	$10,556.25

© 2013 Cengage Learning. All Rights Reserved. May not be scanned, copied, duplicated, or posted to a publicly accessible website, in whole or in part.

DEMONSTRATION PROBLEM 2—SALES JOURNAL

In September, the Adams Company completed the following selected transactions:

Sept. 16 Sold merchandise on account to Foster Company, invoice no. 1032, $3,742.

20 Sold merchandise on account to King Company, invoice no. 1033, $8,950.

25 Sold merchandise on account to Zimmer Company, invoice no. 1034, $173.

27 King Company returned $982 worth of merchandise relating to invoice no. 1033. Adams Company issued credit memo no. 131.

Instructions

1. Record the transactions in either the sales journal (page 134) or the general journal (page 159), as appropriate.

2. Post the entries from the general journal and the total of the sales journal to the general ledger and the accounts receivable ledger.

3. Prepare a schedule of accounts receivable.

4. Compare the total of the schedule of accounts receivable with the September 30 balance of the Accounts Receivable (controlling) account.

© 2013 Cengage Learning. All Rights Reserved. May not be scanned, copied, duplicated, or posted to a publicly accessible website, in whole or in part.

DEMONSTRATION SOLUTION 2

SALES JOURNAL

PAGE **134**

	DATE		INV. NO.	CUSTOMER'S NAME	POST. REF.	ACCOUNTS RECEIVABLE DR. SALES CR.	
1	20—						1
2	Sept.	16	1032	Foster Company	✓	3,742.00	2
3		20	1033	King Company	✓	8,950.00	3
4		25	1034	Zimmer Company	✓	173.00	4
5		30		Total		12,865.00	5
6						(113) (411)	6
7							7

GENERAL JOURNAL

PAGE **159**

	DATE		DESCRIPTION	POST. REF.	DEBIT	CREDIT	
1	20—						1
2	Sept.	27	Sales Returns and Allowances	412	982.00		2
3			Accounts Receivable, King Company	113/ ✓		982.00	3
4			Issued credit memo no. 131.				4
5							5
6							6

© 2013 Cengage Learning. All Rights Reserved. May not be scanned, copied, duplicated, or posted to a publicly accessible website, in whole or in part.

DEMONSTRATION SOLUTION 2 (continued)

GENERAL LEDGER

ACCOUNT   *Accounts Receivable*   ACCOUNT NO.   *113*

DATE		ITEM	POST. REF.	DEBIT	CREDIT	BALANCE	
						DEBIT	CREDIT
20—							
Sept.	1	Balance	✓			5,390.00	
	27		J159		982.00	4,408.00	
	30		S134	12,865.00		17,273.00	

ACCOUNT   *Sales*   ACCOUNT NO.   *411*

DATE		ITEM	POST. REF.	DEBIT	CREDIT	BALANCE	
						DEBIT	CREDIT
20—							
Sept.	1	Balance	✓				51,597.00
	30		S134		12,865.00		64,462.00

ACCOUNT   *Sales Returns and Allowances*   ACCOUNT NO.   *412*

DATE		ITEM	POST. REF.	DEBIT	CREDIT	BALANCE	
						DEBIT	CREDIT
20—							
Sept.	1	Balance	✓			2,777.00	
	27		J159	982.00		3,759.00	

© 2013 Cengage Learning. All Rights Reserved. May not be scanned, copied, duplicated, or posted to a publicly accessible website, in whole or in part.

DEMONSTRATION SOLUTION 2 (concluded)

ACCOUNTS RECEIVABLE LEDGER

NAME *Foster Company*
ADDRESS *330 Wexler Road, S.W.*
Atlanta, GA 30305

DATE		ITEM	POST. REF.	DEBIT	CREDIT	BALANCE
20—						
Sept.	1	Balance	✓			5,390.00
	16		S134	3,742.00		9,132.00

NAME *King Company*
ADDRESS *1450 Myron Avenue, S.W.*
Atlanta, GA 30307

DATE		ITEM	POST. REF.	DEBIT	CREDIT	BALANCE
20—						
Sept.	20		S134	8,950.00		8,950.00
	27		J159		982.00	7,968.00

NAME *Zimmer Company*
ADDRESS *1226 Euclid Avenue, S.W.*
Atlanta, GA 30309

DATE		ITEM	POST. REF.	DEBIT	CREDIT	BALANCE
20—						
Sept.	25		S134	173.00		173.00

Adams Company
Schedule of Accounts Receivable
September 30, 20—

Foster Company	$ 9,132
King Company	7,968
Zimmer Company	173
Total Accounts Receivable	$17,273

© 2013 Cengage Learning. All Rights Reserved. May not be scanned, copied, duplicated, or posted to a publicly accessible website, in whole or in part.

DEMONSTRATION PROBLEM 3—PURCHASES JOURNAL

Brownfield Company, which is located in San Diego, California, completed the following transactions in August:

Aug.   3   Bought merchandise on account from Keller Company, invoice no. 1998, $5,544; terms 2/10, n/30; dated August 1; FOB Los Angeles, freight prepaid and added to the invoice, $554 (total $6,098).

10   Bought supplies on account from Nichols Company, invoice no. A1120, $572; terms net 30 days; dated August 10; FOB San Diego.

12   Received credit memo no. 170 from Keller Company, $640, for merchandise returned.

15   Bought merchandise on account from Lopez Company, invoice no. 3567C, $3,977; terms 1/10, n/30; dated August 12; FOB Reno; freight prepaid and added to the invoice, $380 (total $4,357).

17   Received credit memo no. 435 from Nichols Company, $52, for allowance on damaged supplies purchased August 10.

Instructions

1.   Record the transactions in either the three-column purchases journal (page 81) or the general journal (page 105), as appropriate.

2.   Post the entries from the general journal and the totals from the three-column purchases journal to the general ledger and the accounts payable ledger.

3.   Prepare a schedule of accounts payable.

4.   Compare the total of the schedule of accounts payable with the August 31 balance of the Accounts Payable (controlling) account.

© 2013 Cengage Learning. All Rights Reserved. May not be scanned, copied, duplicated, or posted to a publicly accessible website, in whole or in part.

DEMONSTRATION SOLUTION 3

PURCHASES JOURNAL

DATE		SUPPLIER'S NAME	INV. NO.	INV. DATE	TERMS	POST. REF.	ACCOUNTS PAYABLE CREDIT	FREIGHT IN DEBIT	PURCHASES DEBIT	
20—										1
Aug.	3	Keller Company	1998	8/1	2/10, n/30	✓	6,098.00	554.00	5,544.00	2
	15	Lopez Company	3567C	8/12	1/10, n/30	✓	4,357.00	380.00	3,977.00	3
	31	Totals					10,455.00	934.00	9,521.00	4
							(212)	(514)	(511)	5
										6

© 2013 Cengage Learning. All Rights Reserved. May not be scanned, copied, duplicated, or posted to a publicly accessible website, in whole or in part.

DEMONSTRATION SOLUTION 3 (continued)

GENERAL JOURNAL   PAGE _____ *105*_____

	DATE		DESCRIPTION	POST. REF.	DEBIT	CREDIT	
1	20—						1
2	Aug.	10	Supplies	114	572.00		2
3			Accounts Payable, Nichols Company	212/ ✓		572.00	3
4			Purchased supplies on account,				4
5			invoice no. A1120, invoice dated				5
6			8/10, terms net 30 days.				6
7							7
8		12	Accounts Payable, Keller Company	212/ ✓	640.00		8
9			Purchases Returns and Allowances	512		640.00	9
10			Credit memo no. 170 for return of				10
11			merchandise.				11
12							12
13		17	Accounts Payable, Nichols Company	212/ ✓	52.00		13
14			Supplies	114		52.00	14
15			Credit memo no. 435 for allowance				15
16			on damaged supplies.				16
17							17

© 2013 Cengage Learning. All Rights Reserved. May not be scanned, copied, duplicated, or posted to a publicly accessible website, in whole or in part.

DEMONSTRATION SOLUTION 3 (continued)

GENERAL LEDGER

ACCOUNT _Supplies_   ACCOUNT NO. __114__

DATE		ITEM	POST. REF.	DEBIT	CREDIT	BALANCE DEBIT	BALANCE CREDIT
20—							
Aug.	1	Balance	✓			5,790.00	
	10		J105	572.00		6,362.00	
	17		J105		52.00	6,310.00	

ACCOUNT _Accounts Payable_   ACCOUNT NO. __212__

DATE		ITEM	POST. REF.	DEBIT	CREDIT	BALANCE DEBIT	BALANCE CREDIT
20—							
Aug.	1	Balance	✓				3,780.00
	10		J105		572.00		4,352.00
	12		J105	640.00			3,712.00
	17		J105	52.00			3,660.00
	31		P81		10,455.00		14,115.00

ACCOUNT _Purchases_   ACCOUNT NO. __511__

DATE		ITEM	POST. REF.	DEBIT	CREDIT	BALANCE DEBIT	BALANCE CREDIT
20—							
Aug.	1	Balance	✓			73,185.00	
	31		P81	9,521.00		82,706.00	

ACCOUNT _Purchases Returns and Allowances_   ACCOUNT NO. __512__

DATE		ITEM	POST. REF.	DEBIT	CREDIT	BALANCE DEBIT	BALANCE CREDIT
20—							
Aug.	1	Balance	✓				2,035.00
	12		J105		640.00		2,675.00

ACCOUNT _Freight In_   ACCOUNT NO. __514__

DATE		ITEM	POST. REF.	DEBIT	CREDIT	BALANCE DEBIT	BALANCE CREDIT
20—							
Aug.	1	Balance	✓			7,459.00	
	31		P81	934.00		8,393.00	

© 2013 Cengage Learning. All Rights Reserved. May not be scanned, copied, duplicated, or posted to a publicly accessible website, in whole or in part.

DEMONSTRATION SOLUTION 3 (concluded)

ACCOUNTS PAYABLE LEDGER

NAME   Keller Company

ADDRESS   679 Gurnard Ave.

            Los Angeles, CA 90015

DATE		ITEM	POST. REF.	DEBIT	CREDIT	BALANCE
20—						
Aug.	1	Balance	✓			1,970.00
	3		P81		6,098.00	8,068.00
	12		J105	640.00		7,428.00

NAME   Lopez Company

ADDRESS   482 Jeffries Way

            Reno, NV 89501

DATE		ITEM	POST. REF.	DEBIT	CREDIT	BALANCE
20—						
Aug.	1	Balance	✓			1,810.00
	15		P81		4,357.00	6,167.00

NAME   Nichols Company

ADDRESS   3864 Silva Ave.

            Los Angeles, CA 90015

DATE		ITEM	POST. REF.	DEBIT	CREDIT	BALANCE
20—						
Aug.	10		J105		572.00	572.00
	17		J105	52.00		520.00

Brownfield Company

Schedule of Accounts Payable

August 31, 20—

Keller Company	$ 7,428
Lopez Company	6,167
Nichols Company	520
Total Accounts Payable	$14,115

© 2013 Cengage Learning. All Rights Reserved. May not be scanned, copied, duplicated, or posted to a publicly accessible website, in whole or in part.

EXERCISES AND PROBLEMS

Exercise 9-1

GENERAL JOURNAL   PAGE _____

	DATE		DESCRIPTION	POST. REF.	DEBIT	CREDIT	
1							1
2							2
3							3
4							4
5							5
6							6
7							7
8							8
9							9
10							10
11							11
12							12
13							13
14							14
15							15
16							16
17							17
18							18
19							19
20							20
21							21
22							22
23							23

© 2013 Cengage Learning. All Rights Reserved. May not be scanned, copied, duplicated, or posted to a publicly accessible website, in whole or in part.

Exercise 9-2

GENERAL JOURNAL

PAGE _52_

	DATE		DESCRIPTION	POST. REF.	DEBIT	CREDIT	
1	20—						1
2	June	16	Sales Returns and Allowances		241.27		2
3			Accounts Receivable, F. E. Dixon			241.27	3
4			Issued credit memo no. 131.				4
5							5

GENERAL LEDGER

ACCOUNT **Accounts Receivable**

ACCOUNT NO. _113_

	DATE		ITEM	POST. REF.	DEBIT	CREDIT	BALANCE		
							DEBIT	CREDIT	
	20—								
	June	1	Balance	✓			6,511.19		

ACCOUNT **Sales Returns and Allowances**

ACCOUNT NO. _412_

	DATE		ITEM	POST. REF.	DEBIT	CREDIT	BALANCE		
							DEBIT	CREDIT	
	20—								
	June	1	Balance	✓			314.60		

ACCOUNTS RECEIVABLE LEDGER

NAME **F. E. Dixon**
ADDRESS **416 Fifth Avenue**
Dallas, TX 75204

	DATE		ITEM	POST. REF.	DEBIT	CREDIT	BALANCE	
	20—							
	May	31		J51	312.60		312.60	

© 2013 Cengage Learning. All Rights Reserved. May not be scanned, copied, duplicated, or posted to a publicly accessible website, in whole or in part.

Exercise 9-3

GENERAL JOURNAL

PAGE _____

	DATE		DESCRIPTION	POST. REF.	DEBIT	CREDIT	
1							1
2							2
3							3
4							4
5							5
6							6
7							7
8							8
9							9
10							10
11							11

Exercise 9-4

GENERAL JOURNAL

PAGE _____

	DATE		DESCRIPTION	POST. REF.	DEBIT	CREDIT	
1							1
2							2
3							3
4							4
5							5
6							6
7							7
8							8
9							9
10							10
11							11

© 2013 Cengage Learning. All Rights Reserved. May not be scanned, copied, duplicated, or posted to a publicly accessible website, in whole or in part.

Exercise 9-5

GENERAL JOURNAL   PAGE ___92___

	DATE		DESCRIPTION	POST. REF.	DEBIT	CREDIT	
1	20—						1
2	July	14	Accounts Payable, Jensen and Silva		192.30		2
3			Purchases Returns and Allowances			192.30	3
4			Credit memo no. 942 for return				4
5			of merchandise.				5
6							6
7							7

GENERAL LEDGER

ACCOUNT *Accounts Payable*   ACCOUNT NO. ___212___

DATE		ITEM	POST. REF.	DEBIT	CREDIT	BALANCE DEBIT	BALANCE CREDIT
20—							
July	1	Balance	✓				2,761.24

ACCOUNT *Purchases Returns and Allowances*   ACCOUNT NO. ___512___

DATE		ITEM	POST. REF.	DEBIT	CREDIT	BALANCE DEBIT	BALANCE CREDIT
20—							
July	1	Balance	✓				230.16

ACCOUNTS PAYABLE LEDGER

NAME   *Jensen and Silva*

ADDRESS *542 Roselle Blvd.*

Chicago, IL 60141

DATE		ITEM	POST. REF.	DEBIT	CREDIT	BALANCE	
20—							
July	5	Balance	✓		218.00	218.00	

© 2013 Cengage Learning. All Rights Reserved. May not be scanned, copied, duplicated, or posted to a publicly accessible website, in whole or in part.

Exercise 9-6

Ford Education Outfitters

GENERAL JOURNAL   PAGE _____

	DATE	DESCRIPTION	POST. REF.	DEBIT	CREDIT	
1						1
2						2
3						3
4						4
5						5
6						6
7						7
8						8
9						9
10						10
11						11
12						12
13						13

Romero Textbooks, Inc.

GENERAL JOURNAL   PAGE _____

	DATE	DESCRIPTION	POST. REF.	DEBIT	CREDIT	
1						1
2						2
3						3
4						4
5						5
6						6
7						7
8						8
9						9
10						10
11						11
12						12
13						13
14						14
15						15

© 2013 Cengage Learning. All Rights Reserved. May not be scanned, copied, duplicated, or posted to a publicly accessible website, in whole or in part.

Exercise 9-7

GENERAL JOURNAL

PAGE _____

	DATE		DESCRIPTION	POST. REF.	DEBIT	CREDIT	
1							1
2							2
3							3
4							4
5							5
6							6
7							7
8							8
9							9
10							10
11							11
12							12
13							13
14							14
15							15
16							16
17							17
18							18
19							19
20							20
21							21
22							22
23							23
24							24
25							25
26							26
27							27
28							28
29							29
30							30
31							31
32							32
33							33
34							34
35							35
36							36
37							37

© 2013 Cengage Learning. All Rights Reserved. May not be scanned, copied, duplicated, or posted to a publicly accessible website, in whole or in part.

Exercise 9-8

SALES JOURNAL   PAGE _____ *24* _____

	DATE	INV. NO.	CUSTOMER'S NAME	POST. REF.	ACCOUNTS RECEIVABLE DR. SALES CR.	
1						1
2						2
3						3
4						4
5						5
6						6
7						7
8						8

GENERAL LEDGER

ACCOUNT *Accounts Receivable* _____ ACCOUNT NO. _____ *113* _____

DATE		ITEM	POST. REF.	DEBIT	CREDIT	BALANCE DEBIT	BALANCE CREDIT	
20—								
Mar.	*1*	*Balance*	✓			*2,450.39*		

ACCOUNT *Sales* _____ ACCOUNT NO. _____ *411* _____

DATE		ITEM	POST. REF.	DEBIT	CREDIT	BALANCE DEBIT	BALANCE CREDIT	
20—								
Mar.	*1*	*Balance*	✓				*3,569.80*	

331

© 2013 Cengage Learning. All Rights Reserved. May not be scanned, copied, duplicated, or posted to a publicly accessible website, in whole or in part.

Exercise 9-9

PURCHASES JOURNAL

	DATE	SUPPLIER'S NAME	INV. NO.	INV. DATE	TERMS	POST. REF.	ACCOUNTS PAYABLE CREDIT	FREIGHT IN DEBIT	PURCHASES DEBIT	
1										1
2										2
3										3
4										4
5										5
6										6
7										7
8										8

© 2013 Cengage Learning. All Rights Reserved. May not be scanned, copied, duplicated, or posted to a publicly accessible website, in whole or in part.

Exercise 9-9 *(concluded)*

GENERAL LEDGER

ACCOUNT *Accounts Payable*   ACCOUNT NO. *212*

DATE		ITEM	POST. REF.	DEBIT	CREDIT	BALANCE	
						DEBIT	CREDIT
20—							
May	1	Balance	✓				3,492.29

ACCOUNT *Purchases*   ACCOUNT NO. *511*

DATE		ITEM	POST. REF.	DEBIT	CREDIT	BALANCE	
						DEBIT	CREDIT
20—							
May	1	Balance	✓			4,239.49	

ACCOUNT *Freight In*   ACCOUNT NO. *514*

DATE		ITEM	POST. REF.	DEBIT	CREDIT	BALANCE	
						DEBIT	CREDIT
20—							
May	1	Balance	✓			234.89	

© 2013 Cengage Learning. All Rights Reserved. May not be scanned, copied, duplicated, or posted to a publicly accessible website, in whole or in part.

Exercise 9-10

SALES JOURNAL

PAGE 18

DATE		INV. NO.	CUSTOMER'S NAME	POST. REF.	ACCOUNTS RECEIVABLE DR. SALES CR.	
20—						1
Oct.	3	414	Anderson Company	✓	443.24	2
	4	415	R. T. Holcomb	✓	1,426.90	3
	7	416	Gray and Malo	✓	1,647.00	4
	11	417	Mercer Mobil	✓	3,112.16	5
	16	418	J. L. Anthony	✓	2,130.00	6
	22	419	C. A. Goldschmidt	✓	1,944.05	7
	31	420	F. A. Baumann	✓	2,791.00	8
						9
						10
						11

PURCHASES JOURNAL

PAGE 10

DATE		SUPPLIER'S NAME	INV. NO.	INV. DATE	TERMS	POST. REF.	ACCOUNTS PAYABLE CREDIT	FREIGHT IN DEBIT	PURCHASES DEBIT	
20—										1
Oct.	2	Colter, Inc.	2706	7/31	2/10, n/30	✓	759.00	49.00	710.00	2
	3	Thomas and Son	982	8/2	n/30	✓	829.00	57.00	772.00	3
	5	Archer Mfg. Co.	10611	8/3	2/10, n/30	✓	564.00		564.00	4
	9	Spence Products Co.	B643	8/6	1/10, n/30	✓	165.00	10.00	155.00	5
	18	L. C. Walter	46812	8/17	n/60	✓	228.00		228.00	6
	25	Delaney and Cox	1024	8/23	2/10, n/30	✓	376.00	14.00	362.00	7
	26	Colter, Inc.	2801	8/25	2/10, n/30	✓	406.00	22.00	384.00	8
										9
										10
										11

© 2013 Cengage Learning. All Rights Reserved. May not be scanned, copied, duplicated, or posted to a publicly accessible website, in whole or in part.

Exercise 9-10 *(continued)*

ACCOUNTS RECEIVABLE LEDGER

Anderson Company	J. L. Anthony	F. A. Baumann
+ −	+ −	+ −

C. A. Goldschmidt	Gray and Malo	R. T. Holcomb	Mercer Mobil
+ −	+ −	+ −	+ −

GENERAL LEDGER

Accounts Receivable 113	Accounts Payable 212	Sales 411
+ −	− +	− +

		Purchases 511
		+ −

		Freight In 514
		+ −

ACCOUNTS PAYABLE LEDGER

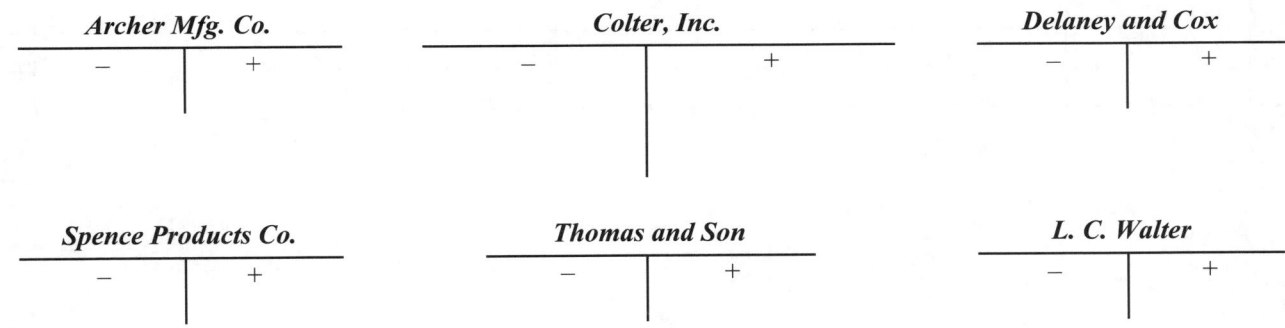

Archer Mfg. Co.	Colter, Inc.	Delaney and Cox
− +	− +	− +

Spence Products Co.	Thomas and Son	L. C. Walter
− +	− +	− +

© 2013 Cengage Learning. All Rights Reserved. May not be scanned, copied, duplicated, or posted to a publicly accessible website, in whole or in part.

Exercise 9-10 *(concluded)*

© 2013 Cengage Learning. All Rights Reserved. May not be scanned, copied, duplicated, or posted to a publicly accessible website, in whole or in part.

Problem 9-1A or 9-1B

GENERAL JOURNAL

PAGE _____

	DATE		DESCRIPTION	POST. REF.	DEBIT	CREDIT	
1							1
2							2
3							3
4							4
5							5
6							6
7							7
8							8
9							9
10							10
11							11
12							12
13							13
14							14
15							15
16							16
17							17
18							18
19							19
20							20
21							21
22							22
23							23
24							24
25							25
26							26
27							27
28							28
29							29
30							30
31							31
32							32
33							33
34							34
35							35
36							36
37							37
38							38
39							39

© 2013 Cengage Learning. All Rights Reserved. May not be scanned, copied, duplicated, or posted to a publicly accessible website, in whole or in part.

Problem 9-1A or 9-1B (continued)

GENERAL JOURNAL

PAGE _____

	DATE		DESCRIPTION	POST. REF.	DEBIT	CREDIT	
1							1
2							2
3							3
4							4
5							5
6							6
7							7
8							8
9							9
10							10
11							11
12							12
13							13
14							14
15							15
16							16

GENERAL LEDGER

ACCOUNT   *Accounts Receivable*   ACCOUNT NO. ___*113*___

DATE		ITEM	POST. REF.	DEBIT	CREDIT	BALANCE DEBIT	BALANCE CREDIT	
20—								
Mar.	*1*	*Balance*	✓			*111.22*		

© 2013 Cengage Learning. All Rights Reserved. May not be scanned, copied, duplicated, or posted to a publicly accessible website, in whole or in part.

Problem 9-1A or 9-1B (continued)

ACCOUNT   *Sales Tax Payable*   ACCOUNT NO.   *214*

DATE		ITEM	POST. REF.	DEBIT	CREDIT	BALANCE DEBIT	BALANCE CREDIT
20—							
Mar.	1	Balance	✓				72.84

ACCOUNT   *Sales*   ACCOUNT NO.   *411*

DATE		ITEM	POST. REF.	DEBIT	CREDIT	BALANCE DEBIT	BALANCE CREDIT

ACCOUNT   *Sales Returns and Allowances*   ACCOUNT NO.   *412*

DATE		ITEM	POST. REF.	DEBIT	CREDIT	BALANCE DEBIT	BALANCE CREDIT

© 2013 Cengage Learning. All Rights Reserved. May not be scanned, copied, duplicated, or posted to a publicly accessible website, in whole or in part.

Problem 9-1A or 9-1B (continued)

ACCOUNTS RECEIVABLE LEDGER

NAME

ADDRESS

DATE		ITEM	POST. REF.	DEBIT	CREDIT	BALANCE
20—						
Mar.	1	Balance	✓			34.22

NAME

ADDRESS

DATE		ITEM	POST. REF.	DEBIT	CREDIT	BALANCE

NAME

ADDRESS

DATE		ITEM	POST. REF.	DEBIT	CREDIT	BALANCE

NAME

ADDRESS

DATE		ITEM	POST. REF.	DEBIT	CREDIT	BALANCE
20—						
Mar.	1	Balance	✓			19.50

© 2013 Cengage Learning. All Rights Reserved. May not be scanned, copied, duplicated, or posted to a publicly accessible website, in whole or in part.

Problem 9-1A or 9-1B (concluded)

NAME _____

ADDRESS _____

DATE		ITEM	POST. REF.	DEBIT	CREDIT	BALANCE	
20—							
Mar.	1	Balance	✓			57.50	

NAME _____

ADDRESS _____

DATE		ITEM	POST. REF.	DEBIT	CREDIT	BALANCE	

© 2013 Cengage Learning. All Rights Reserved. May not be scanned, copied, duplicated, or posted to a publicly accessible website, in whole or in part.

Problem 9-2A or 9-2B

GENERAL JOURNAL

	DATE		DESCRIPTION	POST. REF.	DEBIT	CREDIT	
1							1
2							2
3							3
4							4
5							5
6							6
7							7
8							8
9							9
10							10
11							11
12							12
13							13
14							14
15							15
16							16
17							17
18							18
19							19
20							20
21							21
22							22
23							23
24							24
25							25
26							26
27							27
28							28
29							29
30							30
31							31
32							32
33							33
34							34
35							35
36							36
37							37
38							38
39							39

© 2013 Cengage Learning. All Rights Reserved. May not be scanned, copied, duplicated, or posted to a publicly accessible website, in whole or in part.

Problem 9-2A or 9-2B (continued)

GENERAL JOURNAL   PAGE _____

	DATE		DESCRIPTION	POST. REF.	DEBIT	CREDIT	
1							1
2							2
3							3
4							4
5							5
6							6
7							7
8							8
9							9
10							10
11							11
12							12
13							13
14							14
15							15
16							16
17							17
18							18
19							19
20							20
21							21
22							22
23							23
24							24
25							25
26							26

© 2013 Cengage Learning. All Rights Reserved. May not be scanned, copied, duplicated, or posted to a publicly accessible website, in whole or in part.

Problem 9-2A or 9-2B (continued)

GENERAL LEDGER

ACCOUNT _Accounts Payable_   ACCOUNT NO. _212_

DATE	ITEM	POST. REF.	DEBIT	CREDIT	BALANCE	
					DEBIT	CREDIT

ACCOUNT _Purchases_   ACCOUNT NO. _511_

DATE	ITEM	POST. REF.	DEBIT	CREDIT	BALANCE	
					DEBIT	CREDIT

ACCOUNT _Purchases Returns and Allowances_   ACCOUNT NO. _512_

DATE	ITEM	POST. REF.	DEBIT	CREDIT	BALANCE	
					DEBIT	CREDIT

ACCOUNT _Freight In_   ACCOUNT NO. _514_

DATE	ITEM	POST. REF.	DEBIT	CREDIT	BALANCE	
					DEBIT	CREDIT

© 2013 Cengage Learning. All Rights Reserved. May not be scanned, copied, duplicated, or posted to a publicly accessible website, in whole or in part.

Problem 9-2A or 9-2B (continued)

ACCOUNTS PAYABLE LEDGER

NAME _____

ADDRESS _____

DATE		ITEM	POST. REF.	DEBIT	CREDIT	BALANCE

NAME _____

ADDRESS _____

DATE		ITEM	POST. REF.	DEBIT	CREDIT	BALANCE

NAME _____

ADDRESS _____

DATE		ITEM	POST. REF.	DEBIT	CREDIT	BALANCE

NAME _____

ADDRESS _____

DATE		ITEM	POST. REF.	DEBIT	CREDIT	BALANCE

© 2013 Cengage Learning. All Rights Reserved. May not be scanned, copied, duplicated, or posted to a publicly accessible website, in whole or in part.

Problem 9-2A or 9-2B (concluded)

NAME _____

ADDRESS _____

_____

DATE		ITEM	POST. REF.	DEBIT	CREDIT	BALANCE

NAME _____

ADDRESS _____

_____

DATE		ITEM	POST. REF.	DEBIT	CREDIT	BALANCE

© 2013 Cengage Learning. All Rights Reserved. May not be scanned, copied, duplicated, or posted to a publicly accessible website, in whole or in part.

Problem 9-3A or 9-3B

GENERAL JOURNAL

PAGE _____

	DATE		DESCRIPTION	POST. REF.	DEBIT	CREDIT	
1							1
2							2
3							3
4							4
5							5
6							6
7							7
8							8
9							9
10							10
11							11
12							12
13							13
14							14
15							15
16							16
17							17
18							18
19							19
20							20
21							21
22							22
23							23
24							24
25							25
26							26
27							27
28							28
29							29
30							30
31							31
32							32
33							33
34							34
35							35
36							36
37							37
38							38
39							39
40							40
41							41
42							42
43							43
44							44
45							45
46							46

© 2013 Cengage Learning. All Rights Reserved. May not be scanned, copied, duplicated, or posted to a publicly accessible website, in whole or in part.

Problem 9-3A or 9-3B (continued)

GENERAL LEDGER

ACCOUNT   *Accounts Receivable*   ACCOUNT NO.   *113*

DATE		ITEM	POST. REF.	DEBIT	CREDIT	BALANCE	
						DEBIT	CREDIT

ACCOUNT   *Accounts Payable*   ACCOUNT NO.   *212*

DATE		ITEM	POST. REF.	DEBIT	CREDIT	BALANCE	
						DEBIT	CREDIT

ACCOUNT   *Sales Tax Payable*   ACCOUNT NO.   *214*

DATE		ITEM	POST. REF.	DEBIT	CREDIT	BALANCE	
						DEBIT	CREDIT

ACCOUNT   *Sales*   ACCOUNT NO.   *411*

DATE		ITEM	POST. REF.	DEBIT	CREDIT	BALANCE	
						DEBIT	CREDIT

ACCOUNT   *Sales Returns and Allowances*   ACCOUNT NO.   *412*

DATE		ITEM	POST. REF.	DEBIT	CREDIT	BALANCE	
						DEBIT	CREDIT

© 2013 Cengage Learning. All Rights Reserved. May not be scanned, copied, duplicated, or posted to a publicly accessible website, in whole or in part.

Problem 9-3A or 9-3B (continued)

ACCOUNT   *Purchases*   ACCOUNT NO. ___511___

DATE		ITEM	POST. REF.	DEBIT	CREDIT	BALANCE	
						DEBIT	CREDIT

ACCOUNT   *Purchases Returns and Allowances*   ACCOUNT NO. ___512___

DATE		ITEM	POST. REF.	DEBIT	CREDIT	BALANCE	
						DEBIT	CREDIT

ACCOUNT   *Freight In*   ACCOUNT NO. ___514___

DATE		ITEM	POST. REF.	DEBIT	CREDIT	BALANCE	
						DEBIT	CREDIT

© 2013 Cengage Learning. All Rights Reserved. May not be scanned, copied, duplicated, or posted to a publicly accessible website, in whole or in part.

Problem 9-3A or 9-3B (continued)

ACCOUNTS RECEIVABLE LEDGER

NAME _____

ADDRESS _____
_____

DATE		ITEM	POST. REF.	DEBIT	CREDIT	BALANCE

NAME _____

ADDRESS _____
_____

DATE		ITEM	POST. REF.	DEBIT	CREDIT	BALANCE

© 2013 Cengage Learning. All Rights Reserved. May not be scanned, copied, duplicated, or posted to a publicly accessible website, in whole or in part.

Problem 9-3A or 9-3B (continued)

ACCOUNTS PAYABLE LEDGER

NAME _____

ADDRESS _____

DATE		ITEM	POST. REF.	DEBIT	CREDIT	BALANCE

NAME _____

ADDRESS _____

DATE		ITEM	POST. REF.	DEBIT	CREDIT	BALANCE

NAME _____

ADDRESS _____

DATE		ITEM	POST. REF.	DEBIT	CREDIT	BALANCE

© 2013 Cengage Learning. All Rights Reserved. May not be scanned, copied, duplicated, or posted to a publicly accessible website, in whole or in part.

Problem 9-3A or 9-3B (concluded)

© 2013 Cengage Learning. All Rights Reserved. May not be scanned, copied, duplicated, or posted to a publicly accessible website, in whole or in part.

Problem 9-4A or 9-4B

GENERAL JOURNAL   PAGE _____

	DATE		DESCRIPTION	POST. REF.	DEBIT	CREDIT	
1							1
2							2
3							3
4							4
5							5
6							6
7							7
8							8
9							9
10							10
11							11
12							12
13							13
14							14
15							15
16							16
17							17
18							18
19							19
20							20
21							21
22							22
23							23
24							24
25							25
26							26
27							27
28							28
29							29
30							30
31							31
32							32
33							33
34							34
35							35
36							36
37							37
38							38
39							39

© 2013 Cengage Learning. All Rights Reserved. May not be scanned, copied, duplicated, or posted to a publicly accessible website, in whole or in part.

Problem 9-4A or 9-4B (concluded)

GENERAL JOURNAL   PAGE _____

	DATE		DESCRIPTION	POST. REF.	DEBIT	CREDIT	
1							1
2							2
3							3
4							4
5							5
6							6
7							7
8							8
9							9
10							10
11							11
12							12
13							13
14							14
15							15
16							16
17							17
18							18
19							19
20							20
21							21
22							22
23							23
24							24
25							25
26							26
27							27
28							28
29							29
30							30
31							31
32							32
33							33
34							34
35							35
36							36
37							37
38							38
39							39

© 2013 Cengage Learning. All Rights Reserved. May not be scanned, copied, duplicated, or posted to a publicly accessible website, in whole or in part.

Problem 9-5A or 9-5B

SALES JOURNAL   PAGE _____

	DATE	INV. NO.	CUSTOMER'S NAME	POST. REF.	ACCOUNTS RECEIVABLE DR. SALES CR.	
1						1
2						2
3						3
4						4
5						5
6						6
7						7
8						8
9						9
10						10
11						11

GENERAL JOURNAL   PAGE _____

	DATE	DESCRIPTION	POST. REF.	DEBIT	CREDIT	
1						1
2						2
3						3
4						4
5						5
6						6
7						7
8						8
9						9
10						10
11						11
12						12
13						13
14						14
15						15
16						16

© 2013 Cengage Learning. All Rights Reserved. May not be scanned, copied, duplicated, or posted to a publicly accessible website, in whole or in part.

Problem 9-5A or 9-5B (continued)

GENERAL LEDGER

ACCOUNT   *Accounts Receivable*   ACCOUNT NO.   *113*

DATE		ITEM	POST. REF.	DEBIT	CREDIT	BALANCE	
						DEBIT	CREDIT
20—							
Apr.	1	Balance	✓			1,169.42	

ACCOUNT   *Sales*   ACCOUNT NO.   *411*

DATE		ITEM	POST. REF.	DEBIT	CREDIT	BALANCE	
						DEBIT	CREDIT
20—							
Apr.	1	Balance	✓				11,260.44

ACCOUNT   *Sales Returns and Allowances*   ACCOUNT NO.   *412*

DATE		ITEM	POST. REF.	DEBIT	CREDIT	BALANCE	
						DEBIT	CREDIT
20—							
Apr.	1	Balance	✓			396.42	

ACCOUNTS RECEIVABLE LEDGER

NAME   _____

ADDRESS _____

_____

DATE		ITEM	POST. REF.	DEBIT	CREDIT	BALANCE
20—						
Apr.	1	Balance	✓			927.76

© 2013 Cengage Learning. All Rights Reserved. May not be scanned, copied, duplicated, or posted to a publicly accessible website, in whole or in part.

Problem 9-5A or 9-5B (continued)

NAME _____

ADDRESS _____

_____

DATE		ITEM	POST. REF.	DEBIT	CREDIT	BALANCE

NAME _____

ADDRESS _____

_____

DATE		ITEM	POST. REF.	DEBIT	CREDIT	BALANCE

NAME _____

ADDRESS _____

_____

_____

DATE		ITEM	POST. REF.	DEBIT	CREDIT	BALANCE
20—						
Apr.	1	Balance	✓			241.66

NAME _____

ADDRESS _____

_____

DATE		ITEM	POST. REF.	DEBIT	CREDIT	BALANCE

© 2013 Cengage Learning. All Rights Reserved. May not be scanned, copied, duplicated, or posted to a publicly accessible website, in whole or in part.

Problem 9-5A or 9-5B (concluded)

NAME _____

ADDRESS _____

_____

DATE		ITEM	POST. REF.	DEBIT	CREDIT	BALANCE

© 2013 Cengage Learning. All Rights Reserved. May not be scanned, copied, duplicated, or posted to a publicly accessible website, in whole or in part.

Problem 9-6A or 9-6B

PURCHASES JOURNAL

DATE	SUPPLIER'S NAME	INV. NO.	INV. DATE	TERMS	POST. REF.	ACCOUNTS PAYABLE CREDIT	FREIGHT IN DEBIT	PURCHASES DEBIT	
									1
									2
									3
									4
									5
									6
									7
									8
									9
									10
									11
									12
									13
									14
									15

© 2013 Cengage Learning. All Rights Reserved. May not be scanned, copied, duplicated, or posted to a publicly accessible website, in whole or in part.

Problem 9-6A or 9-6B (continued)

GENERAL LEDGER

ACCOUNT   *Accounts Payable*   ACCOUNT NO.   *212*

DATE		ITEM	POST. REF.	DEBIT	CREDIT	BALANCE	
						DEBIT	CREDIT

ACCOUNT   *Purchases*   ACCOUNT NO.   *511*

DATE		ITEM	POST. REF.	DEBIT	CREDIT	BALANCE	
						DEBIT	CREDIT

ACCOUNT   *Freight In*   ACCOUNT NO.   *514*

DATE		ITEM	POST. REF.	DEBIT	CREDIT	BALANCE	
						DEBIT	CREDIT

© 2013 Cengage Learning. All Rights Reserved. May not be scanned, copied, duplicated, or posted to a publicly accessible website, in whole or in part.

Problem 9-6A or 9-6B (continued)

ACCOUNTS PAYABLE LEDGER

NAME _____

ADDRESS _____

_____

DATE		ITEM	POST. REF.	DEBIT	CREDIT	BALANCE

NAME _____

ADDRESS _____

_____

DATE		ITEM	POST. REF.	DEBIT	CREDIT	BALANCE

NAME _____

ADDRESS _____

_____

DATE		ITEM	POST. REF.	DEBIT	CREDIT	BALANCE

NAME _____

ADDRESS _____

_____

DATE		ITEM	POST. REF.	DEBIT	CREDIT	BALANCE

© 2013 Cengage Learning. All Rights Reserved. May not be scanned, copied, duplicated, or posted to a publicly accessible website, in whole or in part.

Problem 9-6A or 9-6B (concluded)

NAME _____

ADDRESS _____

_____

DATE		ITEM	POST. REF.	DEBIT	CREDIT	BALANCE

NAME _____

ADDRESS _____

_____

DATE		ITEM	POST. REF.	DEBIT	CREDIT	BALANCE

© 2013 Cengage Learning. All Rights Reserved. May not be scanned, copied, duplicated, or posted to a publicly accessible website, in whole or in part.

Continuing Problem: Chapter 9

ALL ABOUT YOU SPA: Sales and Purchases

GENERAL JOURNAL

PAGE _____

	DATE		DESCRIPTION	POST. REF.	DEBIT	CREDIT	
1							1
2							2
3							3
4							4
5							5
6							6
7							7
8							8
9							9
10							10
11							11
12							12
13							13
14							14
15							15
16							16
17							17
18							18
19							19
20							20
21							21
22							22
23							23
24							24
25							25
26							26
27							27
28							28
29							29
30							30
31							31
32							32
33							33
34							34
35							35
36							36
37							37
38							38
39							39
40							40

© 2013 Cengage Learning. All Rights Reserved. May not be scanned, copied, duplicated, or posted to a publicly accessible website, in whole or in part.

ALL ABOUT YOU SPA (continued)

GENERAL JOURNAL

PAGE _____

	DATE		DESCRIPTION	POST. REF.	DEBIT	CREDIT	
1							1
2							2
3							3
4							4
5							5
6							6
7							7
8							8
9							9
10							10
11							11
12							12
13							13
14							14
15							15
16							16
17							17
18							18
19							19
20							20
21							21
22							22
23							23
24							24
25							25
26							26
27							27
28							28
29							29
30							30
31							31
32							32
33							33
34							34
35							35
36							36
37							37
38							38
39							39
40							40
41							41
42							42
43							43
44							44
45							45
46							46
47							47

© 2013 Cengage Learning. All Rights Reserved. May not be scanned, copied, duplicated, or posted to a publicly accessible website, in whole or in part.

ALL ABOUT YOU SPA (continued)

GENERAL JOURNAL   PAGE _____

	DATE		DESCRIPTION	POST. REF.	DEBIT	CREDIT	
1							1
2							2
3							3
4							4
5							5
6							6
7							7
8							8
9							9
10							10
11							11
12							12
13							13
14							14
15							15
16							16
17							17
18							18
19							19
20							20
21							21
22							22
23							23
24							24
25							25
26							26
27							27
28							28
29							29
30							30
31							31
32							32
33							33
34							34
35							35
36							36
37							37
38							38
39							39
40							40
41							41
42							42
43							43
44							44

© 2013 Cengage Learning. All Rights Reserved. May not be scanned, copied, duplicated, or posted to a publicly accessible website, in whole or in part.

ALL ABOUT YOU SPA (continued)

GENERAL JOURNAL

PAGE _____

	DATE		DESCRIPTION	POST. REF.	DEBIT	CREDIT	
1							1
2							2
3							3
4							4
5							5
6							6
7							7
8							8
9							9
10							10
11							11
12							12
13							13
14							14
15							15
16							16
17							17
18							18
19							19
20							20
21							21
22							22
23							23
24							24
25							25
26							26
27							27
28							28
29							29
30							30
31							31
32							32
33							33
34							34
35							35
36							36
37							37
38							38
39							39
40							40
41							41
42							42
43							43
44							44
45							45
46							46
47							47

© 2013 Cengage Learning. All Rights Reserved. May not be scanned, copied, duplicated, or posted to a publicly accessible website, in whole or in part.

ALL ABOUT YOU SPA (continued)

GENERAL JOURNAL   PAGE _____

	DATE		DESCRIPTION	POST. REF.	DEBIT	CREDIT	
1							1
2							2
3							3
4							4
5							5
6							6
7							7
8							8
9							9
10							10
11							11
12							12
13							13
14							14
15							15
16							16
17							17
18							18
19							19
20							20
21							21
22							22
23							23
24							24
25							25
26							26

© 2013 Cengage Learning. All Rights Reserved. May not be scanned, copied, duplicated, or posted to a publicly accessible website, in whole or in part.

ALL ABOUT YOU SPA (continued)

SALES JOURNAL   PAGE _____

	DATE	INV. NO.	CUSTOMER'S NAME	POST. REF.	ACCOUNTS RECEIVABLE DEBIT	SALES TAX PAYABLE CREDIT	MERCHANDISE SALES CREDIT	
1								1
2								2
3								3
4								4
5								5
6								6
7								7
8								8
9								9
10								10
11								11
12								12
13								13
14								14
15								15
16								16
17								17

© 2013 Cengage Learning. All Rights Reserved. May not be scanned, copied, duplicated, or posted to a publicly accessible website, in whole or in part.

ALL ABOUT YOU SPA (continued)

PURCHASES JOURNAL

	DATE	SUPPLIER'S NAME	INV. NO.	INV. DATE	TERMS	POST. REF.	ACCOUNTS PAYABLE CREDIT	FREIGHT IN DEBIT	PURCHASES DEBIT	
1										1
2										2
3										3
4										4
5										5
6										6
7										7
8										8
9										9
10										10
11										11
12										12
13										13
14										14
15										15

© 2013 Cengage Learning. All Rights Reserved. May not be scanned, copied, duplicated, or posted to a publicly accessible website, in whole or in part.

ALL ABOUT YOU SPA (continued)

GENERAL LEDGER

ACCOUNT *Cash* ACCOUNT NO. *111*

DATE		ITEM	POST. REF.	DEBIT	CREDIT	BALANCE DEBIT	BALANCE CREDIT
20—							
July	1	Balance	✓			15,170.00	

© 2013 Cengage Learning. All Rights Reserved. May not be scanned, copied, duplicated, or posted to a publicly accessible website, in whole or in part.

ALL ABOUT YOU SPA (continued)

ACCOUNT   *Accounts Receivable*   ACCOUNT NO.   *113*

DATE		ITEM	POST. REF.	DEBIT	CREDIT	BALANCE DEBIT	BALANCE CREDIT
20—							
July	1	Balance	✓			1,264.00	

ACCOUNT   *Office Supplies*   ACCOUNT NO.   *114*

DATE		ITEM	POST. REF.	DEBIT	CREDIT	BALANCE DEBIT	BALANCE CREDIT
20—							
July	1	Balance	✓			130.00	

ACCOUNT   *Spa Supplies*   ACCOUNT NO.   *115*

DATE		ITEM	POST. REF.	DEBIT	CREDIT	BALANCE DEBIT	BALANCE CREDIT
20—							
July	1	Balance	✓			205.00	

ACCOUNT   *Prepaid Insurance*   ACCOUNT NO.   *117*

DATE		ITEM	POST. REF.	DEBIT	CREDIT	BALANCE DEBIT	BALANCE CREDIT
20—							
July	1	Balance	✓			800.00	

© 2013 Cengage Learning. All Rights Reserved. May not be scanned, copied, duplicated, or posted to a publicly accessible website, in whole or in part.

ALL ABOUT YOU SPA (continued)

ACCOUNT   *Office Equipment*   ACCOUNT NO. **124**

DATE		ITEM	POST. REF.	DEBIT	CREDIT	BALANCE	
						DEBIT	CREDIT
20—							
July	1	Balance	✓			1,150.00	

ACCOUNT   *Accumulated Depreciation, Office Equipment*   ACCOUNT NO. **125**

DATE		ITEM	POST. REF.	DEBIT	CREDIT	BALANCE	
						DEBIT	CREDIT
20—							
July	1	Balance	✓				10.00

ACCOUNT   *Spa Equipment*   ACCOUNT NO. **128**

DATE		ITEM	POST. REF.	DEBIT	CREDIT	BALANCE	
						DEBIT	CREDIT
20—							
July	1	Balance	✓			7,393.00	

ACCOUNT   *Accumulated Depreciation, Spa Equipment*   ACCOUNT NO. **129**

DATE		ITEM	POST. REF.	DEBIT	CREDIT	BALANCE	
						DEBIT	CREDIT
20—							
July	1	Balance	✓				64.88

© 2013 Cengage Learning. All Rights Reserved. May not be scanned, copied, duplicated, or posted to a publicly accessible website, in whole or in part.

ALL ABOUT YOU SPA (continued)

ACCOUNT *Accounts Payable*   ACCOUNT NO. *211*

DATE		ITEM	POST. REF.	DEBIT	CREDIT	BALANCE DEBIT	BALANCE CREDIT
20—							
July	1	Balance	✓				2,248.00

ACCOUNT *Wages Payable*   ACCOUNT NO. *212*

DATE		ITEM	POST. REF.	DEBIT	CREDIT	BALANCE DEBIT	BALANCE CREDIT
20—							
July	1	Balance	✓				369.50

© 2013 Cengage Learning. All Rights Reserved. May not be scanned, copied, duplicated, or posted to a publicly accessible website, in whole or in part.

ALL ABOUT YOU SPA (continued)

ACCOUNT *Sales Tax Payable*   ACCOUNT NO.   *215*

DATE		ITEM	POST. REF.	DEBIT	CREDIT	BALANCE DEBIT	BALANCE CREDIT

ACCOUNT *A. Valli, Capital*   ACCOUNT NO.   *311*

DATE		ITEM	POST. REF.	DEBIT	CREDIT	BALANCE DEBIT	BALANCE CREDIT
20—							
July	1	Balance	✓				23,419.62

ACCOUNT *A. Valli, Drawing*   ACCOUNT NO.   *312*

DATE		ITEM	POST. REF.	DEBIT	CREDIT	BALANCE DEBIT	BALANCE CREDIT

ACCOUNT *Income Summary*   ACCOUNT NO.   *313*

DATE		ITEM	POST. REF.	DEBIT	CREDIT	BALANCE DEBIT	BALANCE CREDIT

© 2013 Cengage Learning. All Rights Reserved. May not be scanned, copied, duplicated, or posted to a publicly accessible website, in whole or in part.

ALL ABOUT YOU SPA (continued)

ACCOUNT   *Income from Services*   ACCOUNT NO.   *411*

DATE	ITEM	POST. REF.	DEBIT	CREDIT	BALANCE DEBIT	CREDIT

ACCOUNT   *Merchandise Sales*   ACCOUNT NO.   *412*

DATE	ITEM	POST. REF.	DEBIT	CREDIT	BALANCE DEBIT	CREDIT

ACCOUNT   *Purchases*   ACCOUNT NO.   *511*

DATE	ITEM	POST. REF.	DEBIT	CREDIT	BALANCE DEBIT	CREDIT

© 2013 Cengage Learning. All Rights Reserved. May not be scanned, copied, duplicated, or posted to a publicly accessible website, in whole or in part.

ALL ABOUT YOU SPA (continued)

ACCOUNT *Freight In*   ACCOUNT NO. *515*

DATE	ITEM	POST. REF.	DEBIT	CREDIT	BALANCE DEBIT	CREDIT

ACCOUNT *Wages Expense*   ACCOUNT NO. *611*

DATE	ITEM	POST. REF.	DEBIT	CREDIT	BALANCE DEBIT	CREDIT

ACCOUNT *Rent Expense*   ACCOUNT NO. *612*

DATE	ITEM	POST. REF.	DEBIT	CREDIT	BALANCE DEBIT	CREDIT

ACCOUNT *Office Supplies Expense*   ACCOUNT NO. *613*

DATE	ITEM	POST. REF.	DEBIT	CREDIT	BALANCE DEBIT	CREDIT

ACCOUNT *Spa Supplies Expense*   ACCOUNT NO. *614*

DATE	ITEM	POST. REF.	DEBIT	CREDIT	BALANCE DEBIT	CREDIT

© 2013 Cengage Learning. All Rights Reserved. May not be scanned, copied, duplicated, or posted to a publicly accessible website, in whole or in part.

ALL ABOUT YOU SPA (continued)

ACCOUNT _Laundry Expense_ ACCOUNT NO. _615_

DATE	ITEM	POST. REF.	DEBIT	CREDIT	BALANCE DEBIT	BALANCE CREDIT

ACCOUNT _Advertising Expense_ ACCOUNT NO. _616_

DATE	ITEM	POST. REF.	DEBIT	CREDIT	BALANCE DEBIT	BALANCE CREDIT

ACCOUNT _Utilities Expense_ ACCOUNT NO. _617_

DATE	ITEM	POST. REF.	DEBIT	CREDIT	BALANCE DEBIT	BALANCE CREDIT

ACCOUNT _Insurance Expense_ ACCOUNT NO. _618_

DATE	ITEM	POST. REF.	DEBIT	CREDIT	BALANCE DEBIT	BALANCE CREDIT

ACCOUNT _Depreciation Expense, Office Equipment_ ACCOUNT NO. _619_

DATE	ITEM	POST. REF.	DEBIT	CREDIT	BALANCE DEBIT	BALANCE CREDIT

ACCOUNT _Depreciation Expense, Spa Equipment_ ACCOUNT NO. _620_

DATE	ITEM	POST. REF.	DEBIT	CREDIT	BALANCE DEBIT	BALANCE CREDIT

© 2013 Cengage Learning. All Rights Reserved. May not be scanned, copied, duplicated, or posted to a publicly accessible website, in whole or in part.

ALL ABOUT YOU SPA (continued)

ACCOUNT   *Miscellaneous Expense*   ACCOUNT NO.   *630*

DATE		ITEM	POST. REF.	DEBIT	CREDIT	BALANCE	
						DEBIT	CREDIT

© 2013 Cengage Learning. All Rights Reserved. May not be scanned, copied, duplicated, or posted to a publicly accessible website, in whole or in part.

ALL ABOUT YOU SPA (continued)

ACCOUNTS RECEIVABLE LEDGER

NAME   *About Face Spa*

ADDRESS

DATE		ITEM	POST. REF.	DEBIT	CREDIT	BALANCE

NAME   *Jill Anson*

ADDRESS

DATE		ITEM	POST. REF.	DEBIT	CREDIT	BALANCE
20—						
July	1	Balance	✓			325.00

NAME   *Chaco's*

ADDRESS

DATE		ITEM	POST. REF.	DEBIT	CREDIT	BALANCE

NAME   *Holmes Condos*

ADDRESS

DATE		ITEM	POST. REF.	DEBIT	CREDIT	BALANCE

© 2013 Cengage Learning. All Rights Reserved. May not be scanned, copied, duplicated, or posted to a publicly accessible website, in whole or in part.

ALL ABOUT YOU SPA (continued)

NAME   *Tory Ligman*

ADDRESS

DATE		ITEM	POST. REF.	DEBIT	CREDIT	BALANCE
20—						
July	1	Balance	✓			344.00

NAME   *Los Obrigados Lodge*

ADDRESS

DATE		ITEM	POST. REF.	DEBIT	CREDIT	BALANCE

NAME   *Mini Spa*

ADDRESS

DATE		ITEM	POST. REF.	DEBIT	CREDIT	BALANCE

NAME   *Jack Morgan*

ADDRESS

DATE		ITEM	POST. REF.	DEBIT	CREDIT	BALANCE
20—						
July	1	Balance	✓			486.00

© 2013 Cengage Learning. All Rights Reserved. May not be scanned, copied, duplicated, or posted to a publicly accessible website, in whole or in part.

ALL ABOUT YOU SPA (continued)

NAME   *Pleasant Spa*

ADDRESS

DATE	ITEM	POST. REF.	DEBIT	CREDIT	BALANCE

NAME   *Judy Wilcox*

ADDRESS

DATE		ITEM	POST. REF.	DEBIT	CREDIT	BALANCE
20—						
July	1	Balance	✓			109.00

© 2013 Cengage Learning. All Rights Reserved. May not be scanned, copied, duplicated, or posted to a publicly accessible website, in whole or in part.

ALL ABOUT YOU SPA (continued)

ACCOUNTS PAYABLE LEDGER

NAME **Adco, Inc.**
ADDRESS

DATE		ITEM	POST. REF.	DEBIT	CREDIT	BALANCE
20—						
July	1	Balance	✓			397.00

NAME **Giftco**
ADDRESS

DATE		ITEM	POST. REF.	DEBIT	CREDIT	BALANCE

NAME **Golden Spa Supplies**
ADDRESS

DATE		ITEM	POST. REF.	DEBIT	CREDIT	BALANCE
20—						
July	1	Balance	✓			492.00

NAME **Logo Products**
ADDRESS

DATE		ITEM	POST. REF.	DEBIT	CREDIT	BALANCE

© 2013 Cengage Learning. All Rights Reserved. May not be scanned, copied, duplicated, or posted to a publicly accessible website, in whole or in part.

ALL ABOUT YOU SPA (continued)

NAME *Office Staples*

ADDRESS

DATE		ITEM	POST. REF.	DEBIT	CREDIT	BALANCE
20—						
July	1	Balance	✓			120.00

NAME *Spa Equipment, Inc.*

ADDRESS

DATE		ITEM	POST. REF.	DEBIT	CREDIT	BALANCE
20—						
July	1	Balance	✓			89.00

NAME *Spa Goods*

ADDRESS

DATE		ITEM	POST. REF.	DEBIT	CREDIT	BALANCE

NAME *Spa Magic*

ADDRESS

DATE		ITEM	POST. REF.	DEBIT	CREDIT	BALANCE

© 2013 Cengage Learning. All Rights Reserved. May not be scanned, copied, duplicated, or posted to a publicly accessible website, in whole or in part.

ALL ABOUT YOU SPA (continued)

NAME   *Superior Equipment*

ADDRESS

DATE		ITEM	POST. REF.	DEBIT	CREDIT	BALANCE	
20—							
July	1	Balance	✓			1,150.00	

© 2013 Cengage Learning. All Rights Reserved. May not be scanned, copied, duplicated, or posted to a publicly accessible website, in whole or in part.

ALL ABOUT YOU SPA (continued)

ACCOUNT NAME	DEBIT	CREDIT

© 2013 Cengage Learning. All Rights Reserved. May not be scanned, copied, duplicated, or posted to a publicly accessible website, in whole or in part.

ALL ABOUT YOU SPA (concluded)

© 2013 Cengage Learning. All Rights Reserved. May not be scanned, copied, duplicated, or posted to a publicly accessible website, in whole or in part.

Answers to Study Guide Questions

CHAPTER 9

GENERAL JOURNAL AND SALES

PART 1   True/False

1.	T	6.	F
2.	F	7.	F
3.	T	8.	T
4.	T	9.	T
5.	F	10.	F

PART 2   Completion—Accounting Language

1. merchandise inventory
2. controlling account
3. subsidiary ledger
4. credit memorandum

GENERAL JOURNAL AND PURCHASES

PART 1   True/False

1.	F	6.	F
2.	T	7.	T
3.	F	8.	F
4.	T	9.	T
5.	T	10.	T

PART 2   Completion—Accounting Language

1. purchase order
2. FOB shipping point
3. invoice
4. FOB destination

SALES JOURNAL

PART 1   True/False

1. T
2. F
3. F
4. F
5. F

PART 2   Completion—Accounting Language

1. sales journal
2. special journals
3. Credit, Credit

© 2013 Cengage Learning. All Rights Reserved. May not be scanned, copied, duplicated, or posted to a publicly accessible website, in whole or in part.

Answers to Study Guide Questions (concluded)

PURCHASES JOURNAL

PART 1   True/False

1.   F
2.   F
3.   T
4.   F
5.   F

PART 2   Completion—Accounting Language

1.   P
2.   Check marks
3.   account numbers

© 2013 Cengage Learning. All Rights Reserved. May not be scanned, copied, duplicated, or posted to a publicly accessible website, in whole or in part.

Cash Receipts and Cash Payments

LEARNING OBJECTIVES

1. Determine cash discounts according to credit terms.

2. In the general journal, record sales transactions involving cash receipts and cash discounts.

3. In the general journal, record purchase transactions involving cash payments and cash discounts.

4. Record transactions involving trade discounts.

5. In the cash receipts journal, record transactions for a merchandising business and post from a cash receipts journal to a general ledger and an accounts receivable ledger.

6. In the cash payments journal, record transactions for a merchandising business and post from a cash payments journal to a general ledger and an accounts payable ledger.

ACCOUNTING LANGUAGE

Cash discount
Cash payments journal
Cash receipts journal
Credit period
Notes payable

Promissory note
Purchases discount
Sales discount
Trade discount

STUDY GUIDE QUESTIONS

PART 1   True/False—General Journal

For each of the following statements, circle T if the statement is true and F if the statement is false.

T   F   1.   The normal balance of the Sales Discounts account is on the debit side.

T   F   2.   The Purchases Discounts account is classified as a revenue account.

T   F   3.   Credit terms of 1/10, n/30 indicate that a discount of 30 percent may be deducted if the bill is paid in 30 days.

T   F   4.   The buyer records the purchases discount when payment is made.

T   F   5.   Trade discounts are not recorded on the books of either the buyer or the seller.

© 2013 Cengage Learning. All Rights Reserved. May not be scanned, copied, duplicated, or posted to a publicly accessible website, in whole or in part.

PART 2   True/False—Cash Receipts and Cash Payments Journals

For each of the following statements, circle T if the statement is true and F if the statement is false.

T   F   1.   An investment of cash by the owner is always recorded in the general journal.

T   F   2.   In a cash receipts journal, the individual amounts in the Other Accounts Credit column are posted at the end of the month.

T   F   3.   Entries in the Accounts Payable Debit column of a cash payments journal are posted daily to the accounts payable ledger.

T   F   4.   The cash receipts journal contains all transactions in which cash is decreased.

T   F   5.   The cash payments journal contains a Cash Debit column.

PART 3   Completion—Accounting Language

Complete each of the following statements by writing the appropriate words in the spaces provided.

1.   Large deductions from the list prices of merchandise are referred to as _____ _____.

2.   The account _____ is used to represent the amount owed on a promissory note.

3.   The _____ is the amount a customer may deduct for paying a bill within a specified period of time.

4.   A _____ is a written promise to pay a specified amount at a specified time.

5.   The time the seller allows the buyer before full payment on a charge sale has to be made is called the _____.

PART 4   Matching

For each numbered item, choose the appropriate journal and write the identifying letter.

_____	1.	Bought merchandise on account	**S** Sales journal
_____	2.	Sold merchandise for cash	**P** Purchases journal (3 columns)
_____	3.	Bought merchandise for cash	**CR** Cash receipts journal
_____	4.	Collected accounts receivable and allowed a cash discount	**CP** Cash payments journal
_____	5.	Bought store equipment on credit	**J** General journal
_____	6.	Recorded accrued wages	
_____	7.	Received credit memo for merchandise returned	
_____	8.	Paid freight bill on merchandise purchased	
_____	9.	Sold merchandise on account	
_____	10.	Paid state unemployment taxes	

© 2013 Cengage Learning. All Rights Reserved. May not be scanned, copied, duplicated, or posted to a publicly accessible website, in whole or in part.

PART 5   Cash Receipts Journal

Label the cash receipts journal columns as Debit or Credit.

CASH	SALES DISCOUNTS	ACCOUNTS RECEIVABLE	SALES	OTHER ACCOUNTS

PART 6   Cash Payments Journal

Label the cash payments journal columns as Debit or Credit.

OTHER ACCOUNTS	ACCOUNTS PAYABLE	PURCHASES DISCOUNTS	CASH

© 2013 Cengage Learning. All Rights Reserved. May not be scanned, copied, duplicated, or posted to a publicly accessible website, in whole or in part.

DEMONSTRATION PROBLEM—SPECIAL JOURNALS

Elegant Jewelry, a retail store, sells merchandise (1) for cash, (2) on charge accounts, and (3) on credit cards. The store uses a sales journal (page 67), purchases journal (page 79), cash receipts journal (page 53), cash payments journal (page 40), and general journal (page 17). The store engaged in the following selected transactions:

June 16   Sold merchandise on account to T. Morgan, sales invoice no. 1230, $9,757, plus $790.32 sales tax.

17   Sold merchandise paid by bank credit cards, $2,271, plus $183.95 sales tax. The bank charges 4 percent of the total sales plus sales tax.

18   Bought merchandise on account from Gem Central, invoice no. D109, $4,542; dated June 16; terms 1/10, n/30; FOB shipping point, freight prepaid and added to the invoice, $60 (total $4,602).

19   Received credit memorandum no. 926, $529, from Gem Central for merchandise returned.

22   Paid Gem Central, invoice no. D109, Ck. No. 5901, $4,032.87 ($4,542 less $529 return and less 1 percent cash discount: $4,542 − $529 = $4,013; $4,013 × 0.01 = $40.13; $4,013 − $40.13 = $3,972.87; $3,972.87 + $60 freight = $4,032.87).

24   Bought packaging supplies on account from The Box Company, invoice no. 990, $459; dated June 22; net 30 days.

29   Paid rent for the month, Ck. No. 5902, $1,980.

30   Bought merchandise on account from Todd Company, invoice no. 1002, dated June 29; list price $2,950 less 40 percent trade discount; terms 2/10, n/30; FOB shipping point.

30   Paid freight bill to Fast Freight, Ck. No. 5903, $110, for merchandise received from Todd Company.

30   Issued Ck. No. 5904, $258.36, to customer L. O. Sherry, for merchandise returned, $239, plus $19.36 sales tax.

Instructions

1.   Journalize the transactions.
2.   Total and rule the journals.
3.   Prove the equality of the debits and the credits at the bottom of each journal.

© 2013 Cengage Learning. All Rights Reserved. May not be scanned, copied, duplicated, or posted to a publicly accessible website, in whole or in part.

SOLUTION

SALES JOURNAL   PAGE ___67___

	DATE	INV. NO.	CUSTOMER'S NAME	POST. REF.	ACCOUNTS RECEIVABLE DEBIT	SALES TAX PAYABLE CREDIT	SALES CREDIT	
1	20—							1
2	June	16	1230	T. Morgan		10,547.32	790.32	9,757.00	2
3		30		Totals		10,547.32	790.32	9,757.00	3
4									4

Debits	**Credits**
$10,547.32	$ 790.32
	9,757.00
$10,547.32	$10,547.32

PURCHASES JOURNAL   PAGE ___79___

	DATE	SUPPLIER'S NAME	INV. NO.	INV. DATE	TERMS	POST. REF.	ACCOUNTS PAYABLE CREDIT	FREIGHT IN DEBIT	PURCHASES DEBIT	
1	20—									1
2	June	18	Gem Central	D109	6/16	1/10, n/30		4,602.00	60.00	4,542.00	2
3		30	Todd Company	1002	6/29	2/10, n/30		1,770.00		1,770.00	3
4		30	Totals					6,372.00	60.00	6,312.00	4
5											5

Debits	**Credits**
$ 60.00	$6,372.00
6,312.00	
$6,372.00	$6,372.00

© 2013 Cengage Learning. All Rights Reserved. May not be scanned, copied, duplicated, or posted to a publicly accessible website, in whole or in part.

SOLUTION (continued)

CASH RECEIPTS JOURNAL   PAGE ___53___

	DATE		ACCOUNT CREDITED	POST. REF.	CASH DEBIT	CREDIT CARD EXPENSE DEBIT	ACCOUNTS RECEIVABLE CREDIT	SALES CREDIT	SALES TAX PAYABLE CREDIT	OTHER ACCOUNTS CREDIT	
1	20—										1
2	June	17			2,356.75	98.20		2,271.00	183.95		2
3		30	Totals		2,356.75	98.20		2,271.00	183.95		3
4											4

Debits	Credits
$ 98.20	$2,271.00
2,356.75	183.95
$2,454.95	$2,454.95

CASH PAYMENTS JOURNAL   PAGE ___40___

	DATE		CK. NO.	ACCOUNT DEBITED	POST. REF.	OTHER ACCOUNTS DEBIT	ACCOUNTS PAYABLE DEBIT	PURCHASES DISCOUNTS CREDIT	CASH CREDIT	
1	20—									1
2	June	22	5901	Gem Central			4,073.00	40.13	4,032.87	2
3		29	5902	Rent Expense		1,980.00			1,980.00	3
4		30	5903	Freight In		110.00			110.00	4
5		30	5904	Sales Returns and Allowances		239.00				5
6				Sales Tax Payable		19.36			258.36	6
7		30		Totals		2,348.36	4,073.00	40.13	6,381.23	7
8										8

Debits	Credits
$2,348.36	$ 40.13
4,073.00	6,381.23
$6,421.36	$6,421.36

© 2013 Cengage Learning. All Rights Reserved. May not be scanned, copied, duplicated, or posted to a publicly accessible website, in whole or in part.

SOLUTION (concluded)

GENERAL JOURNAL   PAGE ____17____

	DATE		DESCRIPTION	POST. REF.	DEBIT	CREDIT	
1	20—						1
2	June	19	Accounts Payable, Gem Central		529.00		2
3			Purchases Returns and Allowances			529.00	3
4			Credit memo no. 926 for return of				4
5			merchandise.				5
6							6
7		24	Packing Supplies		459.00		7
8			Accounts Payable, The Box Company			459.00	8
9			Purchased packing supplies from The Box				9
10			Company, invoice no. 990, dated June 22,				10
11			terms net 30.				11
12							12
13							13
14							14
15							15
16							16

© 2013 Cengage Learning. All Rights Reserved. May not be scanned, copied, duplicated, or posted to a publicly accessible website, in whole or in part.

EXERCISES AND PROBLEMS

Exercise 10-1

a. _____

b. _____

c. _____

d. _____

e. _____

Exercise 10-2

a. _____

b. _____

c. _____

Exercise 10-3

a. _____

b. _____

c. _____

© 2013 Cengage Learning. All Rights Reserved. May not be scanned, copied, duplicated, or posted to a publicly accessible website, in whole or in part.

Exercise 10-4

GENERAL JOURNAL   PAGE _____

	DATE		DESCRIPTION	POST. REF.	DEBIT	CREDIT	
1							1
2							2
3							3
4							4
5							5
6							6
7							7
8							8
9							9
10							10
11							11
12							12
13							13
14							14
15							15
16							16
17							17
18							18
19							19
20							20
21							21
22							22
23							23
24							24
25							25
26							26
27							27
28							28
29							29
30							30
31							31
32							32
33							33
34							34
35							35
36							36
37							37
38							38

© 2013 Cengage Learning. All Rights Reserved. May not be scanned, copied, duplicated, or posted to a publicly accessible website, in whole or in part.

Exercise 10-5

Seller's Books (Fuentes Company)

GENERAL JOURNAL   PAGE _____

	DATE		DESCRIPTION	POST. REF.	DEBIT	CREDIT	
1							1
2							2
3							3
4							4
5							5
6							6
7							7
8							8
9							9
10							10
11							11
12							12
13							13
14							14
15							15

Buyer's Books (Lowe Company)

GENERAL JOURNAL   PAGE _____

	DATE		DESCRIPTION	POST. REF.	DEBIT	CREDIT	
1							1
2							2
3							3
4							4
5							5
6							6
7							7
8							8
9							9
10							10
11							11
12							12
13							13
14							14
15							15

© 2013 Cengage Learning. All Rights Reserved. May not be scanned, copied, duplicated, or posted to a publicly accessible website, in whole or in part.

Exercise 10-6

GENERAL JOURNAL   PAGE _____

	DATE		DESCRIPTION	POST. REF.	DEBIT	CREDIT	
1							1
2							2
3							3
4							4
5							5
6							6
7							7
8							8
9							9
10							10
11							11
12							12
13							13
14							14
15							15
16							16
17							17
18							18
19							19
20							20
21							21
22							22
23							23
24							24
25							25
26							26
27							27
28							28
29							29

© 2013 Cengage Learning. All Rights Reserved. May not be scanned, copied, duplicated, or posted to a publicly accessible website, in whole or in part.

Exercise 10-7

CASH RECEIPTS JOURNAL   PAGE _____

	DATE		ACCOUNT CREDITED	POST. REF.	CASH	SALES DISCOUNTS	ACCOUNTS RECEIVABLE	SALES	OTHER ACCOUNTS	
1										1
2										2
3										3

Exercise 10-8

_____

_____

_____

_____

_____

Exercise 10-9

CASH PAYMENTS JOURNAL   PAGE _____

	DATE		CK. NO.	ACCOUNT DEBITED	POST. REF.	OTHER ACCOUNTS	ACCOUNTS PAYABLE	PURCHASES DISCOUNTS	CASH	
1										1
2										2
3										3

© 2013 Cengage Learning. All Rights Reserved. May not be scanned, copied, duplicated, or posted to a publicly accessible website, in whole or in part.

Exercise 10-10

TRANSACTION	JOURNAL				
	S	P	CR	CP	J
a. Paid a creditor on account.					
b. Bought merchandise on account.					
c. Sold merchandise for cash.					
d. Adjusted for insurance expired.					
e. Received payment on account from a charge customer.					
f. Received a credit memo for merchandise returned.					
g. Bought equipment on credit.					
h. Sold merchandise on account.					
i. Recorded a customer's NSF check.					
j. Invested personal noncash assets in the business.					
k. Withdrew cash for personal use.					

© 2013 Cengage Learning. All Rights Reserved. May not be scanned, copied, duplicated, or posted to a publicly accessible website, in whole or in part.

Problem 10-1A or 10-1B

GENERAL JOURNAL

PAGE _____1_____

	DATE	DESCRIPTION	POST. REF.	DEBIT	CREDIT	
1						1
2						2
3						3
4						4
5						5
6						6
7						7
8						8
9						9
10						10
11						11
12						12
13						13
14						14
15						15
16						16
17						17
18						18
19						19
20						20
21						21
22						22
23						23
24						24
25						25
26						26
27						27
28						28
29						29
30						30
31						31
32						32
33						33
34						34
35						35
36						36
37						37
38						38
39						39
40						40
41						41
42						42
43						43
44						44

© 2013 Cengage Learning. All Rights Reserved. May not be scanned, copied, duplicated, or posted to a publicly accessible website, in whole or in part.

Problem 10-1A or 10-1B (continued)

GENERAL JOURNAL   PAGE _____2_____

	DATE		DESCRIPTION	POST. REF.	DEBIT	CREDIT	
1							1
2							2
3							3
4							4
5							5
6							6
7							7
8							8
9							9
10							10
11							11
12							12
13							13
14							14
15							15
16							16
17							17
18							18
19							19
20							20
21							21
22							22
23							23
24							24
25							25
26							26
27							27
28							28
29							29
30							30
31							31
32							32
33							33
34							34
35							35
36							36
37							37
38							38
39							39
40							40
41							41
42							42
43							43
44							44
45							45

© 2013 Cengage Learning. All Rights Reserved. May not be scanned, copied, duplicated, or posted to a publicly accessible website, in whole or in part.

Problem 10-1A or 10-1B (continued)

GENERAL JOURNAL   PAGE _____3_____

	DATE		DESCRIPTION	POST. REF.	DEBIT	CREDIT	
1							1
2							2
3							3
4							4
5							5
6							6
7							7
8							8
9							9
10							10
11							11
12							12
13							13
14							14
15							15
16							16
17							17
18							18
19							19
20							20
21							21
22							22
23							23
24							24
25							25
26							26
27							27
28							28
29							29
30							30
31							31
32							32
33							33
34							34
35							35
36							36
37							37
38							38
39							39
40							40
41							41
42							42
43							43
44							44

© 2013 Cengage Learning. All Rights Reserved. May not be scanned, copied, duplicated, or posted to a publicly accessible website, in whole or in part.

Problem 10-1A or 10-1B (continued)

GENERAL LEDGER

ACCOUNT **Cash**   ACCOUNT NO. **111**

DATE		ITEM	POST. REF.	DEBIT	CREDIT	BALANCE DEBIT	BALANCE CREDIT
20—							
Jan.	1	Balance	✓			8,740.00	

ACCOUNT **Accounts Receivable**   ACCOUNT NO. **113**

DATE		ITEM	POST. REF.	DEBIT	CREDIT	BALANCE DEBIT	BALANCE CREDIT
20—							
Jan.	1	Balance	✓			1,650.00	

ACCOUNT **Merchandise Inventory**   ACCOUNT NO. **114**

DATE		ITEM	POST. REF.	DEBIT	CREDIT	BALANCE DEBIT	BALANCE CREDIT
20—							
Jan.	1	Balance	✓			20,584.00	

© 2013 Cengage Learning. All Rights Reserved. May not be scanned, copied, duplicated, or posted to a publicly accessible website, in whole or in part.

Problem 10-1A or 10-1B (continued)

ACCOUNT   *Supplies*   ACCOUNT NO.   *115*

DATE		ITEM	POST. REF.	DEBIT	CREDIT	BALANCE	
						DEBIT	CREDIT
20—							
Jan.	1	Balance	✓			592.00	

ACCOUNT   *Prepaid Insurance*   ACCOUNT NO.   *116*

DATE		ITEM	POST. REF.	DEBIT	CREDIT	BALANCE	
						DEBIT	CREDIT
20—							
Jan.	1	Balance	✓			390.00	

ACCOUNT   *Equipment*   ACCOUNT NO.   *121*

DATE		ITEM	POST. REF.	DEBIT	CREDIT	BALANCE	
						DEBIT	CREDIT
20—							
Jan.	1	Balance	✓			3,644.00	

ACCOUNT   *Accounts Payable*   ACCOUNT NO.   *212*

DATE		ITEM	POST. REF.	DEBIT	CREDIT	BALANCE	
						DEBIT	CREDIT
20—							
Jan.	1	Balance	✓				600.00

ACCOUNT   *Salaries Payable*   ACCOUNT NO.   *215*

DATE		ITEM	POST. REF.	DEBIT	CREDIT	BALANCE	
						DEBIT	CREDIT

© 2013 Cengage Learning. All Rights Reserved. May not be scanned, copied, duplicated, or posted to a publicly accessible website, in whole or in part.

Problem 10-1A or 10-1B (continued)

ACCOUNT   *Employees' Federal Income Tax Payable*   ACCOUNT NO.   216

DATE	ITEM	POST. REF.	DEBIT	CREDIT	BALANCE DEBIT	BALANCE CREDIT

ACCOUNT   *FICA Taxes Payable*   ACCOUNT NO.   217

DATE	ITEM	POST. REF.	DEBIT	CREDIT	BALANCE DEBIT	BALANCE CREDIT

ACCOUNT   *State Unemployment Tax Payable*   ACCOUNT NO.   218

DATE	ITEM	POST. REF.	DEBIT	CREDIT	BALANCE DEBIT	BALANCE CREDIT

ACCOUNT   *Federal Unemployment Tax Payable*   ACCOUNT NO.   219

DATE	ITEM	POST. REF.	DEBIT	CREDIT	BALANCE DEBIT	BALANCE CREDIT

ACCOUNT   *, Capital*   ACCOUNT NO.   311

DATE	ITEM	POST. REF.	DEBIT	CREDIT	BALANCE DEBIT	BALANCE CREDIT
20—						
Jan.	1	✓				35,000.00

ACCOUNT   *, Drawing*   ACCOUNT NO.   312

DATE	ITEM	POST. REF.	DEBIT	CREDIT	BALANCE DEBIT	BALANCE CREDIT

© 2013 Cengage Learning. All Rights Reserved. May not be scanned, copied, duplicated, or posted to a publicly accessible website, in whole or in part.

Problem 10-1A or 10-1B (continued)

ACCOUNT   *Sales*   ACCOUNT NO.   *411*

DATE		ITEM	POST. REF.	DEBIT	CREDIT	BALANCE	
						DEBIT	CREDIT

ACCOUNT   *Sales Returns and Allowances*   ACCOUNT NO.   *412*

DATE		ITEM	POST. REF.	DEBIT	CREDIT	BALANCE	
						DEBIT	CREDIT

ACCOUNT   *Sales Discounts*   ACCOUNT NO.   *413*

DATE		ITEM	POST. REF.	DEBIT	CREDIT	BALANCE	
						DEBIT	CREDIT

ACCOUNT   *Purchases*   ACCOUNT NO.   *511*

DATE		ITEM	POST. REF.	DEBIT	CREDIT	BALANCE	
						DEBIT	CREDIT

© 2013 Cengage Learning. All Rights Reserved. May not be scanned, copied, duplicated, or posted to a publicly accessible website, in whole or in part.

Problem 10-1A or 10-1B (continued)

ACCOUNT _Purchases Returns and Allowances_   ACCOUNT NO. _512_

DATE	ITEM	POST. REF.	DEBIT	CREDIT	BALANCE DEBIT	BALANCE CREDIT

ACCOUNT _Purchases Discounts_   ACCOUNT NO. _513_

DATE	ITEM	POST. REF.	DEBIT	CREDIT	BALANCE DEBIT	BALANCE CREDIT

ACCOUNT _Freight In_   ACCOUNT NO. _514_

DATE	ITEM	POST. REF.	DEBIT	CREDIT	BALANCE DEBIT	BALANCE CREDIT

ACCOUNT _Salary Expense_   ACCOUNT NO. _621_

DATE	ITEM	POST. REF.	DEBIT	CREDIT	BALANCE DEBIT	BALANCE CREDIT

ACCOUNT _Payroll Tax Expense_   ACCOUNT NO. _622_

DATE	ITEM	POST. REF.	DEBIT	CREDIT	BALANCE DEBIT	BALANCE CREDIT

© 2013 Cengage Learning. All Rights Reserved. May not be scanned, copied, duplicated, or posted to a publicly accessible website, in whole or in part.

Problem 10-1A or 10-1B (continued)

ACCOUNT   *Rent Expense*   ACCOUNT NO.   *627*

DATE	ITEM	POST. REF.	DEBIT	CREDIT	BALANCE	
					DEBIT	CREDIT

ACCOUNT   *Miscellaneous Expense*   ACCOUNT NO.   *631*

DATE	ITEM	POST. REF.	DEBIT	CREDIT	BALANCE	
					DEBIT	CREDIT

© 2013 Cengage Learning. All Rights Reserved. May not be scanned, copied, duplicated, or posted to a publicly accessible website, in whole or in part.

Problem 10-1A or 10-1B (continued)

ACCOUNTS RECEIVABLE LEDGER

NAME _____

ADDRESS _____

DATE		ITEM	POST. REF.	DEBIT	CREDIT	BALANCE

NAME _____

ADDRESS _____

DATE		ITEM	POST. REF.	DEBIT	CREDIT	BALANCE

NAME _____

ADDRESS _____

DATE		ITEM	POST. REF.	DEBIT	CREDIT	BALANCE

NAME _____

ADDRESS _____

DATE		ITEM	POST. REF.	DEBIT	CREDIT	BALANCE
20—						
Jan.	1	Balance	✓			650.00

NAME _____

ADDRESS _____

DATE		ITEM	POST. REF.	DEBIT	CREDIT	BALANCE
20—						
Jan.	1	Balance	✓			1,000.00

© 2013 Cengage Learning. All Rights Reserved. May not be scanned, copied, duplicated, or posted to a publicly accessible website, in whole or in part.

Problem 10-1A or 10-1B (continued)

ACCOUNTS PAYABLE LEDGER

NAME _____
ADDRESS _____
_____

DATE		ITEM	POST. REF.	DEBIT	CREDIT	BALANCE

NAME _____
ADDRESS _____
_____

DATE		ITEM	POST. REF.	DEBIT	CREDIT	BALANCE

NAME _____
ADDRESS _____
_____

DATE		ITEM	POST. REF.	DEBIT	CREDIT	BALANCE
20—						
Jan.	1	Balance	✓			600.00

NAME _____
ADDRESS _____
_____

DATE		ITEM	POST. REF.	DEBIT	CREDIT	BALANCE

© 2013 Cengage Learning. All Rights Reserved. May not be scanned, copied, duplicated, or posted to a publicly accessible website, in whole or in part.

Problem 10-1A or 10-1B (continued)

ACCOUNT NAME	DEBIT	CREDIT

© 2013 Cengage Learning. All Rights Reserved. May not be scanned, copied, duplicated, or posted to a publicly accessible website, in whole or in part.

Problem 10-1A or 10-1B (concluded)

© 2013 Cengage Learning. All Rights Reserved. May not be scanned, copied, duplicated, or posted to a publicly accessible website, in whole or in part.

Problem 10-2A or 10-2B

PAGE _____

CASH RECEIPTS JOURNAL

	DATE	ACCOUNT CREDITED	POST. REF.	CASH DEBIT	SALES DISCOUNTS DEBIT	ACCOUNTS RECEIVABLE CREDIT	SALES CREDIT	OTHER ACCOUNTS CREDIT	
1									1
2									2
3									3
4									4
5									5
6									6
7									7
8									8
9									9
10									10
11									11
12									12

PAGE _____

SALES JOURNAL

	DATE	INV. NO.	CUSTOMER'S NAME	POST. REF.	ACCOUNTS RECEIVABLE DR. SALES CR.	
1						1
2						2
3						3
4						4
5						5
6						6

EQUALITY OF DEBITS AND CREDITS

DEBITS	CREDITS
$	$
$	$

© 2013 Cengage Learning. All Rights Reserved. May not be scanned, copied, duplicated, or posted to a publicly accessible website, in whole or in part.

Problem 10-3A or 10-3B

CASH PAYMENTS JOURNAL

PAGE _____

DATE	CK. NO.	ACCOUNT DEBITED	POST. REF.	OTHER ACCOUNTS DEBIT	ACCOUNTS PAYABLE DEBIT	PURCHASES DISCOUNTS CREDIT	CASH CREDIT	
								1
								2
								3
								4
								5
								6
								7
								8
								9
								10
								11
								12
								13
								14
								15
								16

EQUALITY OF DEBITS AND CREDITS

DEBITS	CREDITS
$	$
$	$

© 2013 Cengage Learning. All Rights Reserved. May not be scanned, copied, duplicated, or posted to a publicly accessible website, in whole or in part.

Problem 10-4A or 10-4B

SALES JOURNAL

PAGE _____

DATE	INV. NO.	CUSTOMER'S NAME	POST. REF.	ACCOUNTS RECEIVABLE DR. SALES CR.	
					1
					2
					3
					4
					5
					6
					7
					8
					9

PURCHASES JOURNAL

PAGE _____

DATE	INV. NO.	INV. DATE	TERMS	SUPPLIER'S NAME	POST. REF.	ACCOUNTS PAYABLE CREDIT	FREIGHT IN DEBIT	PURCHASES DEBIT	
									1
									2
									3
									4
									5
									6
									7

EQUALITY OF DEBITS AND CREDITS

DEBITS	CREDITS
$	$
$	$

417

© 2013 Cengage Learning. All Rights Reserved. May not be scanned, copied, duplicated, or posted to a publicly accessible website, in whole or in part.

Problem 10-4A or 10-4B (continued)

CASH RECEIPTS JOURNAL

PAGE _____

DATE	ACCOUNT CREDITED	POST. REF.	CASH DEBIT	SALES DISCOUNTS DEBIT	ACCOUNTS RECEIVABLE CREDIT	SALES CREDIT	OTHER ACCOUNTS CREDIT	
								1
								2
								3
								4
								5
								6
								7
								8
								9
								10
								11
								12
								13

EQUALITY OF DEBITS AND CREDITS

DEBITS   CREDITS

$ _____ $ _____

$ _____ $ _____

© 2013 Cengage Learning. All Rights Reserved. May not be scanned, copied, duplicated, or posted to a publicly accessible website, in whole or in part.

Problem 10-4A or 10-4B (continued)

CASH PAYMENTS JOURNAL

PAGE _____

	DATE	CK. NO.	ACCOUNT DEBITED	POST. REF.	OTHER ACCOUNTS DEBIT	ACCOUNTS PAYABLE DEBIT	PURCHASES DISCOUNTS CREDIT	CASH CREDIT	
1									1
2									2
3									3
4									4
5									5
6									6
7									7
8									8
9									9
10									10
11									11
12									12

EQUALITY OF DEBITS AND CREDITS

DEBITS   CREDITS

$ _____ $ _____

$ _____ $ _____

© 2013 Cengage Learning. All Rights Reserved. May not be scanned, copied, duplicated, or posted to a publicly accessible website, in whole or in part.

Problem 10-4A or 10-4B (continued)

GENERAL JOURNAL   PAGE _____

	DATE		DESCRIPTION	POST. REF.	DEBIT	CREDIT	
1							1
2							2
3							3
4							4
5							5
6							6
7							7
8							8
9							9
10							10
11							11
12							12
13							13
14							14
15							15
16							16
17							17
18							18
19							19
20							20
21							21
22							22
23							23
24							24
25							25
26							26
27							27
28							28
29							29
30							30
31							31
32							32
33							33
34							34
35							35

© 2013 Cengage Learning. All Rights Reserved. May not be scanned, copied, duplicated, or posted to a publicly accessible website, in whole or in part.

Problem 10-4A or 10-4B (continued)

GENERAL LEDGER

ACCOUNT *Cash*   ACCOUNT NO. *111*

DATE		ITEM	POST. REF.	DEBIT	CREDIT	BALANCE DEBIT	BALANCE CREDIT	
20—								
Jan.	1	Balance	✓			8,740.00		

ACCOUNT *Accounts Receivable*   ACCOUNT NO. *113*

DATE		ITEM	POST. REF.	DEBIT	CREDIT	BALANCE DEBIT	BALANCE CREDIT	
20—								
Jan.	1	Balance	✓			1,650.00		

ACCOUNT *Merchandise Inventory*   ACCOUNT NO. *114*

DATE		ITEM	POST. REF.	DEBIT	CREDIT	BALANCE DEBIT	BALANCE CREDIT	
20—								
Jan.	1	Balance	✓			20,584.00		

© 2013 Cengage Learning. All Rights Reserved. May not be scanned, copied, duplicated, or posted to a publicly accessible website, in whole or in part.

Problem 10-4A or 10-4B (continued)

ACCOUNT *Supplies* ACCOUNT NO. *115*

DATE		ITEM	POST. REF.	DEBIT	CREDIT	BALANCE	
						DEBIT	CREDIT
20—							
Jan.	1	Balance	✓			592.00	

ACCOUNT *Prepaid Insurance* ACCOUNT NO. *116*

DATE		ITEM	POST. REF.	DEBIT	CREDIT	BALANCE	
						DEBIT	CREDIT
20—							
Jan.	1	Balance	✓			390.00	

ACCOUNT *Equipment* ACCOUNT NO. *121*

DATE		ITEM	POST. REF.	DEBIT	CREDIT	BALANCE	
						DEBIT	CREDIT
20—							
Jan.	1	Balance	✓			3,644.00	

ACCOUNT *Accounts Payable* ACCOUNT NO. *212*

DATE		ITEM	POST. REF.	DEBIT	CREDIT	BALANCE	
						DEBIT	CREDIT
20—							
Jan.	1		✓				600.00

ACCOUNT *Salaries Payable* ACCOUNT NO. *215*

DATE		ITEM	POST. REF.	DEBIT	CREDIT	BALANCE	
						DEBIT	CREDIT

© 2013 Cengage Learning. All Rights Reserved. May not be scanned, copied, duplicated, or posted to a publicly accessible website, in whole or in part.

Problem 10-4A or 10-4B (continued)

ACCOUNT   **Employees' Federal Income Tax Payable**   ACCOUNT NO.   216

DATE		ITEM	POST. REF.	DEBIT	CREDIT	BALANCE	
						DEBIT	CREDIT

ACCOUNT   **FICA Taxes Payable**   ACCOUNT NO.   217

DATE		ITEM	POST. REF.	DEBIT	CREDIT	BALANCE	
						DEBIT	CREDIT

ACCOUNT   **State Unemployment Tax Payable**   ACCOUNT NO.   218

DATE		ITEM	POST. REF.	DEBIT	CREDIT	BALANCE	
						DEBIT	CREDIT

ACCOUNT   **Federal Unemployment Tax Payable**   ACCOUNT NO.   219

DATE		ITEM	POST. REF.	DEBIT	CREDIT	BALANCE	
						DEBIT	CREDIT

ACCOUNT   **, Capital**   ACCOUNT NO.   311

DATE		ITEM	POST. REF.	DEBIT	CREDIT	BALANCE	
						DEBIT	CREDIT
20—							
Jan.	1	Balance	✓				35,000.00

© 2013 Cengage Learning. All Rights Reserved. May not be scanned, copied, duplicated, or posted to a publicly accessible website, in whole or in part.

Problem 10-4A or 10-4B (continued)

ACCOUNT _____, *Drawing* _____   ACCOUNT NO. _____ *312*

DATE		ITEM	POST. REF.	DEBIT	CREDIT	BALANCE	
						DEBIT	CREDIT

ACCOUNT _____ *Sales* _____   ACCOUNT NO. _____ *411*

DATE		ITEM	POST. REF.	DEBIT	CREDIT	BALANCE	
						DEBIT	CREDIT

ACCOUNT _____ *Sales Returns and Allowances* _____   ACCOUNT NO. _____ *412*

DATE		ITEM	POST. REF.	DEBIT	CREDIT	BALANCE	
						DEBIT	CREDIT

ACCOUNT _____ *Sales Discounts* _____   ACCOUNT NO. _____ *413*

DATE		ITEM	POST. REF.	DEBIT	CREDIT	BALANCE	
						DEBIT	CREDIT

ACCOUNT _____ *Purchases* _____   ACCOUNT NO. _____ *511*

DATE		ITEM	POST. REF.	DEBIT	CREDIT	BALANCE	
						DEBIT	CREDIT

© 2013 Cengage Learning. All Rights Reserved. May not be scanned, copied, duplicated, or posted to a publicly accessible website, in whole or in part.

Problem 10-4A or 10-4B (continued)

ACCOUNT   *Purchases Returns and Allowances*   ACCOUNT NO.   *512*

DATE		ITEM	POST. REF.	DEBIT	CREDIT	BALANCE	
						DEBIT	CREDIT

ACCOUNT   *Purchases Discounts*   ACCOUNT NO.   *513*

DATE		ITEM	POST. REF.	DEBIT	CREDIT	BALANCE	
						DEBIT	CREDIT

ACCOUNT   *Freight In*   ACCOUNT NO.   *514*

DATE		ITEM	POST. REF.	DEBIT	CREDIT	BALANCE	
						DEBIT	CREDIT

ACCOUNT   *Salary Expense*   ACCOUNT NO.   *621*

DATE		ITEM	POST. REF.	DEBIT	CREDIT	BALANCE	
						DEBIT	CREDIT

ACCOUNT   *Payroll Tax Expense*   ACCOUNT NO.   *622*

DATE		ITEM	POST. REF.	DEBIT	CREDIT	BALANCE	
						DEBIT	CREDIT

© 2013 Cengage Learning. All Rights Reserved. May not be scanned, copied, duplicated, or posted to a publicly accessible website, in whole or in part.

Problem 10-4A or 10-4B (continued)

ACCOUNT   *Rent Expense*   ACCOUNT NO.   *627*

DATE	ITEM	POST. REF.	DEBIT	CREDIT	BALANCE DEBIT	CREDIT

ACCOUNT   *Miscellaneous Expense*   ACCOUNT NO.   *631*

DATE	ITEM	POST. REF.	DEBIT	CREDIT	BALANCE DEBIT	CREDIT

ACCOUNTS RECEIVABLE LEDGER

NAME _____
ADDRESS _____

DATE	ITEM	POST. REF.	DEBIT	CREDIT	BALANCE

NAME _____
ADDRESS _____

DATE	ITEM	POST. REF.	DEBIT	CREDIT	BALANCE

© 2013 Cengage Learning. All Rights Reserved. May not be scanned, copied, duplicated, or posted to a publicly accessible website, in whole or in part.

Problem 10-4A or 10-4B (continued)

NAME _____

ADDRESS _____

_____

DATE		ITEM	POST. REF.	DEBIT	CREDIT	BALANCE

NAME _____

ADDRESS _____

_____

DATE		ITEM	POST. REF.	DEBIT	CREDIT	BALANCE
20—						
Jan.	1	Balance	✓			650.00

NAME _____

ADDRESS _____

_____

DATE		ITEM	POST. REF.	DEBIT	CREDIT	BALANCE
20—						
Jan.	1	Balance	✓			1,000.00

© 2013 Cengage Learning. All Rights Reserved. May not be scanned, copied, duplicated, or posted to a publicly accessible website, in whole or in part.

Problem 10-4A or 10-4B (continued)

ACCOUNTS PAYABLE LEDGER

NAME _____

ADDRESS _____

DATE		ITEM	POST. REF.	DEBIT	CREDIT	BALANCE

NAME _____

ADDRESS _____

DATE		ITEM	POST. REF.	DEBIT	CREDIT	BALANCE

NAME _____

ADDRESS _____

DATE		ITEM	POST. REF.	DEBIT	CREDIT	BALANCE
20—						
Jan.	1	Balance	✓			600.00

NAME _____

ADDRESS _____

DATE		ITEM	POST. REF.	DEBIT	CREDIT	BALANCE

© 2013 Cengage Learning. All Rights Reserved. May not be scanned, copied, duplicated, or posted to a publicly accessible website, in whole or in part.

Problem 10-4A or 10-4B (continued)

ACCOUNT NAME	DEBIT	CREDIT

© 2013 Cengage Learning. All Rights Reserved. May not be scanned, copied, duplicated, or posted to a publicly accessible website, in whole or in part.

Problem 10-4A or 10-4B (concluded)

© 2013 Cengage Learning. All Rights Reserved. May not be scanned, copied, duplicated, or posted to a publicly accessible website, in whole or in part.

Problem 10-5A or 10-5B

CASH RECEIPTS JOURNAL

PAGE _____

DATE	ACCOUNT CREDITED	POST. REF.	CASH DEBIT	SALES DISCOUNTS DEBIT	ACCOUNTS RECEIVABLE CREDIT	SALES CREDIT	OTHER ACCOUNTS CREDIT	
								1
								2
								3
								4
								5
								6
								7

GENERAL JOURNAL

PAGE _____

DATE	DESCRIPTION	POST. REF.	DEBIT	CREDIT	
					1
					2
					3
					4
					5
					6
					7
					8
					9

EQUALITY OF DEBITS AND CREDITS

DEBITS	CREDITS
$	$
$	$

© 2013 Cengage Learning. All Rights Reserved. May not be scanned, copied, duplicated, or posted to a publicly accessible website, in whole or in part.

Problem 10-5A or 10-5B (concluded)

CASH PAYMENTS JOURNAL

PAGE _____

DATE	CK. NO.	ACCOUNT DEBITED	POST. REF.	OTHER ACCOUNTS DEBIT	ACCOUNTS PAYABLE DEBIT	PURCHASES DISCOUNTS CREDIT	CASH CREDIT	
								1
								2
								3
								4
								5
								6
								7
								8
								9

EQUALITY OF DEBITS AND CREDITS

DEBITS   CREDITS

$ _____ $ _____

$ _____ $ _____

© 2013 Cengage Learning. All Rights Reserved. May not be scanned, copied, duplicated, or posted to a publicly accessible website, in whole or in part.

ALL ABOUT YOU SPA: Cash Receipts and Cash Payments

General Journal Only (If special journals are used, skip to page 439.)

GENERAL JOURNAL   PAGE _____

	DATE		DESCRIPTION	POST. REF.	DEBIT	CREDIT	
1							1
2							2
3							3
4							4
5							5
6							6
7							7
8							8
9							9
10							10
11							11
12							12
13							13
14							14
15							15
16							16
17							17
18							18
19							19
20							20
21							21
22							22
23							23
24							24
25							25
26							26
27							27
28							28
29							29
30							30
31							31
32							32
33							33
34							34
35							35
36							36
37							37
38							38
39							39
40							40
41							41
42							42
43							43
44							44
45							45

© 2013 Cengage Learning. All Rights Reserved. May not be scanned, copied, duplicated, or posted to a publicly accessible website, in whole or in part.

ALL ABOUT YOU SPA (continued)

GENERAL JOURNAL   PAGE _____

	DATE		DESCRIPTION	POST. REF.	DEBIT	CREDIT	
1							1
2							2
3							3
4							4
5							5
6							6
7							7
8							8
9							9
10							10
11							11
12							12
13							13
14							14
15							15
16							16
17							17
18							18
19							19
20							20
21							21
22							22
23							23
24							24
25							25
26							26
27							27
28							28
29							29
30							30
31							31
32							32
33							33
34							34
35							35
36							36
37							37
38							38
39							39
40							40
41							41
42							42
43							43
44							44
45							45

© 2013 Cengage Learning. All Rights Reserved. May not be scanned, copied, duplicated, or posted to a publicly accessible website, in whole or in part.

ALL ABOUT YOU SPA (continued)

GENERAL JOURNAL   PAGE _____

	DATE		DESCRIPTION	POST. REF.	DEBIT	CREDIT	
1							1
2							2
3							3
4							4
5							5
6							6
7							7
8							8
9							9
10							10
11							11
12							12
13							13
14							14
15							15
16							16
17							17
18							18
19							19
20							20
21							21
22							22
23							23
24							24
25							25
26							26
27							27
28							28
29							29
30							30
31							31
32							32
33							33
34							34
35							35
36							36
37							37
38							38
39							39
40							40
41							41
42							42
43							43
44							44
45							45

© 2013 Cengage Learning. All Rights Reserved. May not be scanned, copied, duplicated, or posted to a publicly accessible website, in whole or in part.

ALL ABOUT YOU SPA (continued)

GENERAL JOURNAL   PAGE _____

	DATE		DESCRIPTION	POST. REF.	DEBIT	CREDIT	
1							1
2							2
3							3
4							4
5							5
6							6
7							7
8							8
9							9
10							10
11							11
12							12
13							13
14							14
15							15
16							16
17							17
18							18
19							19
20							20
21							21
22							22
23							23
24							24
25							25
26							26
27							27
28							28
29							29
30							30
31							31
32							32
33							33
34							34
35							35
36							36
37							37
38							38
39							39
40							40
41							41
42							42
43							43
44							44
45							45

© 2013 Cengage Learning. All Rights Reserved. May not be scanned, copied, duplicated, or posted to a publicly accessible website, in whole or in part.

ALL ABOUT YOU SPA (continued)

GENERAL JOURNAL   PAGE _____

	DATE		DESCRIPTION	POST. REF.	DEBIT	CREDIT	
1							1
2							2
3							3
4							4
5							5
6							6
7							7
8							8
9							9
10							10
11							11
12							12
13							13
14							14
15							15
16							16
17							17
18							18
19							19
20							20
21							21
22							22
23							23
24							24
25							25
26							26
27							27
28							28
29							29
30							30
31							31
32							32
33							33
34							34
35							35
36							36
37							37
38							38
39							39
40							40
41							41
42							42
43							43
44							44
45							45

© 2013 Cengage Learning. All Rights Reserved. May not be scanned, copied, duplicated, or posted to a publicly accessible website, in whole or in part.

ALL ABOUT YOU SPA (continued)

GENERAL JOURNAL

PAGE _____

	DATE	DESCRIPTION	POST. REF.	DEBIT	CREDIT	
1						1
2						2
3						3
4						4
5						5
6						6
7						7
8						8
9						9
10						10
11						11
12						12
13						13
14						14
15						15
16						16
17						17
18						18
19						19
20						20
21						21
22						22
23						23
24						24
25						25
26						26

© 2013 Cengage Learning. All Rights Reserved. May not be scanned, copied, duplicated, or posted to a publicly accessible website, in whole or in part.

ALL ABOUT YOU SPA (continued)
General Journal and Special Journals

PAGE _____

CASH RECEIPTS JOURNAL

	DATE	ACCOUNT CREDITED	POST. REF.	CASH DEBIT	SALES DISCOUNTS DEBIT	ACCOUNTS RECEIVABLE CREDIT	INCOME FROM SERVICES CREDIT	MERCHANDISE SALES CREDIT	SALES TAX PAYABLE CREDIT	OTHER ACCOUNTS CREDIT	
1											1
2											2
3											3
4											4
5											5
6											6
7											7
8											8
9											9
10											10
11											11
12											12
13											13
14											14
15											15
16											16
17											17
18											18

EQUALITY OF DEBITS AND CREDITS

DEBITS   CREDITS

$ _____ $ _____

$ _____ $ _____

© 2013 Cengage Learning. All Rights Reserved. May not be scanned, copied, duplicated, or posted to a publicly accessible website, in whole or in part.

ALL ABOUT YOU SPA (continued)

CASH PAYMENTS JOURNAL

PAGE ___

DATE	CK. NO.	ACCOUNT DEBITED	POST. REF.	OTHER ACCOUNTS DEBIT	ACCOUNTS PAYABLE DEBIT	PURCHASES DISCOUNTS CREDIT	CASH CREDIT	
								1
								2
								3
								4
								5
								6
								7
								8
								9
								10
								11
								12
								13
								14
								15
								16
								17
								18
								19
								20
								21
								22
								23
								24
								25
								26
								27
								28

EQUALITY OF DEBITS AND CREDITS

DEBITS $_____   CREDITS $_____

$_____ $_____

440

© 2013 Cengage Learning. All Rights Reserved. May not be scanned, copied, duplicated, or posted to a publicly accessible website, in whole or in part.

ALL ABOUT YOU SPA (continued)

PURCHASES JOURNAL

PAGE _____

DATE	SUPPLIER'S NAME	INV. NO.	INV. DATE	TERMS	POST. REF.	ACCOUNTS PAYABLE CREDIT	FREIGHT IN DEBIT	PURCHASES DEBIT	
									1
									2
									3
									4
									5
									6
									7
									8

EQUALITY OF DEBITS AND CREDITS

DEBITS   CREDITS

$ _____ $ _____

$ _____ $ _____

SALES JOURNAL

PAGE _____

DATE	CUSTOMER'S NAME	INV. NO.	POST. REF.	ACCOUNTS RECEIVABLE DEBIT	SALES TAX PAYABLE CREDIT	MERCHANDISE SALES CREDIT	
							1
							2
							3
							4
							5
							6
							7
							8
							9
							10

EQUALITY OF DEBITS AND CREDITS

DEBITS   CREDITS

$ _____ $ _____

$ _____ $ _____

441

© 2013 Cengage Learning. All Rights Reserved. May not be scanned, copied, duplicated, or posted to a publicly accessible website, in whole or in part.

ALL ABOUT YOU SPA (continued)

GENERAL JOURNAL   PAGE _____

	DATE		DESCRIPTION	POST. REF.	DEBIT	CREDIT	
1							1
2							2
3							3
4							4
5							5
6							6
7							7
8							8
9							9
10							10
11							11
12							12
13							13
14							14
15							15
16							16
17							17
18							18
19							19
20							20
21							21
22							22
23							23
24							24
25							25
26							26

© 2013 Cengage Learning. All Rights Reserved. May not be scanned, copied, duplicated, or posted to a publicly accessible website, in whole or in part.

ALL ABOUT YOU SPA (continued)

GENERAL LEDGER

ACCOUNT **Cash**   ACCOUNT NO. **111**

DATE		ITEM	POST. REF.	DEBIT	CREDIT	BALANCE	
						DEBIT	CREDIT
20—							
Aug.	1	Balance	✓			44,969.26	

© 2013 Cengage Learning. All Rights Reserved. May not be scanned, copied, duplicated, or posted to a publicly accessible website, in whole or in part.

ALL ABOUT YOU SPA (continued)

ACCOUNT   *Accounts Receivable*   ACCOUNT NO.   *113*

DATE		ITEM	POST. REF.	DEBIT	CREDIT	BALANCE	
						DEBIT	CREDIT
20—							
Aug.	1	Balance	✓			4,568.79	

ACCOUNT   *Office Supplies*   ACCOUNT NO.   *114*

DATE		ITEM	POST. REF.	DEBIT	CREDIT	BALANCE	
						DEBIT	CREDIT
20—							
Aug.	1	Balance	✓			248.00	

© 2013 Cengage Learning. All Rights Reserved. May not be scanned, copied, duplicated, or posted to a publicly accessible website, in whole or in part.

ALL ABOUT YOU SPA (continued)

ACCOUNT *Spa Supplies*   ACCOUNT NO. **115**

DATE		ITEM	POST. REF.	DEBIT	CREDIT	BALANCE DEBIT	BALANCE CREDIT
20—							
Aug.	1	Balance	✓			695.00	

ACCOUNT *Prepaid Insurance*   ACCOUNT NO. **117**

DATE		ITEM	POST. REF.	DEBIT	CREDIT	BALANCE DEBIT	BALANCE CREDIT
20—							
Aug.	1	Balance	✓			800.00	

ACCOUNT *Office Equipment*   ACCOUNT NO. **128**

DATE		ITEM	POST. REF.	DEBIT	CREDIT	BALANCE DEBIT	BALANCE CREDIT
20—							
Aug.	1	Balance	✓			1,570.00	

ACCOUNT *Accumulated Depreciation, Office Equipment*   ACCOUNT NO. **129**

DATE		ITEM	POST. REF.	DEBIT	CREDIT	BALANCE DEBIT	BALANCE CREDIT
20—							
Aug.	1	Balance	✓				10.00

© 2013 Cengage Learning. All Rights Reserved. May not be scanned, copied, duplicated, or posted to a publicly accessible website, in whole or in part.

ALL ABOUT YOU SPA (continued)

ACCOUNT *Spa Equipment*   ACCOUNT NO. *128*

DATE		ITEM	POST. REF.	DEBIT	CREDIT	BALANCE DEBIT	BALANCE CREDIT
20—							
Aug.	*1*	*Balance*	✓			*17,601.00*	

ACCOUNT *Accumulated Depreciation, Spa Equipment*   ACCOUNT NO. *129*

DATE		ITEM	POST. REF.	DEBIT	CREDIT	BALANCE DEBIT	BALANCE CREDIT
20—							
Aug.	*1*	*Balance*	✓				*64.88*

ACCOUNT *Accounts Payable*   ACCOUNT NO. *211*

DATE		ITEM	POST. REF.	DEBIT	CREDIT	BALANCE DEBIT	BALANCE CREDIT
20—							
Aug.	*1*	*Balance*	✓				*20,720.00*

ACCOUNT *Wages Payable*   ACCOUNT NO. *212*

DATE		ITEM	POST. REF.	DEBIT	CREDIT	BALANCE DEBIT	BALANCE CREDIT

© 2013 Cengage Learning. All Rights Reserved. May not be scanned, copied, duplicated, or posted to a publicly accessible website, in whole or in part.

ALL ABOUT YOU SPA (continued)

ACCOUNT   *Sales Tax Payable*   ACCOUNT NO.   **215**

DATE		ITEM	POST. REF.	DEBIT	CREDIT	BALANCE	
						DEBIT	CREDIT
20—							
Aug.	1	Balance	✓				1,829.90

ACCOUNT   *A. Valli, Capital*   ACCOUNT NO.   **311**

DATE		ITEM	POST. REF.	DEBIT	CREDIT	BALANCE	
						DEBIT	CREDIT
20—							
Aug.	1	Balance	✓				50,219.62

ACCOUNT   *A. Valli, Drawing*   ACCOUNT NO.   **312**

DATE		ITEM	POST. REF.	DEBIT	CREDIT	BALANCE	
						DEBIT	CREDIT
20—							
Aug.	1	Balance	✓			2,500.00	

ACCOUNT   *Income Summary*   ACCOUNT NO.   **313**

DATE		ITEM	POST. REF.	DEBIT	CREDIT	BALANCE	
						DEBIT	CREDIT

© 2013 Cengage Learning. All Rights Reserved. May not be scanned, copied, duplicated, or posted to a publicly accessible website, in whole or in part.

ALL ABOUT YOU SPA (continued)

ACCOUNT   *Income from Services*   ACCOUNT NO. *411*

DATE		ITEM	POST. REF.	DEBIT	CREDIT	BALANCE DEBIT	BALANCE CREDIT
20—							
Aug.	1	Balance	✓				12,722.00

ACCOUNT   *Merchandise Sales*   ACCOUNT NO. *412*

DATE		ITEM	POST. REF.	DEBIT	CREDIT	BALANCE DEBIT	BALANCE CREDIT
20—							
Aug.	1	Balance	✓				10,151.65

ACCOUNT   _____   ACCOUNT NO. _____

DATE		ITEM	POST. REF.	DEBIT	CREDIT	BALANCE DEBIT	BALANCE CREDIT

ACCOUNT   _____   ACCOUNT NO. _____

DATE		ITEM	POST. REF.	DEBIT	CREDIT	BALANCE DEBIT	BALANCE CREDIT

© 2013 Cengage Learning. All Rights Reserved. May not be scanned, copied, duplicated, or posted to a publicly accessible website, in whole or in part.

ALL ABOUT YOU SPA (continued)

ACCOUNT *Purchases*   ACCOUNT NO. *511*

DATE		ITEM	POST. REF.	DEBIT	CREDIT	BALANCE DEBIT	BALANCE CREDIT
20—							
Aug.	1	Balance	✓			12,868.00	

ACCOUNT *Purchases Discounts*   ACCOUNT NO. *512*

DATE		ITEM	POST. REF.	DEBIT	CREDIT	BALANCE DEBIT	BALANCE CREDIT

ACCOUNT *Purchases Returns and Allowances*   ACCOUNT NO. *513*

DATE		ITEM	POST. REF.	DEBIT	CREDIT	BALANCE DEBIT	BALANCE CREDIT

ACCOUNT *Freight In*   ACCOUNT NO. *515*

DATE		ITEM	POST. REF.	DEBIT	CREDIT	BALANCE DEBIT	BALANCE CREDIT
20—							
Aug.	1	Balance	✓			403.00	

© 2013 Cengage Learning. All Rights Reserved. May not be scanned, copied, duplicated, or posted to a publicly accessible website, in whole or in part.

ALL ABOUT YOU SPA (continued)

ACCOUNT **Wages Expense** ACCOUNT NO. **611**

DATE		ITEM	POST. REF.	DEBIT	CREDIT	BALANCE	
						DEBIT	CREDIT
20—							
Aug.	1	Balance	✓			7,004.00	

ACCOUNT **Rent Expense** ACCOUNT NO. **612**

DATE		ITEM	POST. REF.	DEBIT	CREDIT	BALANCE	
						DEBIT	CREDIT
20—							
Aug.	1	Balance	✓			1,650.00	

ACCOUNT **Office Supplies Expense** ACCOUNT NO. **613**

DATE		ITEM	POST. REF.	DEBIT	CREDIT	BALANCE	
						DEBIT	CREDIT

ACCOUNT **Spa Supplies Expense** ACCOUNT NO. **614**

DATE		ITEM	POST. REF.	DEBIT	CREDIT	BALANCE	
						DEBIT	CREDIT

ACCOUNT **Laundry Expense** ACCOUNT NO. **615**

DATE		ITEM	POST. REF.	DEBIT	CREDIT	BALANCE	
						DEBIT	CREDIT
20—							
Aug.	1	Balance	✓			84.00	

© 2013 Cengage Learning. All Rights Reserved. May not be scanned, copied, duplicated, or posted to a publicly accessible website, in whole or in part.

ALL ABOUT YOU SPA (continued)

ACCOUNT   *Advertising Expense*   ACCOUNT NO.   *616*

DATE		ITEM	POST. REF.	DEBIT	CREDIT	BALANCE	
						DEBIT	CREDIT

ACCOUNT   *Utilities Expense*   ACCOUNT NO.   *617*

DATE		ITEM	POST. REF.	DEBIT	CREDIT	BALANCE	
						DEBIT	CREDIT
20—							
Aug.	1	Balance	✓			473.00	

ACCOUNT   *Insurance Expense*   ACCOUNT NO.   *618*

DATE		ITEM	POST. REF.	DEBIT	CREDIT	BALANCE	
						DEBIT	CREDIT

ACCOUNT   *Depreciation Expense, Office Equipment*   ACCOUNT NO.   *619*

DATE		ITEM	POST. REF.	DEBIT	CREDIT	BALANCE	
						DEBIT	CREDIT

ACCOUNT   *Depreciation Expense, Spa Equipment*   ACCOUNT NO.   *620*

DATE		ITEM	POST. REF.	DEBIT	CREDIT	BALANCE	
						DEBIT	CREDIT

ACCOUNT   *Miscellaneous Expense*   ACCOUNT NO.   *630*

DATE		ITEM	POST. REF.	DEBIT	CREDIT	BALANCE	
						DEBIT	CREDIT
20—							
Aug.	1	Balance	✓			284.00	

© 2013 Cengage Learning. All Rights Reserved. May not be scanned, copied, duplicated, or posted to a publicly accessible website, in whole or in part.

ALL ABOUT YOU SPA (continued)

ACCOUNTS RECEIVABLE LEDGER

NAME   *About Face Spa*
ADDRESS

DATE		ITEM	POST. REF.	DEBIT	CREDIT	BALANCE
20—						
Aug.	1	Balance	✓			521.59

NAME   *Jill Anson*
ADDRESS

DATE		ITEM	POST. REF.	DEBIT	CREDIT	BALANCE
20—						
Aug.	1	Balance	✓			175.00

NAME   *Chaco's*
ADDRESS

DATE		ITEM	POST. REF.	DEBIT	CREDIT	BALANCE
20—						
Aug.	1	Balance	✓			520.02

NAME   *Holmes Condos*
ADDRESS

DATE		ITEM	POST. REF.	DEBIT	CREDIT	BALANCE
20—						
Aug.	1	Balance	✓			367.47

© 2013 Cengage Learning. All Rights Reserved. May not be scanned, copied, duplicated, or posted to a publicly accessible website, in whole or in part.

ALL ABOUT YOU SPA (continued)

NAME   **Tory Ligman**

ADDRESS

DATE		ITEM	POST. REF.	DEBIT	CREDIT	BALANCE
20—						
Aug.	1	Balance	✓			164.00

NAME   **Los Obrigados Lodge**

ADDRESS

DATE		ITEM	POST. REF.	DEBIT	CREDIT	BALANCE
20—						
Aug.	1	Balance	✓			351.00

NAME   **Mini Spa**

ADDRESS

DATE		ITEM	POST. REF.	DEBIT	CREDIT	BALANCE
20—						
Aug.	1	Balance	✓			222.48

NAME   **Jack Morgan**

ADDRESS

DATE		ITEM	POST. REF.	DEBIT	CREDIT	BALANCE
20—						
Aug.	1	Balance	✓			286.00

© 2013 Cengage Learning. All Rights Reserved. May not be scanned, copied, duplicated, or posted to a publicly accessible website, in whole or in part.

ALL ABOUT YOU SPA (continued)

NAME   *Pleasant Spa*

ADDRESS

DATE		ITEM	POST. REF.	DEBIT	CREDIT	BALANCE
20—						
Aug.	1	Balance	✓			1,961.23

NAME   *Judy Wilcox*

ADDRESS

DATE		ITEM	POST. REF.	DEBIT	CREDIT	BALANCE

© 2013 Cengage Learning. All Rights Reserved. May not be scanned, copied, duplicated, or posted to a publicly accessible website, in whole or in part.

ALL ABOUT YOU SPA (continued)

ACCOUNTS PAYABLE LEDGER

NAME   *Adco, Inc.*

ADDRESS

	DATE		ITEM	POST. REF.	DEBIT	CREDIT	BALANCE

NAME   *Giftco*

ADDRESS

	DATE		ITEM	POST. REF.	DEBIT	CREDIT	BALANCE
20—							
Aug.	1		Balance	✓			1,309.00

NAME   *Golden Spa Supplies*

ADDRESS

	DATE		ITEM	POST. REF.	DEBIT	CREDIT	BALANCE
20—							
Aug.	1		Balance	✓			490.00

NAME   *Logo Products*

ADDRESS

	DATE		ITEM	POST. REF.	DEBIT	CREDIT	BALANCE
20—							
Aug.	1		Balance	✓			3,796.00

© 2013 Cengage Learning. All Rights Reserved. May not be scanned, copied, duplicated, or posted to a publicly accessible website, in whole or in part.

ALL ABOUT YOU SPA (continued)

NAME   *Office Staples*

ADDRESS

DATE		ITEM	POST. REF.	DEBIT	CREDIT	BALANCE
20—						
Aug.	1	Balance	✓			304.00

NAME   *Spa Equipment, Inc.*

ADDRESS

DATE		ITEM	POST. REF.	DEBIT	CREDIT	BALANCE
20—						
Aug.	1	Balance	✓			6,235.00

NAME   *Spa Goods*

ADDRESS

DATE		ITEM	POST. REF.	DEBIT	CREDIT	BALANCE
20—						
Aug.	1	Balance	✓			5,445.00

NAME   *Spa Magic*

ADDRESS

DATE		ITEM	POST. REF.	DEBIT	CREDIT	BALANCE
20—						
Aug.	1	Balance	✓			2,721.00

© 2013 Cengage Learning. All Rights Reserved. May not be scanned, copied, duplicated, or posted to a publicly accessible website, in whole or in part.

ALL ABOUT YOU SPA (continued)

NAME *Superior Equipment*
ADDRESS

DATE		ITEM	POST. REF.	DEBIT	CREDIT	BALANCE
20—						
Aug.	1	Balance	✓			420.00

© 2013 Cengage Learning. All Rights Reserved. May not be scanned, copied, duplicated, or posted to a publicly accessible website, in whole or in part.

ALL ABOUT YOU SPA (continued)

ACCOUNT NAME	DEBIT	CREDIT

ALL ABOUT YOU SPA (concluded)

© 2013 Cengage Learning. All Rights Reserved. May not be scanned, copied, duplicated, or posted to a publicly accessible website, in whole or in part.

CHAPTER 10: Appendix

Problem 10A-1

VOUCHER REGISTER

	DATE		VOU. NO.	CREDITOR	PAYMENT		VOUCHERS PAYABLE CREDIT	PURCHASES DEBIT	FREIGHT IN DEBIT
					DATE	CK. NO.			
1									
2									
3									
4									
5									
6									
7									
8									
9									
10									
11									
12									
13									
14									
15									
16									
17									
18									
19									
20									

EQUALITY OF DEBITS AND CREDITS

DEBITS   CREDITS

$ _____ $ _____

$ _____

© 2013 Cengage Learning. All Rights Reserved. May not be scanned, copied, duplicated, or posted to a publicly accessible website, in whole or in part.

Problem 10A-1 (concluded)

PAGE _____ *65*

WAGES PAYABLE DEBIT	ADVERTISING EXPENSE DEBIT	MISC. EXPENSE DEBIT	OTHER ACCOUNTS DEBIT			
			ACCOUNT	POST. REF.	AMOUNT	
						1
						2
						3
						4
						5
						6
						7
						8
						9
						10
						11
						12
						13
						14
						15
						16
						17
						18
						19
						20

CHECK REGISTER

PAGE _____ *71*

DATE	CK. NO.	PAYEE	VOU. NO.	VOUCHERS PAYABLE DEBIT	PURCHASES DISCOUNTS CREDIT	CASH CREDIT

EQUALITY OF DEBITS AND CREDITS

DEBITS   CREDITS

$ _____ $

$ _____

© 2013 Cengage Learning. All Rights Reserved. May not be scanned, copied, duplicated, or posted to a publicly accessible website, in whole or in part.

Problem 10A-2

VOUCHER REGISTER

	DATE	VOU. NO.	CREDITOR	PAYMENT DATE	CK. NO.	VOUCHERS PAYABLE CREDIT	PURCHASES DEBIT	FREIGHT IN DEBIT
1								
2								
3								
4								
5								
6								
7								
8								
9								
10								
11								
12								
13								
14								
15								
16								
17								

EQUALITY OF DEBITS AND CREDITS

DEBITS   CREDITS

$ $ _____

$ _____

© 2013 Cengage Learning. All Rights Reserved. May not be scanned, copied, duplicated, or posted to a publicly accessible website, in whole or in part.

Problem 10A-2 (continued)

PAGE _____ 75 _____

WAGES PAYABLE DEBIT	SUPPLIES EXPENSE DEBIT	MISC. EXPENSE DEBIT	OTHER ACCOUNTS DEBIT			
			ACCOUNT	POST. REF.	AMOUNT	
						1
						2
						3
						4
						5
						6
						7
						8
						9
						10
						11
						12
						13
						14
						15
						16
						17

CHECK REGISTER

PAGE _____ 86 _____

DATE	CK. NO.	PAYEE	VOU. NO.	VOUCHERS PAYABLE DEBIT	PURCHASES DISCOUNTS CREDIT	CASH CREDIT

EQUALITY OF DEBITS AND CREDITS

DEBITS   CREDITS

$ _____ $ _____

$ _____

© 2013 Cengage Learning. All Rights Reserved. May not be scanned, copied, duplicated, or posted to a publicly accessible website, in whole or in part.

Problem 10A-2 (concluded)

GENERAL JOURNAL   PAGE _____ *41* _____

	DATE		DESCRIPTION	POST. REF.	DEBIT	CREDIT	
1							1
2							2
3							3
4							4
5							5
6							6
7							7
8							8
9							9
10							10
11							11
12							12
13							13
14							14
15							15
16							16
17							17
18							18
19							19
20							20
21							21
22							22
23							23
24							24
25							25
26							26

© 2013 Cengage Learning. All Rights Reserved. May not be scanned, copied, duplicated, or posted to a publicly accessible website, in whole or in part.

Extra Form

GENERAL JOURNAL   PAGE _____

	DATE		DESCRIPTION	POST. REF.	DEBIT	CREDIT	
1							1
2							2
3							3
4							4
5							5
6							6
7							7
8							8
9							9
10							10
11							11
12							12
13							13
14							14
15							15
16							16
17							17
18							18
19							19
20							20
21							21
22							22
23							23
24							24
25							25
26							26

© 2013 Cengage Learning. All Rights Reserved. May not be scanned, copied, duplicated, or posted to a publicly accessible website, in whole or in part.

Problem 10A-3

VOUCHER REGISTER

	DATE		VOU. NO.	CREDITOR	PAYMENT		VOUCHERS PAYABLE CREDIT	PURCHASES DEBIT	FREIGHT IN DEBIT
					DATE	CK. NO.			
1									
2									
3									
4									
5									
6									
7									
8									
9									
10									
11									
12									
13									
14									
15									
16									
17									
18									
19									

EQUALITY OF DEBITS AND CREDITS

DEBITS   CREDITS

$ _____ $ _____

$ _____

© 2013 Cengage Learning. All Rights Reserved. May not be scanned, copied, duplicated, or posted to a publicly accessible website, in whole or in part.

Problem 10A-3 (continued)

PAGE _____ *32*

WAGES PAYABLE DEBIT	SUPPLIES EXPENSE DEBIT	MISC. EXPENSE DEBIT	OTHER ACCOUNTS DEBIT		
			ACCOUNT	POST. REF.	AMOUNT
						1
						2
						3
						4
						5
						6
						7
						8
						9
						10
						11
						12
						13
						14
						15
						16
						17
						18
						19

CHECK REGISTER

PAGE _____ *34*

DATE	CK. NO.	PAYEE	VOU. NO.	VOUCHERS PAYABLE DEBIT	PURCHASES DISCOUNTS CREDIT	CASH CREDIT

EQUALITY OF DEBITS AND CREDITS

DEBITS   CREDITS

$ _____ $ _____

$ _____

© 2013 Cengage Learning. All Rights Reserved. May not be scanned, copied, duplicated, or posted to a publicly accessible website, in whole or in part.

Problem 10A-3 (continued)

GENERAL JOURNAL   PAGE _____ *18* _____

	DATE		DESCRIPTION	POST. REF.	DEBIT	CREDIT	
1							1
2							2
3							3
4							4
5							5
6							6
7							7
8							8
9							9
10							10
11							11
12							12
13							13
14							14
15							15
16							16
17							17
18							18
19							19
20							20
21							21
22							22
23							23
24							24
25							25
26							26

© 2013 Cengage Learning. All Rights Reserved. May not be scanned, copied, duplicated, or posted to a publicly accessible website, in whole or in part.

Problem 10A-3 (concluded)

GENERAL LEDGER

ACCOUNT   *Vouchers Payable*   ACCOUNT NO.   *212*

DATE	ITEM	POST. REF.	DEBIT	CREDIT	BALANCE	
					DEBIT	CREDIT

VOU. NO.	NAME OF CREDITOR	AMOUNT

© 2013 Cengage Learning. All Rights Reserved. May not be scanned, copied, duplicated, or posted to a publicly accessible website, in whole or in part.

Answers to Study Guide Questions

CHAPTER 10

PART 1   True/False—General Journal

1. T
2. F
3. F
4. T
5. T

PART 2   True/False—Cash Receipts and Cash Payments Journals

1. F
2. F
3. T
4. F
5. F

PART 3   Completion—Accounting Language

1. trade discounts
2. Notes Payable
3. cash discount
4. promissory note
5. credit period

PART 4   Matching

1. P
2. CR
3. CP
4. CR
5. J
6. J
7. J
8. CP
9. S
10. CP

PART 5   Cash Receipts Journal

Cash Debit
Sales Discounts Debit
Accounts Receivable Credit
Sales Credit
Other Accounts Credit

PART 6   Cash Payments Journal

Other Accounts Debit
Accounts Payable Debit
Purchases Discounts Credit
Cash Credit

© 2013 Cengage Learning. All Rights Reserved. May not be scanned, copied, duplicated, or posted to a publicly accessible website, in whole or in part.

Work Sheet and Adjusting Entries

LEARNING OBJECTIVES

1. Prepare an adjustment for unearned revenue.

2. Prepare an adjustment for merchandise inventory under the periodic inventory system.

3. Record the adjustment data in a work sheet including merchandise inventory, unearned revenue, supplies used, expired insurance, depreciation, and accrued wages or salaries.

4. Complete the work sheet.

5. Journalize the adjusting entries for a merchandising business under the periodic inventory system.

6. Prepare and journalize the adjusting entry for merchandise inventory under the perpetual inventory system.

ACCOUNTING LANGUAGE

Inventory shrinkage
Physical inventory
Revenue recognition principle
Unearned revenue

STUDY GUIDE QUESTIONS

PART 1   True/False

For each of the following statements, circle T if the statement is true and F if the statement is false.

T	F	1.	An actual count of a stock of goods on hand is called a physical inventory.
T	F	2.	The balance of the Sales Discounts account appears in the Income Statement Credit column.
T	F	3.	The balance of the Unearned Revenue account appears in the Balance Sheet Credit column.
T	F	4.	The first adjustment for Merchandise Inventory is to debit Merchandise Inventory for the amount of the beginning inventory.
T	F	5.	Under the periodic inventory system, entries are recorded in the Merchandise Inventory account at the end of the fiscal period only.
T	F	6.	When a business receives cash for a product or service that is to be delivered in the future, the Unearned Revenue account is credited.
T	F	7.	The value of the ending Merchandise Inventory appears in the Balance Sheet Credit column of the work sheet.
T	F	8.	The balance of the Purchases Discounts account appears in the Income Statement Credit column.

© 2013 Cengage Learning. All Rights Reserved. May not be scanned, copied, duplicated, or posted to a publicly accessible website, in whole or in part.

T   F   9. In the Balance Sheet columns of the work sheet, Income Summary is shown in two figures.

T   F   10. If Income Summary has a debit of $80,000 and a credit of $70,000 in the Adjustments columns of the work sheet, these will be combined into a debit of $10,000 in the Income Statement Debit column.

PART 2   Identifying Work Sheet Columns

Below is a list of selected accounts. Using a check mark, identify the columns in which the balance of each of the accounts would appear.

ACCOUNT NAME	INCOME STATEMENT		BALANCE SHEET	
	DEBIT	CREDIT	DEBIT	CREDIT
Example:				
0. *Rent Income*		✓		
1. Sales				
2. Sales Returns and Allowances				
3. Supplies				
4. Sales Discounts				
5. Salaries Payable				
6. Purchases Returns and Allowances				
7. Income Summary				
8. Unearned Rent				
9. Accumulated Depreciation, Equipment				
10. Purchases				
11. S. Walker, Drawing				
12. Purchases Discounts				
13. S. Walker, Capital				
14. Merchandise Inventory				

© 2013 Cengage Learning. All Rights Reserved. May not be scanned, copied, duplicated, or posted to a publicly accessible website, in whole or in part.

DEMONSTRATION PROBLEM

Office Specialists sells and services copiers and fax machines. The trial balance as of December 31, the end of its fiscal year, is as follows:

Office Specialists
Trial Balance
December 31, 20—

ACCOUNT NAME	DEBIT	CREDIT
Cash	4,000	
Merchandise Inventory	151,000	
Supplies	2,000	
Prepaid Insurance	1,000	
Store Equipment	26,000	
Accumulated Depreciation, Store Equipment		12,500
Accounts Payable		50,000
Employees' Income Tax Payable		3,000
Payroll Taxes and Employees' Withholding Payable		1,500
Unearned Service Contracts		15,000
L. Griswald, Capital		44,100
L. Griswald, Drawing	60,000	
Sales		453,000
Service Contract Income		56,000
Purchases	280,000	
Purchases Discounts		3,800
Freight In	3,900	
Salary Expense	80,000	
Payroll Tax Expense	8,000	
Rent Expense	20,000	
Miscellaneous Expense	3,000	
	638,900	638,900

The earnings from short-term contracts completed during the year have been recorded in Service Contract Income. Amounts received in advance for longer-term service contracts have been recorded in Unearned Service Contracts. To save space by reducing the number of accounts, we use the account called Payroll Taxes and Employees' Withholding Payable for the FICA and unemployment tax liabilities. Data for the adjustments are as follows:

a–b. Merchandise inventory at December 31, $139,500.
   c. Supplies inventory (on hand), $1,700.
   d. Insurance expired, $600.
   e. Salaries accrued, $2,000.
   f. Depreciation of store equipment, $5,200.
   g. Unearned service contract income now earned, $4,800.

Instructions

Complete the work sheet.

© 2013 Cengage Learning. All Rights Reserved. May not be scanned, copied, duplicated, or posted to a publicly accessible website, in whole or in part.

SOLUTION

	ACCOUNT NAME	TRIAL BALANCE	
		DEBIT	CREDIT
1	*Office Specialists*		
2	*Work Sheet*		
3	*For Year Ended December 31, 20—*		
4			
5			
6	ACCOUNT NAME	DEBIT	CREDIT
7	Cash	4,000.00	
8	Merchandise Inventory	151,000.00	
9	Supplies	2,000.00	
10	Prepaid Insurance	1,000.00	
11	Store Equipment	26,000.00	
12	Accumulated Depreciation, Store Equipment		12,500.00
13	Accounts Payable		50,000.00
14	Employees' Income Tax Payable		3,000.00
15	Payroll Taxes and Employees' Withholding Payable		1,500.00
16	Unearned Service Contracts		15,000.00
17	L. Griswald, Capital		44,100.00
18	L. Griswald, Drawing	60,000.00	
19	Sales		453,000.00
20	Service Contract Income		56,000.00
21	Purchases	280,000.00	
22	Purchases Discounts		3,800.00
23	Freight In	3,900.00	
24	Salary Expense	80,000.00	
25	Payroll Tax Expense	8,000.00	
26	Rent Expense	20,000.00	
27	Miscellaneous Expense	3,000.00	
28		638,900.00	638,900.00
29	Income Summary		
30	Supplies Expense		
31	Insurance Expense		
32	Salaries Payable		
33	Depreciation Expense, Store Equipment		
34			
35	Net Income		
36			
37			
38			
39			
40			
41			

© 2013 Cengage Learning. All Rights Reserved. May not be scanned, copied, duplicated, or posted to a publicly accessible website, in whole or in part.

SOLUTION (concluded)

	ADJUSTMENTS			INCOME STATEMENT		BALANCE SHEET		
	DEBIT		CREDIT	DEBIT	CREDIT	DEBIT	CREDIT	
						4,000.00		7
(b)	139,500.00	(a)	151,000.00			139,500.00		8
		(c)	300.00			1,700.00		9
		(d)	600.00			400.00		10
						26,000.00		11
		(f)	5,200.00				17,700.00	12
							50,000.00	13
							3,000.00	14
							1,500.00	15
(g)	4,800.00						10,200.00	16
							44,100.00	17
						60,000.00		18
					453,000.00			19
		(g)	4,800.00		60,800.00			20
				280,000.00				21
					3,800.00			22
				3,900.00				23
(e)	2,000.00			82,000.00				24
				8,000.00				25
				20,000.00				26
				3,000.00				27
								28
(a)	151,000.00	(b)	139,500.00	151,000.00	139,500.00			29
(c)	300.00			300.00				30
(d)	600.00			600.00				31
		(e)	2,000.00				2,000.00	32
(f)	5,200.00			5,200.00				33
	303,400.00		303,400.00	554,000.00	657,100.00	231,600.00	128,500.00	34
				103,100.00			103,100.00	35
				657,100.00	657,100.00	231,600.00	231,600.00	36
								37
								38
								39
								40
								41

© 2013 Cengage Learning. All Rights Reserved. May not be scanned, copied, duplicated, or posted to a publicly accessible website, in whole or in part.

EXERCISES AND PROBLEMS

Exercise 11-1

_____   _____
_____   _____
_____   _____
_____   _____
_____   _____
_____   _____

Exercise 11-2

a.   GENERAL JOURNAL   PAGE _____

	DATE		DESCRIPTION	POST. REF.	DEBIT	CREDIT	
1							1
2							2
3							3
4							4
5							5

b. _____

c. _____

Exercise 11-3

Exercise 11-4

a. _____
b. _____
c. _____
d. _____
e. _____
f. _____
g. _____
h. _____
i. _____
j. _____

© 2013 Cengage Learning. All Rights Reserved. May not be scanned, copied, duplicated, or posted to a publicly accessible website, in whole or in part.

Exercise 11-5

GENERAL JOURNAL   PAGE _____

	DATE	DESCRIPTION	POST. REF.	DEBIT	CREDIT	
1						1
2						2
3						3
4						4
5						5
6						6
7						7
8						8
9						9
10						10
11						11
12						12
13						13
14						14
15						15
16						16
17						17
18						18
19						19
20						20
21						21
22						22
23						23
24						24
25						25
26						26

© 2013 Cengage Learning. All Rights Reserved. May not be scanned, copied, duplicated, or posted to a publicly accessible website, in whole or in part.

Exercise 11-6

GENERAL JOURNAL

PAGE _____

	DATE		DESCRIPTION	POST. REF.	DEBIT	CREDIT	
1							1
2							2
3							3
4							4
5							5
6							6
7							7
8							8
9							9
10							10
11							11
12							12
13							13
14							14
15							15
16							16
17							17
18							18
19							19
20							20
21							21
22							22
23							23
24							24
25							25
26							26

© 2013 Cengage Learning. All Rights Reserved. May not be scanned, copied, duplicated, or posted to a publicly accessible website, in whole or in part.

Exercise 11-7

GENERAL JOURNAL   PAGE _____

	DATE		DESCRIPTION	POST. REF.	DEBIT	CREDIT	
1							1
2							2
3							3
4							4
5							5
6							6
7							7

© 2013 Cengage Learning. All Rights Reserved. May not be scanned, copied, duplicated, or posted to a publicly accessible website, in whole or in part.

Problem 11-1A or 11-1B

	ACCOUNT NAME	TRIAL BALANCE	
		DEBIT	CREDIT
1			
2			
3			
4			
5			
6			
7			
8			
9			
10			
11			
12			
13			
14			
15			
16			
17			
18			
19			
20			
21			
22			
23			
24			
25			
26			
27			
28			
29			
30			
31			
32			
33			
34			
35			
36			
37			
38			
39			
40			
41			

© 2013 Cengage Learning. All Rights Reserved. May not be scanned, copied, duplicated, or posted to a publicly accessible website, in whole or in part.

Problem 11-1A or 11-1B (concluded)

	ADJUSTMENTS		INCOME STATEMENT		BALANCE SHEET		
	DEBIT	CREDIT	DEBIT	CREDIT	DEBIT	CREDIT	
							1
							2
							3
							4
							5
							6
							7
							8
							9
							10
							11
							12
							13
							14
							15
							16
							17
							18
							19
							20
							21
							22
							23
							24
							25
							26
							27
							28
							29
							30
							31
							32
							33
							34
							35
							36
							37
							38
							39
							40
							41

© 2013 Cengage Learning. All Rights Reserved. May not be scanned, copied, duplicated, or posted to a publicly accessible website, in whole or in part.

Problem 11-2A or 11-2B

	ACCOUNT NAME	TRIAL BALANCE	
		DEBIT	CREDIT
1			
2			
3			
4			
5			
6			
7			
8			
9			
10			
11			
12			
13			
14			
15			
16			
17			
18			
19			
20			
21			
22			
23			
24			
25			
26			
27			
28			
29			
30			
31			
32			
33			
34			
35			
36			
37			
38			
39			
40			
41			

© 2013 Cengage Learning. All Rights Reserved. May not be scanned, copied, duplicated, or posted to a publicly accessible website, in whole or in part.

Problem 11-2A or 11-2B (continued)

		ADJUSTMENTS		INCOME STATEMENT		BALANCE SHEET		
	DEBIT	CREDIT	DEBIT	CREDIT	DEBIT	CREDIT	
							1
							2
							3
							4
							5
							6
							7
							8
							9
							10
							11
							12
							13
							14
							15
							16
							17
							18
							19
							20
							21
							22
							23
							24
							25
							26
							27
							28
							29
							30
							31
							32
							33
							34
							35
							36
							37
							38
							39
							40
							41

© 2013 Cengage Learning. All Rights Reserved. May not be scanned, copied, duplicated, or posted to a publicly accessible website, in whole or in part.

Problem 11-2A or 11-2B (concluded)

GENERAL JOURNAL   PAGE _____16_____

	DATE		DESCRIPTION	POST. REF.	DEBIT	CREDIT	
1							1
2							2
3							3
4							4
5							5
6							6
7							7
8							8
9							9
10							10
11							11
12							12
13							13
14							14
15							15
16							16
17							17
18							18
19							19
20							20
21							21
22							22
23							23
24							24
25							25
26							26
27							27
28							28
29							29
30							30
31							31
32							32
33							33
34							34
35							35
36							36

© 2013 Cengage Learning. All Rights Reserved. May not be scanned, copied, duplicated, or posted to a publicly accessible website, in whole or in part.

Problem 11-3A or 11-3B

1.   GENERAL JOURNAL   PAGE _____ *41* _____

	DATE		DESCRIPTION	POST. REF.	DEBIT	CREDIT	
1							1
2							2
3							3
4							4
5							5
6							6
7							7
8							8
9							9
10							10
11							11
12							12
13							13
14							14
15							15
16							16
17							17
18							18
19							19
20							20
21							21
22							22
23							23
24							24
25							25
26							26

2. _____ $ _____

   _____

   _____

   _____ $ _____

3. _____

   _____

   _____ $ _____

   _____ $ _____

   _____   _____

   _____

   _____ $ _____

© 2013 Cengage Learning. All Rights Reserved. May not be scanned, copied, duplicated, or posted to a publicly accessible website, in whole or in part.

Problem 11-4A or 11-4B

	ACCOUNT NAME	TRIAL BALANCE	
		DEBIT	CREDIT
1			
2			
3			
4			
5			
6			
7			
8			
9			
10			
11			
12			
13			
14			
15			
16			
17			
18			
19			
20			
21			
22			
23			
24			
25			
26			
27			
28			
29			
30			
31			
32			
33			
34			
35			
36			
37			
38			
39			
40			
41			

© 2013 Cengage Learning. All Rights Reserved. May not be scanned, copied, duplicated, or posted to a publicly accessible website, in whole or in part.

Problem 11-4A or 11-4B (continued)

		ADJUSTMENTS		INCOME STATEMENT		BALANCE SHEET		
		DEBIT	CREDIT	DEBIT	CREDIT	DEBIT	CREDIT	
								1
								2
								3
								4
								5
								6
								7
								8
								9
								10
								11
								12
								13
								14
								15
								16
								17
								18
								19
								20
								21
								22
								23
								24
								25
								26
								27
								28
								29
								30
								31
								32
								33
								34
								35
								36
								37
								38
								39
								40
								41

© 2013 Cengage Learning. All Rights Reserved. May not be scanned, copied, duplicated, or posted to a publicly accessible website, in whole or in part.

Problem 11-4A or 11-4B (concluded)

GENERAL JOURNAL PAGE _____ *63* _____

	DATE		DESCRIPTION	POST. REF.	DEBIT	CREDIT	
1							1
2							2
3							3
4							4
5							5
6							6
7							7
8							8
9							9
10							10
11							11
12							12
13							13
14							14
15							15
16							16
17							17
18							18
19							19
20							20
21							21
22							22
23							23
24							24
25							25
26							26
27							27
28							28
29							29
30							30
31							31
32							32
33							33

© 2013 Cengage Learning. All Rights Reserved. May not be scanned, copied, duplicated, or posted to a publicly accessible website, in whole or in part.

Problem 11-5A or 11-5B

1.   GENERAL JOURNAL   PAGE _____

	DATE		DESCRIPTION	POST. REF.	DEBIT	CREDIT	
1							1
2							2
3							3
4							4
5							5
6							6
7							7
8							8
9							9
10							10
11							11
12							12
13							13
14							14
15							15
16							16
17							17
18							18
19							19
20							20
21							21

2. _____ $ _____

   _____

   _____ $ _____

   _____

3. _____ $ _____

   _____

   _____ $ _____

   _____   _____

   _____

   _____ $ _____

© 2013 Cengage Learning. All Rights Reserved. May not be scanned, copied, duplicated, or posted to a publicly accessible website, in whole or in part.

ALL ABOUT YOU SPA: Work Sheet and Adjusting Entries

	ACCOUNT NAME	TRIAL BALANCE	
		DEBIT	CREDIT
1			
2			
3			
4			
5			
6			
7			
8			
9			
10			
11			
12			
13			
14			
15			
16			
17			
18			
19			
20			
21			
22			
23			
24			
25			
26			
27			
28			
29			
30			
31			
32			
33			
34			
35			
36			
37			
38			
39			
40			
41			
42			
43			
44			
45			

© 2013 Cengage Learning. All Rights Reserved. May not be scanned, copied, duplicated, or posted to a publicly accessible website, in whole or in part.

ALL ABOUT YOU SPA (continued)

	ADJUSTMENTS		INCOME STATEMENT		BALANCE SHEET		
	DEBIT	CREDIT	DEBIT	CREDIT	DEBIT	CREDIT	
							1
							2
							3
							4
							5
							6
							7
							8
							9
							10
							11
							12
							13
							14
							15
							16
							17
							18
							19
							20
							21
							22
							23
							24
							25
							26
							27
							28
							29
							30
							31
							32
							33
							34
							35
							36
							37
							38
							39
							40
							41
							42
							43
							44
							45

© 2013 Cengage Learning. All Rights Reserved. May not be scanned, copied, duplicated, or posted to a publicly accessible website, in whole or in part.

ALL ABOUT YOU SPA (continued)

GENERAL JOURNAL   PAGE _____ *16* _____

	DATE	DESCRIPTION	POST. REF.	DEBIT	CREDIT	
1						1
2						2
3						3
4						4
5						5
6						6
7						7
8						8
9						9
10						10
11						11
12						12
13						13
14						14
15						15
16						16
17						17
18						18
19						19
20						20
21						21
22						22
23						23
24						24
25						25
26						26

© 2013 Cengage Learning. All Rights Reserved. May not be scanned, copied, duplicated, or posted to a publicly accessible website, in whole or in part.

ALL ABOUT YOU SPA (continued)

GENERAL LEDGER

ACCOUNT **Cash**   ACCOUNT NO. **111**

DATE		ITEM	POST. REF.	DEBIT	CREDIT	BALANCE	
						DEBIT	CREDIT
20—							
Aug.	31	Balance	✓			36,489.12	

ACCOUNT **Accounts Receivable**   ACCOUNT NO. **113**

DATE		ITEM	POST. REF.	DEBIT	CREDIT	BALANCE	
						DEBIT	CREDIT
20—							
Aug.	31	Balance	✓			6,253.79	

ACCOUNT **Office Supplies**   ACCOUNT NO. **114**

DATE		ITEM	POST. REF.	DEBIT	CREDIT	BALANCE	
						DEBIT	CREDIT
20—							
Aug.	31	Balance	✓			248.00	

ACCOUNT **Spa Supplies**   ACCOUNT NO. **115**

DATE		ITEM	POST. REF.	DEBIT	CREDIT	BALANCE	
						DEBIT	CREDIT
20—							
Aug.	31	Balance	✓			740.00	

ACCOUNT **Merchandise Inventory**   ACCOUNT NO. **116**

DATE		ITEM	POST. REF.	DEBIT	CREDIT	BALANCE	
						DEBIT	CREDIT

© 2013 Cengage Learning. All Rights Reserved. May not be scanned, copied, duplicated, or posted to a publicly accessible website, in whole or in part.

ALL ABOUT YOU SPA (continued)

ACCOUNT *Prepaid Insurance*   ACCOUNT NO. *117*

DATE		ITEM	POST. REF.	DEBIT	CREDIT	BALANCE	
						DEBIT	CREDIT
20—							
Aug.	31	Balance	✓			800.00	

ACCOUNT *Office Equipment*   ACCOUNT NO. *124*

DATE		ITEM	POST. REF.	DEBIT	CREDIT	BALANCE	
						DEBIT	CREDIT
20—							
Aug.	31	Balance	✓			1,570.00	

ACCOUNT *Accumulated Depreciation, Office Equipment*   ACCOUNT NO. *125*

DATE		ITEM	POST. REF.	DEBIT	CREDIT	BALANCE	
						DEBIT	CREDIT
20—							
Aug.	31	Balance	✓				10.00

ACCOUNT *Spa Equipment*   ACCOUNT NO. *128*

DATE		ITEM	POST. REF.	DEBIT	CREDIT	BALANCE	
						DEBIT	CREDIT
20—							
Aug.	31	Balance	✓			18,083.00	

ACCOUNT *Accumulated Depreciation, Spa Equipment*   ACCOUNT NO. *129*

DATE		ITEM	POST. REF.	DEBIT	CREDIT	BALANCE	
						DEBIT	CREDIT
20—							
Aug.	31	Balance	✓				64.88

ACCOUNT *Accounts Payable*   ACCOUNT NO. *211*

DATE		ITEM	POST. REF.	DEBIT	CREDIT	BALANCE	
						DEBIT	CREDIT
20—							
Aug.	31	Balance	✓				15,513.00

© 2013 Cengage Learning. All Rights Reserved. May not be scanned, copied, duplicated, or posted to a publicly accessible website, in whole or in part.

ALL ABOUT YOU SPA (continued)

ACCOUNT   *Wages Payable*   ACCOUNT NO.   *212*

DATE		ITEM	POST. REF.	DEBIT	CREDIT	BALANCE	
						DEBIT	CREDIT

ACCOUNT   *Sales Tax Payable*   ACCOUNT NO.   *215*

DATE		ITEM	POST. REF.	DEBIT	CREDIT	BALANCE	
						DEBIT	CREDIT
20—							
Aug.	31	Balance	✓				2,001.12

ACCOUNT   *A. Valli, Capital*   ACCOUNT NO.   *311*

DATE		ITEM	POST. REF.	DEBIT	CREDIT	BALANCE	
						DEBIT	CREDIT
20—							
Aug.	31	Balance	✓				50,219.62

ACCOUNT   *A. Valli, Drawing*   ACCOUNT NO.   *312*

DATE		ITEM	POST. REF.	DEBIT	CREDIT	BALANCE	
						DEBIT	CREDIT
20—							
Aug.	31	Balance	✓			5,000.00	

ACCOUNT   *Income Summary*   ACCOUNT NO.   *313*

DATE		ITEM	POST. REF.	DEBIT	CREDIT	BALANCE	
						DEBIT	CREDIT

ACCOUNT   *Income from Services*   ACCOUNT NO.   *411*

DATE		ITEM	POST. REF.	DEBIT	CREDIT	BALANCE	
						DEBIT	CREDIT
20—							
Aug.	31	Balance	✓				25,398.00

© 2013 Cengage Learning. All Rights Reserved. May not be scanned, copied, duplicated, or posted to a publicly accessible website, in whole or in part.

ALL ABOUT YOU SPA (continued)

ACCOUNT   *Merchandise Sales*   ACCOUNT NO.   *412*

DATE		ITEM	POST. REF.	DEBIT	CREDIT	BALANCE	
						DEBIT	CREDIT
20—							
Aug.	31	Balance	✓				22,489.65

ACCOUNT   *Sales Discounts*   ACCOUNT NO.   *413*

DATE		ITEM	POST. REF.	DEBIT	CREDIT	BALANCE	
						DEBIT	CREDIT
20—							
Aug.	31	Balance	✓			17.46	

ACCOUNT   *Sales Returns and Allowances*   ACCOUNT NO.   *414*

DATE		ITEM	POST. REF.	DEBIT	CREDIT	BALANCE	
						DEBIT	CREDIT
20—							
Aug.	31	Balance	✓			88.00	

ACCOUNT   *Purchases*   ACCOUNT NO.   *511*

DATE		ITEM	POST. REF.	DEBIT	CREDIT	BALANCE	
						DEBIT	CREDIT
20—							
Aug.	31	Balance	✓			24,101.00	

ACCOUNT   *Purchases Discounts*   ACCOUNT NO.   *512*

DATE		ITEM	POST. REF.	DEBIT	CREDIT	BALANCE	
						DEBIT	CREDIT
20—							
Aug.	31	Balance	✓				82.00

ACCOUNT   *Purchases Returns and Allowances*   ACCOUNT NO.   *513*

DATE		ITEM	POST. REF.	DEBIT	CREDIT	BALANCE	
						DEBIT	CREDIT
20—							
Aug.	31	Balance	✓				123.00

© 2013 Cengage Learning. All Rights Reserved. May not be scanned, copied, duplicated, or posted to a publicly accessible website, in whole or in part.

ALL ABOUT YOU SPA (continued)

ACCOUNT **Freight In**   ACCOUNT NO. **515**

DATE		ITEM	POST. REF.	DEBIT	CREDIT	BALANCE	
						DEBIT	CREDIT
20—							
Aug.	31	Balance	✓			992.00	

ACCOUNT **Wages Expense**   ACCOUNT NO. **611**

DATE		ITEM	POST. REF.	DEBIT	CREDIT	BALANCE	
						DEBIT	CREDIT
20—							
Aug.	31	Balance	✓			16,250.00	

ACCOUNT **Rent Expense**   ACCOUNT NO. **612**

DATE		ITEM	POST. REF.	DEBIT	CREDIT	BALANCE	
						DEBIT	CREDIT
20—							
Aug.	31	Balance	✓			3,300.00	

ACCOUNT **Office Supplies Expense**   ACCOUNT NO. **613**

DATE		ITEM	POST. REF.	DEBIT	CREDIT	BALANCE	
						DEBIT	CREDIT

ACCOUNT **Spa Supplies Expense**   ACCOUNT NO. **614**

DATE		ITEM	POST. REF.	DEBIT	CREDIT	BALANCE	
						DEBIT	CREDIT

© 2013 Cengage Learning. All Rights Reserved. May not be scanned, copied, duplicated, or posted to a publicly accessible website, in whole or in part.

ALL ABOUT YOU SPA (continued)

ACCOUNT   *Laundry Expense*   ACCOUNT NO.   *615*

DATE		ITEM	POST. REF.	DEBIT	CREDIT	BALANCE	
						DEBIT	CREDIT
20—							
Aug.	31	Balance	✓			179.00	

ACCOUNT   *Advertising Expense*   ACCOUNT NO.   *616*

DATE		ITEM	POST. REF.	DEBIT	CREDIT	BALANCE	
						DEBIT	CREDIT
20—							
Aug.	31	Balance	✓			455.00	

ACCOUNT   *Utilities Expense*   ACCOUNT NO.   *617*

DATE		ITEM	POST. REF.	DEBIT	CREDIT	BALANCE	
						DEBIT	CREDIT
20—							
Aug.	31	Balance	✓			963.00	

ACCOUNT   *Insurance Expense*   ACCOUNT NO.   *618*

DATE		ITEM	POST. REF.	DEBIT	CREDIT	BALANCE	
						DEBIT	CREDIT

ACCOUNT   *Depreciation Expense, Office Equipment*   ACCOUNT NO.   *619*

DATE		ITEM	POST. REF.	DEBIT	CREDIT	BALANCE	
						DEBIT	CREDIT

© 2013 Cengage Learning. All Rights Reserved. May not be scanned, copied, duplicated, or posted to a publicly accessible website, in whole or in part.

ALL ABOUT YOU SPA (continued)

ACCOUNT _Depreciation Expense, Spa Equipment_   ACCOUNT NO. _620_

DATE		ITEM	POST. REF.	DEBIT	CREDIT	BALANCE DEBIT	BALANCE CREDIT

ACCOUNT _Miscellaneous Expense_   ACCOUNT NO. _630_

DATE		ITEM	POST. REF.	DEBIT	CREDIT	BALANCE DEBIT	BALANCE CREDIT
20—							
Aug.	31	Balance	✓			371.90	

© 2013 Cengage Learning. All Rights Reserved. May not be scanned, copied, duplicated, or posted to a publicly accessible website, in whole or in part.

ALL ABOUT YOU SPA (concluded)

ACCOUNT NAME	DEBIT	CREDIT

© 2013 Cengage Learning. All Rights Reserved. May not be scanned, copied, duplicated, or posted to a publicly accessible website, in whole or in part.

Answers to Study Guide Questions

CHAPTER 11

PART 1   True/False

1.	T	6.	T
2.	F	7.	F
3.	T	8.	T
4.	F	9.	F
5.	T	10.	F

PART 2   Identifying Work Sheet Columns

ACCOUNT NAME	INCOME STATEMENT DEBIT	INCOME STATEMENT CREDIT	BALANCE SHEET DEBIT	BALANCE SHEET CREDIT
Example:				
0. Rent Income		✓		
1. Sales		✓		
2. Sales Returns and Allowances	✓			
3. Supplies			✓	
4. Sales Discounts	✓			
5. Salaries Payable				✓
6. Purchases Returns and Allowances		✓		
7. Income Summary	✓	✓		
8. Unearned Rent				✓
9. Accumulated Depreciation, Equipment				✓
10. Purchases	✓			
11. S. Walker, Drawing			✓	
12. Purchases Discounts		✓		
13. S. Walker, Capital				✓
14. Merchandise Inventory	✓	✓	✓	

© 2013 Cengage Learning. All Rights Reserved. May not be scanned, copied, duplicated, or posted to a publicly accessible website, in whole or in part.

Financial Statements, Closing Entries, and Reversing Entries

LEARNING OBJECTIVES

1. Prepare a classified income statement for a merchandising firm.
2. Prepare a classified balance sheet for any type of business.
3. Compute working capital and current ratio.
4. Record the closing entries for a merchandising firm.
5. Determine which adjusting entries can be reversed and record the reversing entries.

ACCOUNTING LANGUAGE

Current Assets
Current Liabilities
Current ratio
Delivered Cost of Purchases
General Expenses
Gross Profit
Liquidity
Long-Term Liabilities
Net Income or Net Profit

Net Purchases
Net Sales
Notes Receivable (current)
Property and Equipment
Reversing entries
Selling Expenses
Temporary-equity accounts
Working capital

STUDY GUIDE QUESTIONS

PART 1   True/False

For each of the following statements, circle T if the statement is true and F if the statement is false.

T   F   1.   Insurance Expense is classified in the Other Expenses section of an income statement.

T   F   2.   Freight In is classified in the Operating Expenses section of an income statement.

T   F   3.   An increase in Rent Expense results in a decrease in gross profit.

T   F   4.   The cost of goods sold is obtained by subtracting the goods available for sale from the gross sales.

T   F   5.   An increase in Sales Returns and Allowances represents a decrease in gross profit.

T   F   6.   In the Current Liabilities section of a balance sheet, Accounts Payable precedes Notes Payable.

T   F   7.   An unearned revenue account is classified as a current liability.

T   F   8.   Reversing entries are required for all adjusting entries.

T   F   9.   On a balance sheet, Prepaid Insurance is classified in the Property and Equipment section.

T   F   10.   Gross profit is equal to net sales minus goods available for sale.

© 2013 Cengage Learning. All Rights Reserved. May not be scanned, copied, duplicated, or posted to a publicly accessible website, in whole or in part.

PART 2   Completion—Accounting Language

Complete each of the following statements by writing the appropriate words in the spaces provided.

1.   Gross Profit minus Operating Expenses is called _____

     _____.

2.   Net Sales minus Cost of Goods Sold is _____

3.   Gross Purchases minus Purchase Returns and Allowances minus Purchases Discounts

     plus _____ equals Delivered Cost of Purchases.

4.   Current Assets minus Current Liabilities equals _____

5.   Cost of Goods Available for Sale minus ending Merchandise Inventory is called _____

     _____.

PART 3   Financial Statement Classifications

Classify the following accounts according to the title of the financial statement and the statement classification. The first two accounts are provided as examples.

Account Name	Financial Statement	Classification
0. *Example: Wages Expense*	*Income Statement*	*Operating Expenses*
0. *Example: Accounts Payable*	*Balance Sheet*	*Current Liabilities*
1. Freight In		
2. Unearned Subscriptions		
3. Accumulated Depreciation, Equipment		
4. Purchases		
5. Purchases Returns and Allowances		
6. Supplies		
7. Sales Discounts		
8. Accounts Receivable		
9. Building		
10. Interest Expense		

© 2013 Cengage Learning. All Rights Reserved. May not be scanned, copied, duplicated, or posted to a publicly accessible website, in whole or in part.

DEMONSTRATION PROBLEM

Loren's Apparel has a fiscal year extending from January 1 through December 31. Its account balances after adjustments are presented below in random order. The beginning merchandise inventory amounts to $35,870. With regard to the outstanding mortgage, $2,000 is due within the next twelve months.

Notes Receivable	$ 7,000	Freight In	$ 7,040
Interest Income	5,362	Office Salary Expense	11,119
Building	45,400	Accounts Receivable	46,627
Accounts Payable	25,245	Store Supplies	1,094
Prepaid Insurance	1,090	Interest Expense	2,100
Insurance Expense	2,505	Cash	3,305
Accumulated Depreciation,		Depreciation Expense,	
Building	15,133	Building	1,297
Notes Payable (current portion)	10,250	Purchases Discounts	1,335
Sales	267,111	Accumulated Depreciation,	
Sales Salary Expense	60,377	Store Equipment	10,750
Rent Income	2,400	Salaries Payable	3,420
Store Equipment	21,500	C. P. Loren, Drawing	60,000
Mortgage Payable (current		Office Equipment	8,875
portion is $2,000)	31,000	Property Tax Expense	4,006
Land	10,000	Accumulated Depreciation,	
Sales Commission Expense	6,400	Office Equipment	4,438
Sales Discounts	2,671	Miscellaneous General	
Merchandise Inventory,		Expense	1,750
Dec. 31, 20—	41,998	Store Supplies Expense	1,918
Purchases	133,556	C. P. Loren, Capital,	
Advertising Expense	5,342	Jan. 1, 20—	110,980
Sales Returns and		Depreciation Expense, Office	
Allowances	3,149	Equipment	1,775
Purchases Returns		Depreciation Expense,	
and Allowances	2,642	Store Equipment	4,300

Instructions

1. Prepare a classified income statement and subdivide operating expenses.

2. Prepare a statement of owner's equity.

3. Prepare a balance sheet.

4. Determine the amount of working capital and the current ratio.

© 2013 Cengage Learning. All Rights Reserved. May not be scanned, copied, duplicated, or posted to a publicly accessible website, in whole or in part.

SOLUTION

1.

Loren's Apparel				
Income Statement				
For Year Ended December 31, 20—				
Revenue from Sales:				
Sales			$267,111	
Less: Sales Returns and Allowances		$ 3,149		
Sales Discounts		2,671	5,820	
Net Sales				$261,291
Cost of Goods Sold:				
Merchandise Inventory, January 1, 20—			$ 35,870	
Purchases		$133,556		
Less: Purchases Returns and Allowances	$2,642			
Purchases Discounts	1,335	3,977		
Net Purchases		$129,579		
Add Freight In		7,040		
Delivered Cost of Purchases			136,619	
Cost of Goods Available for Sale			$172,489	
Less Merchandise Inventory,				
December 31, 20—			41,998	
Cost of Goods Sold				130,491
Gross Profit				$130,800
Operating Expenses:				
Selling Expenses:				
Sales Salary Expense		$ 60,377		
Sales Commission Expense		6,400		
Advertising Expense		5,342		
Store Supplies Expense		1,918		
Depreciation Expense, Store Equipment		4,300		
Total Selling Expenses			$ 78,337	
General Expenses:				
Insurance Expense		$ 2,505		
Office Salary Expense		11,119		
Depreciation Expense, Building		1,297		
Property Tax Expense		4,006		
Miscellaneous General Expense		1,750		
Depreciation Expense, Office Equipment		1,775		
Total General Expenses			22,452	
Total Operating Expenses				100,789
Income from Operations				$ 30,011
Other Income:				
Interest Income			$ 5,362	
Rent Income			2,400	
Total Other Income			$ 7,762	
Other Expenses:				
Interest Expense			2,100	5,662
Net Income				$ 35,673

© 2013 Cengage Learning. All Rights Reserved. May not be scanned, copied, duplicated, or posted to a publicly accessible website, in whole or in part.

SOLUTION (continued)

2.

Loren's Apparel		
Statement of Owner's Equity		
For Year Ended December 31, 20—		
C. P. Loren, Capital, January 1, 20—		*$110,980*
Net Income for the Year	*$35,673*	
Less Withdrawals for the Year	*60,000*	
Decrease in Capital		*24,327*
C. P. Loren, Capital, December 31, 20—		*$ 86,653*

3.

Loren's Apparel			
Balance Sheet			
December 31, 20—			
Assets			
Current Assets:			
Cash		*$ 3,305*	
Notes Receivable		*7,000*	
Accounts Receivable		*46,627*	
Merchandise Inventory		*41,998*	
Store Supplies		*1,094*	
Prepaid Insurance		*1,090*	
Total Current Assets			*$101,114*
Property and Equipment:			
Land		*$10,000*	
Building	*$45,400*		
Less Accumulated Depreciation	*15,133*	*30,267*	
Office Equipment	*$ 8,875*		
Less Accumulated Depreciation	*4,438*	*4,437*	
Store Equipment	*$21,500*		
Less Accumulated Depreciation	*10,750*	*10,750*	
Total Property and Equipment			*55,454*
Total Assets			*$156,568*
Liabilities			
Current Liabilities:			
Notes Payable		*$10,250*	
Mortgage Payable (current portion)		*2,000*	
Accounts Payable		*25,245*	
Salaries Payable		*3,420*	
Total Current Liabilities			*$ 40,915*
Long-Term Liabilities:			
Mortgage Payable			*29,000*
Total Liabilities			*$ 69,915*
Owner's Equity			
C. P. Loren, Capital			*86,653*
Total Liabilities and Owner's Equity			*$156,568*

© 2013 Cengage Learning. All Rights Reserved. May not be scanned, copied, duplicated, or posted to a publicly accessible website, in whole or in part.

SOLUTION (concluded)

4.   Working Capital = $101,114 − $40,915 = $60,199

$$\text{Current Ratio} = \frac{\$101,114}{\$40,915} = \underline{\underline{2.47}}$$

© 2013 Cengage Learning. All Rights Reserved. May not be scanned, copied, duplicated, or posted to a publicly accessible website, in whole or in part.

EXERCISES AND PROBLEMS

Exercise 12-1

a. _____

b. _____

c. _____

Exercise 12-2

Exercise 12-3

a. _____ f. _____

b. _____ g. _____

c. _____ h. _____

d. _____ i. _____

e. _____ j. _____

© 2013 Cengage Learning. All Rights Reserved. May not be scanned, copied, duplicated, or posted to a publicly accessible website, in whole or in part.

Exercise 12-4

© 2013 Cengage Learning. All Rights Reserved. May not be scanned, copied, duplicated, or posted to a publicly accessible website, in whole or in part.

Exercise 12-5

a. _____   f. _____

b. _____   g. _____

c. _____   h. _____

d. _____   i. _____

e. _____   j. _____

Exercise 12-6

Current Assets:

_____ $ _____

_____

_____

_____

Total $ _____

Current Liabilities:

_____ $ _____

_____

_____

_____

Total $ _____

Working Capital = $ _____ – $ _____ = $ _____

Current Ratio = $\dfrac{\$ _____}{\$ _____}$ = _____

© 2013 Cengage Learning. All Rights Reserved. May not be scanned, copied, duplicated, or posted to a publicly accessible website, in whole or in part.

Exercise 12-7

GENERAL JOURNAL

PAGE _____

	DATE		DESCRIPTION	POST. REF.	DEBIT	CREDIT	
1							1
2							2
3							3
4							4
5							5
6							6
7							7
8							8
9							9
10							10
11							11
12							12
13							13
14							14
15							15
16							16
17							17
18							18
19							19
20							20
21							21
22							22

© 2013 Cengage Learning. All Rights Reserved. May not be scanned, copied, duplicated, or posted to a publicly accessible website, in whole or in part.

Exercise 12-8

GENERAL JOURNAL   PAGE _____

	DATE		DESCRIPTION	POST. REF.	DEBIT	CREDIT	
1							1
2							2
3							3
4							4
5							5
6							6
7							7

© 2013 Cengage Learning. All Rights Reserved. May not be scanned, copied, duplicated, or posted to a publicly accessible website, in whole or in part.

Problem 12-1A or 12-1B

© 2013 Cengage Learning. All Rights Reserved. May not be scanned, copied, duplicated, or posted to a publicly accessible website, in whole or in part.

Problem 12-1A or 12-1B (concluded)

GENERAL JOURNAL   PAGE _____

	DATE		DESCRIPTION	POST. REF.	DEBIT	CREDIT	
1							1
2							2
3							3
4							4
5							5
6							6
7							7
8							8
9							9
10							10
11							11
12							12
13							13
14							14
15							15
16							16
17							17
18							18
19							19
20							20
21							21
22							22
23							23
24							24
25							25
26							26

© 2013 Cengage Learning. All Rights Reserved. May not be scanned, copied, duplicated, or posted to a publicly accessible website, in whole or in part.

Problem 12-2A or 12-2B

© 2013 Cengage Learning. All Rights Reserved. May not be scanned, copied, duplicated, or posted to a publicly accessible website, in whole or in part.

Problem 12-2A or 12-2B (concluded)

Working Capital =

_____ − _____ = _____

Current Ratio =

_____ = _____

© 2013 Cengage Learning. All Rights Reserved. May not be scanned, copied, duplicated, or posted to a publicly accessible website, in whole or in part.

Problem 12-3A or 12-3B

GENERAL JOURNAL

PAGE _____

	DATE		DESCRIPTION	POST. REF.	DEBIT	CREDIT	
1							1
2							2
3							3
4							4
5							5
6							6
7							7
8							8
9							9
10							10
11							11
12							12
13							13
14							14
15							15
16							16
17							17
18							18
19							19
20							20
21							21
22							22
23							23
24							24
25							25
26							26
27							27
28							28
29							29
30							30
31							31
32							32
33							33
34							34
35							35
36							36
37							37
38							38
39							39
40							40

© 2013 Cengage Learning. All Rights Reserved. May not be scanned, copied, duplicated, or posted to a publicly accessible website, in whole or in part.

Problem 12-3A or 12-3B (concluded)

GENERAL JOURNAL   PAGE _____

	DATE		DESCRIPTION	POST. REF.	DEBIT	CREDIT	
1							1
2							2
3							3
4							4
5							5
6							6
7							7
8							8
9							9
10							10
11							11
12							12
13							13
14							14
15							15
16							16
17							17
18							18
19							19
20							20
21							21
22							22
23							23
24							24
25							25
26							26
27							27
28							28
29							29
30							30
31							31
32							32
33							33
34							34
35							35
36							36
37							37
38							38
39							39
40							40

© 2013 Cengage Learning. All Rights Reserved. May not be scanned, copied, duplicated, or posted to a publicly accessible website, in whole or in part.

Problem 12-4A or 12-4B

	ACCOUNT NAME	TRIAL BALANCE	
		DEBIT	CREDIT
1			
2			
3			
4			
5			
6			
7			
8			
9			
10			
11			
12			
13			
14			
15			
16			
17			
18			
19			
20			
21			
22			
23			
24			
25			
26			
27			
28			
29			
30			
31			
32			
33			
34			
35			
36			
37			
38			
39			
40			
41			
42			
43			
44			

© 2013 Cengage Learning. All Rights Reserved. May not be scanned, copied, duplicated, or posted to a publicly accessible website, in whole or in part.

Problem 12-4A or 12-4B (continued)

ADJUSTMENTS		INCOME STATEMENT		BALANCE SHEET		5
DEBIT	CREDIT	DEBIT	CREDIT	DEBIT	CREDIT	6
						7
						8
						9
						10
						11
						12
						13
						14
						15
						16
						17
						18
						19
						20
						21
						22
						23
						24
						25
						26
						27
						28
						29
						30
						31
						32
						33
						34
						35
						36
						37
						38
						39
						40
						41
						42
						43
						44

© 2013 Cengage Learning. All Rights Reserved. May not be scanned, copied, duplicated, or posted to a publicly accessible website, in whole or in part.

Problem 12-4A or 12-4B (continued)

© 2013 Cengage Learning. All Rights Reserved. May not be scanned, copied, duplicated, or posted to a publicly accessible website, in whole or in part.

Problem 12-4A or 12-4B (continued)

© 2013 Cengage Learning. All Rights Reserved. May not be scanned, copied, duplicated, or posted to a publicly accessible website, in whole or in part.

Problem 12-4A or 12-4B (continued)

GENERAL JOURNAL   PAGE _____

	DATE		DESCRIPTION	POST. REF.	DEBIT	CREDIT	
1							1
2							2
3							3
4							4
5							5
6							6
7							7
8							8
9							9
10							10
11							11
12							12
13							13
14							14
15							15
16							16
17							17
18							18
19							19
20							20
21							21
22							22
23							23
24							24
25							25
26							26
27							27
28							28
29							29
30							30
31							31
32							32
33							33
34							34
35							35
36							36
37							37
38							38
39							39
40							40

© 2013 Cengage Learning. All Rights Reserved. May not be scanned, copied, duplicated, or posted to a publicly accessible website, in whole or in part.

Problem 12-4A or 12-4B (concluded)

GENERAL JOURNAL   PAGE _____

	DATE		DESCRIPTION	POST. REF.	DEBIT	CREDIT	
1							1
2							2
3							3
4							4
5							5
6							6
7							7
8							8
9							9
10							10
11							11
12							12
13							13
14							14
15							15
16							16
17							17
18							18
19							19
20							20
21							21
22							22
23							23
24							24
25							25
26							26
27							27
28							28
29							29
30							30
31							31
32							32
33							33
34							34
35							35
36							36
37							37
38							38
39							39
40							40

© 2013 Cengage Learning. All Rights Reserved. May not be scanned, copied, duplicated, or posted to a publicly accessible website, in whole or in part.

COMPREHENSIVE REVIEW PROBLEM (General Journal)

GENERAL JOURNAL   PAGE   *89*

	DATE		DESCRIPTION	POST. REF.	DEBIT	CREDIT	
1							1
2							2
3							3
4							4
5							5
6							6
7							7
8							8
9							9
10							10
11							11
12							12
13							13
14							14
15							15
16							16
17							17
18							18
19							19
20							20
21							21
22							22
23							23
24							24
25							25
26							26
27							27
28							28
29							29
30							30
31							31
32							32
33							33
34							34
35							35
36							36
37							37
38							38
39							39
40							40
41							41
42							42
43							43

526

© 2013 Cengage Learning. All Rights Reserved. May not be scanned, copied, duplicated, or posted to a publicly accessible website, in whole or in part.

COMPREHENSIVE REVIEW PROBLEM (General Journal) (continued)

GENERAL JOURNAL   PAGE _____ *90* _____

	DATE		DESCRIPTION	POST. REF.	DEBIT	CREDIT	
1							1
2							2
3							3
4							4
5							5
6							6
7							7
8							8
9							9
10							10
11							11
12							12
13							13
14							14
15							15
16							16
17							17
18							18
19							19
20							20
21							21
22							22
23							23
24							24
25							25
26							26
27							27
28							28
29							29
30							30
31							31
32							32
33							33
34							34
35							35
36							36
37							37
38							38
39							39
40							40
41							41
42							42
43							43

© 2013 Cengage Learning. All Rights Reserved. May not be scanned, copied, duplicated, or posted to a publicly accessible website, in whole or in part.

COMPREHENSIVE REVIEW PROBLEM (General Journal) (continued)

GENERAL JOURNAL   PAGE   *91*

	DATE		DESCRIPTION	POST. REF.	DEBIT	CREDIT	
1							1
2							2
3							3
4							4
5							5
6							6
7							7
8							8
9							9
10							10
11							11
12							12
13							13
14							14
15							15
16							16
17							17
18							18
19							19
20							20
21							21
22							22
23							23
24							24
25							25
26							26
27							27
28							28
29							29
30							30
31							31
32							32
33							33
34							34
35							35
36							36
37							37
38							38
39							39
40							40
41							41
42							42
43							43

© 2013 Cengage Learning. All Rights Reserved. May not be scanned, copied, duplicated, or posted to a publicly accessible website, in whole or in part.

COMPREHENSIVE REVIEW PROBLEM (General Journal) (continued)

GENERAL JOURNAL   PAGE _____ *92* _____

	DATE		DESCRIPTION	POST. REF.	DEBIT	CREDIT	
1							1
2							2
3							3
4							4
5							5
6							6
7							7
8							8
9							9
10							10
11							11
12							12
13							13
14							14
15							15
16							16
17							17
18							18
19							19
20							20
21							21
22							22
23							23
24							24
25							25
26							26
27							27
28							28
29							29
30							30
31							31
32							32
33							33
34							34
35							35
36							36
37							37
38							38
39							39
40							40
41							41
42							42
43							43

© 2013 Cengage Learning. All Rights Reserved. May not be scanned, copied, duplicated, or posted to a publicly accessible website, in whole or in part.

COMPREHENSIVE REVIEW PROBLEM (General Journal) (continued)

GENERAL JOURNAL   PAGE   *93*

	DATE		DESCRIPTION	POST. REF.	DEBIT	CREDIT	
1							1
2							2
3							3
4							4
5							5
6							6
7							7
8							8
9							9
10							10
11							11
12							12
13							13
14							14
15							15
16							16
17							17
18							18
19							19
20							20
21							21
22							22
23							23
24							24
25							25
26							26

© 2013 Cengage Learning. All Rights Reserved. May not be scanned, copied, duplicated, or posted to a publicly accessible website, in whole or in part.

COMPREHENSIVE REVIEW PROBLEM (General Journal) (continued)

GENERAL JOURNAL   PAGE ___94___

	DATE		DESCRIPTION	POST. REF.	DEBIT	CREDIT	
1							1
2							2
3							3
4							4
5							5
6							6
7							7
8							8
9							9
10							10
11							11
12							12
13							13
14							14
15							15
16							16
17							17
18							18
19							19
20							20
21							21
22							22
23							23
24							24
25							25
26							26

© 2013 Cengage Learning. All Rights Reserved. May not be scanned, copied, duplicated, or posted to a publicly accessible website, in whole or in part.

COMPREHENSIVE REVIEW PROBLEM (General Journal) (continued)

GENERAL JOURNAL   PAGE _____ *95* _____

	DATE		DESCRIPTION	POST. REF.	DEBIT	CREDIT	
1							1
2							2
3							3
4							4
5							5
6							6
7							7
8							8
9							9
10							10
11							11
12							12
13							13
14							14
15							15
16							16
17							17
18							18
19							19
20							20
21							21
22							22
23							23
24							24
25							25
26							26

© 2013 Cengage Learning. All Rights Reserved. May not be scanned, copied, duplicated, or posted to a publicly accessible website, in whole or in part.

COMPREHENSIVE REVIEW PROBLEM (General Journal) (continued)

GENERAL LEDGER

ACCOUNT *Cash*   ACCOUNT NO. __111__

DATE		ITEM	POST. REF.	DEBIT	CREDIT	BALANCE DEBIT	BALANCE CREDIT
20—							
Feb.	1	Balance	✓			34,641.34	

ACCOUNT *Petty Cash Fund*   ACCOUNT NO. __112__

DATE		ITEM	POST. REF.	DEBIT	CREDIT	BALANCE DEBIT	BALANCE CREDIT
20—							
Feb.	1	Balance	✓			70.00	

ACCOUNT *Accounts Receivable*   ACCOUNT NO. __113__

DATE		ITEM	POST. REF.	DEBIT	CREDIT	BALANCE DEBIT	BALANCE CREDIT
20—							
Feb.	1	Balance	✓			15,611.16	

© 2013 Cengage Learning. All Rights Reserved. May not be scanned, copied, duplicated, or posted to a publicly accessible website, in whole or in part.

COMPREHENSIVE REVIEW PROBLEM (General Journal) (continued)

ACCOUNT *Merchandise Inventory*   ACCOUNT NO. **114**

DATE		ITEM	POST. REF.	DEBIT	CREDIT	BALANCE	
						DEBIT	CREDIT
20—							
Feb.	1	Balance	✓			52,640.00	

ACCOUNT *Supplies*   ACCOUNT NO. **116**

DATE		ITEM	POST. REF.	DEBIT	CREDIT	BALANCE	
						DEBIT	CREDIT

ACCOUNT *Prepaid Insurance*   ACCOUNT NO. **118**

DATE		ITEM	POST. REF.	DEBIT	CREDIT	BALANCE	
						DEBIT	CREDIT
20—							
Feb.	1	Balance	✓			2,480.00	

ACCOUNT *Equipment*   ACCOUNT NO. **122**

DATE		ITEM	POST. REF.	DEBIT	CREDIT	BALANCE	
						DEBIT	CREDIT
20—							
Feb.	1	Balance	✓			9,324.00	

ACCOUNT *Accumulated Depreciation, Equipment*   ACCOUNT NO. **123**

DATE		ITEM	POST. REF.	DEBIT	CREDIT	BALANCE	
						DEBIT	CREDIT
20—							
Feb.	1	Balance	✓				5,328.00

© 2013 Cengage Learning. All Rights Reserved. May not be scanned, copied, duplicated, or posted to a publicly accessible website, in whole or in part.

COMPREHENSIVE REVIEW PROBLEM (General Journal) (continued)

ACCOUNT   *Accounts Payable*   ACCOUNT NO. ___221___

DATE		ITEM	POST. REF.	DEBIT	CREDIT	BALANCE DEBIT	BALANCE CREDIT
20—							
Feb.	1	Balance	✓				39,254.10

ACCOUNT   *Employees' Income Tax Payable*   ACCOUNT NO. ___226___

DATE		ITEM	POST. REF.	DEBIT	CREDIT	BALANCE DEBIT	BALANCE CREDIT
20—							
Feb.	1	Balance	✓				1,285.00

ACCOUNT   *FICA Taxes Payable*   ACCOUNT NO. ___227___

DATE		ITEM	POST. REF.	DEBIT	CREDIT	BALANCE DEBIT	BALANCE CREDIT
20—							
Feb.	1	Balance	✓				1,615.80

ACCOUNT   *State Unemployment Tax Payable*   ACCOUNT NO. ___228___

DATE		ITEM	POST. REF.	DEBIT	CREDIT	BALANCE DEBIT	BALANCE CREDIT
20—							
Feb.	1	Balance	✓				536.76

© 2013 Cengage Learning. All Rights Reserved. May not be scanned, copied, duplicated, or posted to a publicly accessible website, in whole or in part.

COMPREHENSIVE REVIEW PROBLEM (General Journal) (continued)

ACCOUNT   *Federal Unemployment Tax Payable*   ACCOUNT NO.   *229*

DATE		ITEM	POST. REF.	DEBIT	CREDIT	BALANCE	
						DEBIT	CREDIT
20—							
Feb.	1	Balance	✓				79.52

ACCOUNT   *Salaries Payable*   ACCOUNT NO.   *230*

DATE		ITEM	POST. REF.	DEBIT	CREDIT	BALANCE	
						DEBIT	CREDIT
20—							
Feb.	1	Balance	✓				620.00

ACCOUNT   *M. L. Langdon, Capital*   ACCOUNT NO.   *311*

DATE		ITEM	POST. REF.	DEBIT	CREDIT	BALANCE	
						DEBIT	CREDIT
20—							
Feb.	1	Balance	✓				66,047.32

ACCOUNT   *M. L. Langdon, Drawing*   ACCOUNT NO.   *312*

DATE		ITEM	POST. REF.	DEBIT	CREDIT	BALANCE	
						DEBIT	CREDIT

© 2013 Cengage Learning. All Rights Reserved. May not be scanned, copied, duplicated, or posted to a publicly accessible website, in whole or in part.

COMPREHENSIVE REVIEW PROBLEM (General Journal) (continued)

ACCOUNT   *Income Summary*   ACCOUNT NO.   *313*

DATE	ITEM	POST. REF.	DEBIT	CREDIT	BALANCE DEBIT	BALANCE CREDIT

ACCOUNT   *Sales*   ACCOUNT NO.   *411*

DATE	ITEM	POST. REF.	DEBIT	CREDIT	BALANCE DEBIT	BALANCE CREDIT

ACCOUNT   *Sales Returns and Allowances*   ACCOUNT NO.   *412*

DATE	ITEM	POST. REF.	DEBIT	CREDIT	BALANCE DEBIT	BALANCE CREDIT

ACCOUNT   *Purchases*   ACCOUNT NO.   *511*

DATE	ITEM	POST. REF.	DEBIT	CREDIT	BALANCE DEBIT	BALANCE CREDIT

© 2013 Cengage Learning. All Rights Reserved. May not be scanned, copied, duplicated, or posted to a publicly accessible website, in whole or in part.

COMPREHENSIVE REVIEW PROBLEM (General Journal) (continued)

ACCOUNT   *Purchases Returns and Allowances*   ACCOUNT NO.   *512*

DATE	ITEM	POST. REF.	DEBIT	CREDIT	BALANCE DEBIT	BALANCE CREDIT

ACCOUNT   *Purchases Discounts*   ACCOUNT NO.   *513*

DATE	ITEM	POST. REF.	DEBIT	CREDIT	BALANCE DEBIT	BALANCE CREDIT

ACCOUNT   *Freight In*   ACCOUNT NO.   *514*

DATE	ITEM	POST. REF.	DEBIT	CREDIT	BALANCE DEBIT	BALANCE CREDIT

ACCOUNT   *Salary Expense*   ACCOUNT NO.   *611*

DATE	ITEM	POST. REF.	DEBIT	CREDIT	BALANCE DEBIT	BALANCE CREDIT

© 2013 Cengage Learning. All Rights Reserved. May not be scanned, copied, duplicated, or posted to a publicly accessible website, in whole or in part.

COMPREHENSIVE REVIEW PROBLEM (General Journal) (continued)

ACCOUNT   *Payroll Tax Expense*   ACCOUNT NO.   *612*

DATE	ITEM	POST. REF.	DEBIT	CREDIT	BALANCE DEBIT	CREDIT

ACCOUNT   *Rent Expense*   ACCOUNT NO.   *613*

DATE	ITEM	POST. REF.	DEBIT	CREDIT	BALANCE DEBIT	CREDIT

ACCOUNT   *Utilities Expense*   ACCOUNT NO.   *614*

DATE	ITEM	POST. REF.	DEBIT	CREDIT	BALANCE DEBIT	CREDIT

ACCOUNT   *Supplies Expense*   ACCOUNT NO.   *616*

DATE	ITEM	POST. REF.	DEBIT	CREDIT	BALANCE DEBIT	CREDIT

ACCOUNT   *Insurance Expense*   ACCOUNT NO.   *617*

DATE	ITEM	POST. REF.	DEBIT	CREDIT	BALANCE DEBIT	CREDIT

© 2013 Cengage Learning. All Rights Reserved. May not be scanned, copied, duplicated, or posted to a publicly accessible website, in whole or in part.

COMPREHENSIVE REVIEW PROBLEM (General Journal) (continued)

ACCOUNT   *Depreciation Expense, Equipment*   ACCOUNT NO.   *618*

DATE		ITEM	POST. REF.	DEBIT	CREDIT	BALANCE	
						DEBIT	CREDIT

ACCOUNT   *Miscellaneous Expense*   ACCOUNT NO.   *619*

DATE		ITEM	POST. REF.	DEBIT	CREDIT	BALANCE	
						DEBIT	CREDIT

© 2013 Cengage Learning. All Rights Reserved. May not be scanned, copied, duplicated, or posted to a publicly accessible website, in whole or in part.

COMPREHENSIVE REVIEW PROBLEM (General Journal) (continued)

ACCOUNTS RECEIVABLE LEDGER

NAME   *Fashion Decor*

ADDRESS   *642 Guthrie St.*

          Dallas, TX 75294

DATE		ITEM	POST. REF.	DEBIT	CREDIT	BALANCE
20—						
Feb.	1	Balance	✓			4,830.65

NAME   *Hotel Beritz*

ADDRESS   *4600 Beaumont Drive*

          Dallas, TX 75294

DATE	ITEM	POST. REF.	DEBIT	CREDIT	BALANCE

NAME   *Jason and Waldon*

ADDRESS   *1420 Favela Road*

          Dallas, TX 75294

DATE		ITEM	POST. REF.	DEBIT	CREDIT	BALANCE
20—						
Feb.	1	Balance	✓			10,780.51

© 2013 Cengage Learning. All Rights Reserved. May not be scanned, copied, duplicated, or posted to a publicly accessible website, in whole or in part.

COMPREHENSIVE REVIEW PROBLEM (General Journal) (continued)

ACCOUNTS PAYABLE LEDGER

NAME *Brandon, Inc.*
ADDRESS *400 W. Tatum St.*
Amarillo, TX 79178

DATE		ITEM	POST. REF.	DEBIT	CREDIT	BALANCE

NAME *Kingston Fabrics*
ADDRESS *1464 Harding Drive*
Dallas, TX 75294

DATE		ITEM	POST. REF.	DEBIT	CREDIT	BALANCE
20—						
Feb.	1	Balance	✓			16,932.10

NAME *Magnuson Textiles*
ADDRESS *620 W. Huber St.*
Corpus Christi, TX 78410

DATE		ITEM	POST. REF.	DEBIT	CREDIT	BALANCE
20—						
Feb.	1	Balance	✓			9,782.00

NAME *Tyson Manufacturing Company*
ADDRESS *842 N. Howard Ave.*
Fort Worth, TX 76196

DATE		ITEM	POST. REF.	DEBIT	CREDIT	BALANCE
20—						
Feb.	1	Balance	✓			12,540.00

© 2013 Cengage Learning. All Rights Reserved. May not be scanned, copied, duplicated, or posted to a publicly accessible website, in whole or in part.

COMPREHENSIVE REVIEW PROBLEM (General Journal) (continued)

Fabulous Furnishings
Schedule of Accounts Receivable
February 28, 20—

Fabulous Furnishings
Schedule of Accounts Payable
February 28, 20—

© 2013 Cengage Learning. All Rights Reserved. May not be scanned, copied, duplicated, or posted to a publicly accessible website, in whole or in part.

COMPREHENSIVE REVIEW PROBLEM (General Journal) (continued)

	ACCOUNT NAME	TRIAL BALANCE	
	Fabulous Furnishings		
	Work Sheet		
	For Month Ended February 28, 20—		
		DEBIT	CREDIT
7	*Cash*		
8	*Petty Cash Fund*		
9	*Accounts Receivable*		
10	*Merchandise Inventory*		
11	*Supplies*		
12	*Prepaid Insurance*		
13	*Equipment*		
14	*Accumulated Depreciation, Equipment*		
15	*Accounts Payable*		
16	*Employees' Income Tax Payable*		
17	*FICA Taxes Payable*		
18	*State Unemployment Tax Payable*		
19	*Federal Unemployment Tax Payable*		
20	*M. L. Langdon, Capital*		
21	*M. L. Langdon, Drawing*		
22	*Sales*		
23	*Sales Returns and Allowances*		
24	*Purchases*		
25	*Purchases Returns and Allowances*		
26	*Purchases Discounts*		
27	*Freight In*		
28	*Salary Expense*		
29	*Payroll Tax Expense*		
30	*Rent Expense*		
31	*Utilities Expense*		
32	*Miscellaneous Expense*		
33			
34			
35			
36			
37			
38			
39			
40			
41			
42			
43			

© 2013 Cengage Learning. All Rights Reserved. May not be scanned, copied, duplicated, or posted to a publicly accessible website, in whole or in part.

COMPREHENSIVE REVIEW PROBLEM (General Journal) (continued)

	ADJUSTMENTS		INCOME STATEMENT		BALANCE SHEET		
	DEBIT	CREDIT	DEBIT	CREDIT	DEBIT	CREDIT	
							1
							2
							3
							4
							5
							6
							7
							8
							9
							10
							11
							12
							13
							14
							15
							16
							17
							18
							19
							20
							21
							22
							23
							24
							25
							26
							27
							28
							29
							30
							31
							32
							33
							34
							35
							36
							37
							38
							39
							40
							41
							42
							43

© 2013 Cengage Learning. All Rights Reserved. May not be scanned, copied, duplicated, or posted to a publicly accessible website, in whole or in part.

COMPREHENSIVE REVIEW PROBLEM (General Journal) (continued)

Fabulous Furnishings

Income Statement

For Month Ended February 28, 20—

© 2013 Cengage Learning. All Rights Reserved. May not be scanned, copied, duplicated, or posted to a publicly accessible website, in whole or in part.

COMPREHENSIVE REVIEW PROBLEM (General Journal) (continued)

Fabulous Furnishings

Statement of Owner's Equity

For Month Ended February 28, 20—

© 2013 Cengage Learning. All Rights Reserved. May not be scanned, copied, duplicated, or posted to a publicly accessible website, in whole or in part.

COMPREHENSIVE REVIEW PROBLEM (General Journal) (continued)

Fabulous Furnishings
Balance Sheet
February 28, 20—

© 2013 Cengage Learning. All Rights Reserved. May not be scanned, copied, duplicated, or posted to a publicly accessible website, in whole or in part.

COMPREHENSIVE REVIEW PROBLEM (General Journal) (continued)

Fabulous Furnishings
Post-Closing Trial Balance
February 28, 20—

ACCOUNT NAME	DEBIT	CREDIT

© 2013 Cengage Learning. All Rights Reserved. May not be scanned, copied, duplicated, or posted to a publicly accessible website, in whole or in part.

COMPREHENSIVE REVIEW PROBLEM (General Journal) (concluded)

PAGE

PAYROLL REGISTER FOR BIWEEKLY PERIOD ENDED

NAME	TOTAL HOURS	BEGINNING CUMULATIVE EARNINGS	TOTAL EARNINGS	ENDING CUMULATIVE EARNINGS	TAXABLE EARNINGS			DEDUCTIONS				PAYMENTS		SALARY EXPENSE DEBIT
					UNEMPLOY-MENT	SOCIAL SECURITY	MEDICARE	FEDERAL INCOME TAX	SOCIAL SECURITY TAX	MEDICARE TAX	TOTAL	NET AMOUNT	CK. NO.	
R. W. Harris	*80*	*5,465.00*												
T. L. Newkirk	*80*	*4,580.00*												
		10,045.00												

PAGE

PAYROLL REGISTER FOR BIWEEKLY PERIOD ENDED

NAME	TOTAL HOURS	BEGINNING CUMULATIVE EARNINGS	TOTAL EARNINGS	ENDING CUMULATIVE EARNINGS	TAXABLE EARNINGS			DEDUCTIONS				PAYMENTS		SALARY EXPENSE DEBIT
					UNEMPLOY-MENT	SOCIAL SECURITY	MEDICARE	FEDERAL INCOME TAX	SOCIAL SECURITY TAX	MEDICARE TAX	TOTAL	NET AMOUNT	CK. NO.	
R. W. Harris	*80*													
T. L. Newkirk	*80*													

© 2013 Cengage Learning. All Rights Reserved. May not be scanned, copied, duplicated, or posted to a publicly accessible website, in whole or in part.

COMPREHENSIVE REVIEW PROBLEM (Special Journals)

SALES JOURNAL   PAGE ___56___

	DATE	INV. NO.	CUSTOMER'S NAME	POST. REF.	ACCOUNTS RECEIVABLE DR. SALES CR.	
1						1
2						2
3						3
4						4
5						5
6						6
7						7
8						8
9						9
10						10
11						11

PURCHASES JOURNAL   PAGE ___62___

	DATE	SUPPLIER'S NAME	INV. NO.	INV. DATE	TERMS	POST. REF.	ACCOUNTS PAYABLE CREDIT	FREIGHT IN DEBIT	PURCHASES DEBIT	
1										1
2										2
3										3
4										4
5										5
6										6
7										7
8										8
9										9
10										10
11										11

© 2013 Cengage Learning. All Rights Reserved. May not be scanned, copied, duplicated, or posted to a publicly accessible website, in whole or in part.

COMPREHENSIVE REVIEW PROBLEM (Special Journals) (continued)

CASH RECEIPTS JOURNAL   PAGE ___69___

	DATE		ACCOUNT CREDITED	POST. REF.	CASH DEBIT	ACCOUNTS RECEIVABLE CREDIT	SALES CREDIT	OTHER ACCOUNTS CREDIT	
1									1
2									2
3									3
4									4
5									5
6									6
7									7
8									8
9									9
10									10
11									11
12									12
13									13

© 2013 Cengage Learning. All Rights Reserved. May not be scanned, copied, duplicated, or posted to a publicly accessible website, in whole or in part.

COMPREHENSIVE REVIEW PROBLEM (Special Journals) (continued)

CASH PAYMENTS JOURNAL   PAGE ___75___

	DATE	CK. NO.	ACCOUNT NAME	POST. REF.	CASH CREDIT	OTHER ACCOUNTS DEBIT	ACCOUNTS PAYABLE DEBIT	PURCHASES DISCOUNTS CREDIT	
1									1
2									2
3									3
4									4
5									5
6									6
7									7
8									8
9									9
10									10
11									11
12									12
13									13
14									14
15									15
16									16
17									17
18									18
19									19
20									20
21									21
22									22
23									23
24									24
25									25
26									26

© 2013 Cengage Learning. All Rights Reserved. May not be scanned, copied, duplicated, or posted to a publicly accessible website, in whole or in part.

COMPREHENSIVE REVIEW PROBLEM (Special Journals) (continued)

GENERAL JOURNAL   PAGE ___89___

	DATE		DESCRIPTION	POST. REF.	DEBIT	CREDIT	
1							1
2							2
3							3
4							4
5							5
6							6
7							7
8							8
9							9
10							10
11							11
12							12
13							13
14							14
15							15
16							16
17							17
18							18
19							19
20							20
21							21
22							22
23							23
24							24
25							25
26							26
27							27
28							28
29							29
30							30
31							31
32							32
33							33
34							34
35							35
36							36
37							37
38							38
39							39
40							40

© 2013 Cengage Learning. All Rights Reserved. May not be scanned, copied, duplicated, or posted to a publicly accessible website, in whole or in part.

COMPREHENSIVE REVIEW PROBLEM (Special Journals) (continued)

GENERAL JOURNAL   PAGE _____ *90* _____

	DATE		DESCRIPTION	POST. REF.	DEBIT	CREDIT	
1							1
2							2
3							3
4							4
5							5
6							6
7							7
8							8
9							9
10							10
11							11
12							12
13							13
14							14
15							15
16							16
17							17
18							18
19							19
20							20
21							21
22							22
23							23
24							24
25							25
26							26

© 2013 Cengage Learning. All Rights Reserved. May not be scanned, copied, duplicated, or posted to a publicly accessible website, in whole or in part.

COMPREHENSIVE REVIEW PROBLEM (Special Journals) (continued)

GENERAL JOURNAL   PAGE _____ *91* _____

	DATE		DESCRIPTION	POST. REF.	DEBIT	CREDIT	
1							1
2							2
3							3
4							4
5							5
6							6
7							7
8							8
9							9
10							10
11							11
12							12
13							13
14							14
15							15
16							16
17							17
18							18
19							19
20							20
21							21
22							22
23							23
24							24
25							25
26							26

© 2013 Cengage Learning. All Rights Reserved. May not be scanned, copied, duplicated, or posted to a publicly accessible website, in whole or in part.

COMPREHENSIVE REVIEW PROBLEM (Special Journals) (continued)

GENERAL JOURNAL   PAGE _____92_____

	DATE		DESCRIPTION	POST. REF.	DEBIT	CREDIT	
1							1
2							2
3							3
4							4
5							5
6							6
7							7
8							8
9							9
10							10
11							11
12							12
13							13
14							14
15							15
16							16
17							17
18							18
19							19
20							20
21							21
22							22
23							23
24							24
25							25
26							26

© 2013 Cengage Learning. All Rights Reserved. May not be scanned, copied, duplicated, or posted to a publicly accessible website, in whole or in part.

COMPREHENSIVE REVIEW PROBLEM (Special Journals) (continued)

GENERAL LEDGER

ACCOUNT   *Cash*   ACCOUNT NO. _____ *111*

DATE		ITEM	POST. REF.	DEBIT	CREDIT	BALANCE DEBIT	BALANCE CREDIT
20—							
Feb.	1	Balance	✓			34,641.34	

ACCOUNT   *Petty Cash Fund*   ACCOUNT NO. _____ *112*

DATE		ITEM	POST. REF.	DEBIT	CREDIT	BALANCE DEBIT	BALANCE CREDIT
20—							
Feb.	1	Balance	✓			70.00	

ACCOUNT   *Accounts Receivable*   ACCOUNT NO. _____ *113*

DATE		ITEM	POST. REF.	DEBIT	CREDIT	BALANCE DEBIT	BALANCE CREDIT
20—							
Feb.	1	Balance	✓			15,611.16	

ACCOUNT   *Merchandise Inventory*   ACCOUNT NO. _____ *114*

DATE		ITEM	POST. REF.	DEBIT	CREDIT	BALANCE DEBIT	BALANCE CREDIT
20—							
Feb.	1	Balance	✓			52,640.00	

ACCOUNT   *Supplies*   ACCOUNT NO. _____ *116*

DATE		ITEM	POST. REF.	DEBIT	CREDIT	BALANCE DEBIT	BALANCE CREDIT

© 2013 Cengage Learning. All Rights Reserved. May not be scanned, copied, duplicated, or posted to a publicly accessible website, in whole or in part.

COMPREHENSIVE REVIEW PROBLEM (Special Journals) (continued)

ACCOUNT   *Prepaid Insurance*   ACCOUNT NO.   *118*

DATE		ITEM	POST. REF.	DEBIT	CREDIT	BALANCE DEBIT	BALANCE CREDIT
20—							
Feb.	1	Balance	✓			2,480.00	

ACCOUNT   *Equipment*   ACCOUNT NO.   *122*

DATE		ITEM	POST. REF.	DEBIT	CREDIT	BALANCE DEBIT	BALANCE CREDIT
20—							
Feb.	1	Balance	✓			9,324.00	

ACCOUNT   *Accumulated Depreciation, Equipment*   ACCOUNT NO.   *123*

DATE		ITEM	POST. REF.	DEBIT	CREDIT	BALANCE DEBIT	BALANCE CREDIT
20—							
Feb.	1	Balance	✓				5,328.00

ACCOUNT   *Accounts Payable*   ACCOUNT NO.   *221*

DATE		ITEM	POST. REF.	DEBIT	CREDIT	BALANCE DEBIT	BALANCE CREDIT
20—							
Feb.	1	Balance	✓				39,254.10

ACCOUNT   *Employees' Income Tax Payable*   ACCOUNT NO.   *226*

DATE		ITEM	POST. REF.	DEBIT	CREDIT	BALANCE DEBIT	BALANCE CREDIT
20—							
Feb.	1	Balance	✓				1,285.00

© 2013 Cengage Learning. All Rights Reserved. May not be scanned, copied, duplicated, or posted to a publicly accessible website, in whole or in part.

COMPREHENSIVE REVIEW PROBLEM (Special Journals) (continued)

ACCOUNT   *FICA Taxes Payable*   ACCOUNT NO.   227

DATE		ITEM	POST. REF.	DEBIT	CREDIT	BALANCE	
						DEBIT	CREDIT
20—							
Feb.	1	Balance	✓				1,615.80

ACCOUNT   *State Unemployment Tax Payable*   ACCOUNT NO.   228

DATE		ITEM	POST. REF.	DEBIT	CREDIT	BALANCE	
						DEBIT	CREDIT
20—							
Feb.	1	Balance	✓				536.76

ACCOUNT   *Federal Unemployment Tax Payable*   ACCOUNT NO.   229

DATE		ITEM	POST. REF.	DEBIT	CREDIT	BALANCE	
						DEBIT	CREDIT
20—							
Feb.	1	Balance	✓				79.52

ACCOUNT   *Salaries Payable*   ACCOUNT NO.   230

DATE		ITEM	POST. REF.	DEBIT	CREDIT	BALANCE	
						DEBIT	CREDIT
20—							
Feb.	1	Balance	✓				620.00

© 2013 Cengage Learning. All Rights Reserved. May not be scanned, copied, duplicated, or posted to a publicly accessible website, in whole or in part.

COMPREHENSIVE REVIEW PROBLEM (Special Journals) (continued)

ACCOUNT   *M. L. Langdon, Capital*   ACCOUNT NO.   *311*

DATE		ITEM	POST. REF.	DEBIT	CREDIT	BALANCE DEBIT	BALANCE CREDIT
20—							
Feb.	1	Balance	✓				66,047.32

ACCOUNT   *M. L. Langdon, Drawing*   ACCOUNT NO.   *312*

DATE		ITEM	POST. REF.	DEBIT	CREDIT	BALANCE DEBIT	BALANCE CREDIT

ACCOUNT   *Income Summary*   ACCOUNT NO.   *313*

DATE		ITEM	POST. REF.	DEBIT	CREDIT	BALANCE DEBIT	BALANCE CREDIT

ACCOUNT   *Sales*   ACCOUNT NO.   *411*

DATE		ITEM	POST. REF.	DEBIT	CREDIT	BALANCE DEBIT	BALANCE CREDIT

ACCOUNT   *Sales Returns and Allowances*   ACCOUNT NO.   *412*

DATE		ITEM	POST. REF.	DEBIT	CREDIT	BALANCE DEBIT	BALANCE CREDIT

© 2013 Cengage Learning. All Rights Reserved. May not be scanned, copied, duplicated, or posted to a publicly accessible website, in whole or in part.

COMPREHENSIVE REVIEW PROBLEM (Special Journals) (continued)

ACCOUNT   *Purchases*   ACCOUNT NO.   *511*

DATE		ITEM	POST. REF.	DEBIT	CREDIT	BALANCE	
						DEBIT	CREDIT

ACCOUNT   *Purchases Returns and Allowances*   ACCOUNT NO.   *512*

DATE		ITEM	POST. REF.	DEBIT	CREDIT	BALANCE	
						DEBIT	CREDIT

ACCOUNT   *Purchases Discounts*   ACCOUNT NO.   *513*

DATE		ITEM	POST. REF.	DEBIT	CREDIT	BALANCE	
						DEBIT	CREDIT

ACCOUNT   *Freight In*   ACCOUNT NO.   *514*

DATE		ITEM	POST. REF.	DEBIT	CREDIT	BALANCE	
						DEBIT	CREDIT

ACCOUNT   *Salary Expense*   ACCOUNT NO.   *611*

DATE		ITEM	POST. REF.	DEBIT	CREDIT	BALANCE	
						DEBIT	CREDIT

© 2013 Cengage Learning. All Rights Reserved. May not be scanned, copied, duplicated, or posted to a publicly accessible website, in whole or in part.

COMPREHENSIVE REVIEW PROBLEM (Special Journals) (continued)

ACCOUNT   *Payroll Tax Expense*   ACCOUNT NO.   *612*

DATE	ITEM	POST. REF.	DEBIT	CREDIT	BALANCE	
					DEBIT	CREDIT

ACCOUNT   *Rent Expense*   ACCOUNT NO.   *613*

DATE	ITEM	POST. REF.	DEBIT	CREDIT	BALANCE	
					DEBIT	CREDIT

ACCOUNT   *Utilities Expense*   ACCOUNT NO.   *614*

DATE	ITEM	POST. REF.	DEBIT	CREDIT	BALANCE	
					DEBIT	CREDIT

ACCOUNT   *Supplies Expense*   ACCOUNT NO.   *616*

DATE	ITEM	POST. REF.	DEBIT	CREDIT	BALANCE	
					DEBIT	CREDIT

ACCOUNT   *Insurance Expense*   ACCOUNT NO.   *617*

DATE	ITEM	POST. REF.	DEBIT	CREDIT	BALANCE	
					DEBIT	CREDIT

© 2013 Cengage Learning. All Rights Reserved. May not be scanned, copied, duplicated, or posted to a publicly accessible website, in whole or in part.

COMPREHENSIVE REVIEW PROBLEM (Special Journals) (continued)

ACCOUNT   *Depreciation Expense, Equipment*   ACCOUNT NO.   *618*

DATE	ITEM	POST. REF.	DEBIT	CREDIT	BALANCE	
					DEBIT	CREDIT

ACCOUNT   *Miscellaneous Expense*   ACCOUNT NO.   *619*

DATE	ITEM	POST. REF.	DEBIT	CREDIT	BALANCE	
					DEBIT	CREDIT

© 2013 Cengage Learning. All Rights Reserved. May not be scanned, copied, duplicated, or posted to a publicly accessible website, in whole or in part.

COMPREHENSIVE REVIEW PROBLEM (Special Journals) (continued)

ACCOUNTS RECEIVABLE LEDGER

NAME   *Fashion Decor*

ADDRESS   *642 Guthrie St.*
Dallas, TX 75294

DATE		ITEM	POST. REF.	DEBIT	CREDIT	BALANCE
20—						
Feb.	*1*	*Balance*	✓			*4,830.65*

NAME   *Hotel Beritz*

ADDRESS   *4600 Beaumont Drive*
Dallas, TX 75294

DATE		ITEM	POST. REF.	DEBIT	CREDIT	BALANCE

NAME   *Jason and Waldon*

ADDRESS   *1420 Favela Road*
Dallas, TX 75294

DATE		ITEM	POST. REF.	DEBIT	CREDIT	BALANCE
20—						
Feb.	*1*	*Balance*	✓			*10,780.51*

© 2013 Cengage Learning. All Rights Reserved. May not be scanned, copied, duplicated, or posted to a publicly accessible website, in whole or in part.

COMPREHENSIVE REVIEW PROBLEM (Special Journals) (continued)

ACCOUNTS PAYABLE LEDGER

NAME   *Brandon, Inc.*
ADDRESS *400 W. Tatum St.*
         Amarillo, TX 79178

DATE		ITEM	POST. REF.	DEBIT	CREDIT	BALANCE

NAME   *Kingston Fabrics*
ADDRESS *1464 Harding Drive*
         Dallas, TX 75294

DATE		ITEM	POST. REF.	DEBIT	CREDIT	BALANCE
20—						
Feb.	*1*	*Balance*	✓			*16,932.10*

NAME   *Magnuson Textiles*
ADDRESS *620 W. Huber St.*
         Corpus Christi, TX 78410

DATE		ITEM	POST. REF.	DEBIT	CREDIT	BALANCE
20—						
Feb.	*1*	*Balance*	✓			*9,782.00*

NAME   *Tyson Manufacturing Company*
ADDRESS *842 N. Howard Ave.*
         Fort Worth, TX 76196

DATE		ITEM	POST. REF.	DEBIT	CREDIT	BALANCE
20—						
Feb.	*1*	*Balance*	✓			*12,540.00*

© 2013 Cengage Learning. All Rights Reserved. May not be scanned, copied, duplicated, or posted to a publicly accessible website, in whole or in part.

COMPREHENSIVE REVIEW PROBLEM (Special Journals) (continued)

Fabulous Furnishings
Schedule of Accounts Receivable
February 28, 20—

Fabulous Furnishings
Schedule of Accounts Payable
February 28, 20—

567

COMPREHENSIVE REVIEW PROBLEM (Special Journals) (continued)

		TRIAL BALANCE	
	Fabulous Furnishings		
	Work Sheet		
	For Month Ended February 28, 20—		
	ACCOUNT NAME	DEBIT	CREDIT
7	*Cash*		
8	*Petty Cash Fund*		
9	*Accounts Receivable*		
10	*Merchandise Inventory*		
11	*Supplies*		
12	*Prepaid Insurance*		
13	*Equipment*		
14	*Accumulated Depreciation, Equipment*		
15	*Accounts Payable*		
16	*Employees' Income Tax Payable*		
17	*FICA Taxes Payable*		
18	*State Unemployment Tax Payable*		
19	*Federal Unemployment Tax Payable*		
20	*M. L. Langdon, Capital*		
21	*M. L. Langdon, Drawing*		
22	*Sales*		
23	*Sales Returns and Allowances*		
24	*Purchases*		
25	*Purchases Returns and Allowances*		
26	*Purchases Discounts*		
27	*Freight In*		
28	*Salary Expense*		
29	*Payroll Tax Expense*		
30	*Rent Expense*		
31	*Utilities Expense*		
32	*Miscellaneous Expense*		
33			
34			
35			
36			
37			
38			
39			
40			
41			
42			
43			

© 2013 Cengage Learning. All Rights Reserved. May not be scanned, copied, duplicated, or posted to a publicly accessible website, in whole or in part.

COMPREHENSIVE REVIEW PROBLEM (Special Journals) (continued)

						1
						2
						3
						4
ADJUSTMENTS		INCOME STATEMENT		BALANCE SHEET		5
DEBIT	CREDIT	DEBIT	CREDIT	DEBIT	CREDIT	6
						7
						8
						9
						10
						11
						12
						13
						14
						15
						16
						17
						18
						19
						20
						21
						22
						23
						24
						25
						26
						27
						28
						29
						30
						31
						32
						33
						34
						35
						36
						37
						38
						39
						40
						41
						42
						43

© 2013 Cengage Learning. All Rights Reserved. May not be scanned, copied, duplicated, or posted to a publicly accessible website, in whole or in part.

COMPREHENSIVE REVIEW PROBLEM (Special Journals) (continued)

Fabulous Furnishings
Income Statement
For Month Ended February 28, 20—

© 2013 Cengage Learning. All Rights Reserved. May not be scanned, copied, duplicated, or posted to a publicly accessible website, in whole or in part.

COMPREHENSIVE REVIEW PROBLEM (Special Journals) (continued)

Fabulous Furnishings

Statement of Owner's Equity

For Month Ended February 28, 20—

© 2013 Cengage Learning. All Rights Reserved. May not be scanned, copied, duplicated, or posted to a publicly accessible website, in whole or in part.

COMPREHENSIVE REVIEW PROBLEM (Special Journals) (continued)

Fabulous Furnishings
Balance Sheet
February 28, 20—

© 2013 Cengage Learning. All Rights Reserved. May not be scanned, copied, duplicated, or posted to a publicly accessible website, in whole or in part.

COMPREHENSIVE REVIEW PROBLEM (Special Journals) (continued)

Fabulous Furnishings

Post-Closing Trial Balance

February 28, 20—

ACCOUNT NAME	DEBIT	CREDIT

© 2013 Cengage Learning. All Rights Reserved. May not be scanned, copied, duplicated, or posted to a publicly accessible website, in whole or in part.

COMPREHENSIVE REVIEW PROBLEM (Special Journals) (concluded)

PAYROLL REGISTER FOR BIWEEKLY PERIOD ENDED _____   PAGE _____

NAME	TOTAL HOURS	BEGINNING CUMULATIVE EARNINGS	TOTAL EARNINGS	ENDING CUMULATIVE EARNINGS	TAXABLE EARNINGS			DEDUCTIONS				PAYMENTS		SALARY EXPENSE DEBIT
					UNEMPLOY-MENT	SOCIAL SECURITY	MEDICARE	FEDERAL INCOME TAX	SOCIAL SECURITY TAX	MEDICARE TAX	TOTAL	NET AMOUNT	CK. NO.	
R. W. Harris	80	5,465.00												
T. L. Newkirk	80	4,580.00												
		10,045.00												

PAYROLL REGISTER FOR BIWEEKLY PERIOD ENDED _____   PAGE _____

NAME	TOTAL HOURS	BEGINNING CUMULATIVE EARNINGS	TOTAL EARNINGS	ENDING CUMULATIVE EARNINGS	TAXABLE EARNINGS			DEDUCTIONS				PAYMENTS		SALARY EXPENSE DEBIT
					UNEMPLOY-MENT	SOCIAL SECURITY	MEDICARE	FEDERAL INCOME TAX	SOCIAL SECURITY TAX	MEDICARE TAX	TOTAL	NET AMOUNT	CK. NO.	
R. W. Harris	80													
T. L. Newkirk	80													

© 2013 Cengage Learning. All Rights Reserved. May not be scanned, copied, duplicated, or posted to a publicly accessible website, in whole or in part.

© 2013 Cengage Learning. All Rights Reserved. May not be scanned, copied, duplicated, or posted to a publicly accessible website, in whole or in part.

ALL ABOUT YOU SPA (continued)

© 2013 Cengage Learning. All Rights Reserved. May not be scanned, copied, duplicated, or posted to a publicly accessible website, in whole or in part.

ALL ABOUT YOU SPA (continued)

© 2013 Cengage Learning. All Rights Reserved. May not be scanned, copied, duplicated, or posted to a publicly accessible website, in whole or in part.

ALL ABOUT YOU SPA (continued)

GENERAL JOURNAL   PAGE _____ 17 _____

	DATE	DESCRIPTION	POST. REF.	DEBIT	CREDIT	
1						1
2						2
3						3
4						4
5						5
6						6
7						7
8						8
9						9
10						10
11						11
12						12
13						13
14						14
15						15
16						16
17						17
18						18
19						19
20						20
21						21
22						22
23						23
24						24
23						23
24						24
25						25
26						26
27						27
28						28
29						29
30						30
31						31
32						32
33						33
34						34

© 2013 Cengage Learning. All Rights Reserved. May not be scanned, copied, duplicated, or posted to a publicly accessible website, in whole or in part.

ALL ABOUT YOU SPA (continued)

ACCOUNT NAME	DEBIT	CREDIT

© 2013 Cengage Learning. All Rights Reserved. May not be scanned, copied, duplicated, or posted to a publicly accessible website, in whole or in part.

Answers to Study Guide Questions

CHAPTER 12

PART 1   True/False

1.	F	6.	F
2.	F	7.	T
3.	F	8.	F
4.	F	9.	F
5.	T	10.	F

PART 2   Completion—Accounting Language

1. Income from Operations
2. Gross Profit
3. Freight In
4. Working Capital
5. Cost of Goods Sold

PART 3   Financial Statement Classifications

	Account Name	Financial Statement	Classification
0.	*Example: Wages Expense*	*Income Statement*	*Operating Expenses*
0.	*Example: Accounts Payable*	*Balance Sheet*	*Current Liabilities*
1.	Freight In	Income Statement	Cost of Goods Sold
2.	Unearned Subscriptions	Balance Sheet	Current Liabilities
3.	Accumulated Depreciation, Equipment	Balance Sheet	Property and Equipment
4.	Purchases	Income Statement	Cost of Goods Sold
5.	Purchases Returns and Allowances	Income Statement	Cost of Goods Sold
6.	Supplies	Balance Sheet	Current Assets
7.	Sales Discounts	Income Statement	Revenue from Sales
8.	Accounts Receivable	Balance Sheet	Current Assets
9.	Building	Balance Sheet	Property and Equipment
10.	Interest Expense	Income Statement	Other Expenses

© 2013 Cengage Learning. All Rights Reserved. May not be scanned, copied, duplicated, or posted to a publicly accessible website, in whole or in part.

A | Methods of Depreciation

LEARNING OBJECTIVES

1. Prepare a schedule of depreciation using the straight-line method.

2. Prepare a schedule of depreciation using the double-declining-balance method.

3. Prepare a schedule of depreciation for five-year property under the Modified Accelerated Cost Recovery System.

ACCOUNTING LANGUAGE

Double-declining-balance method
Modified Accelerated Cost Recovery System (MACRS)
Straight-line method

© 2013 Cengage Learning. All Rights Reserved. May not be scanned, copied, duplicated, or posted to a publicly accessible website, in whole or in part.

Problem A-1

YEAR	DEPRECIATION FOR THE YEAR	ACCUMULATED DEPRECIATION	BOOK VALUE
	$ _____ ÷ _____ = $ _____	$ _____ + $ _____ = $ _____	$ _____ − $ _____ = $ _____
	_____ ÷ _____ = _____	_____ + _____ = _____	_____ − _____ = _____
	_____ ÷ _____ = _____	_____ + _____ = _____	_____ − _____ = _____
	_____ ÷ _____ = _____	_____ + _____ = _____	_____ − _____ = _____
	_____ $ _____		

Problem A-2

YEAR	DEPRECIATION FOR THE YEAR	ACCUMULATED DEPRECIATION	BOOK VALUE
	$ _____ × _____ = $ _____	$ _____ + $ _____ = $ _____	$ _____ − $ _____ = $ _____
	_____ × _____ = _____	_____ + _____ = _____	_____ − _____ = _____
	_____ × _____ = _____	_____ + _____ = _____	_____ − _____ = _____
	_____ − _____ = $ _____		

Problem A-3

YEAR	DEPRECIATION FOR THE YEAR	ACCUMULATED DEPRECIATION	BOOK VALUE
	$ _____ × _____ = $ _____	$ _____ + $ _____ = $ _____	$ _____ − $ _____ = $ _____
	_____ × _____ = _____	_____ + _____ = _____	_____ − _____ = _____
	_____ × _____ = _____	_____ + _____ = _____	_____ − _____ = _____
	_____ × _____ = _____	_____ + _____ = _____	_____ − _____ = _____
	_____ × _____ = _____	_____ + _____ = _____	_____ − _____ = _____
	_____ × _____ = $ _____		

© 2013 Cengage Learning. All Rights Reserved. May not be scanned, copied, duplicated, or posted to a publicly accessible website, in whole or in part.

B | **Bad Debts**

LEARNING OBJECTIVES

1. Prepare the adjusting entry for bad debts using the allowance method, based on a percentage of credit sales.

2. Prepare the entry to write off an account as uncollectible when the allowance method is used.

3. Prepare the entry to write off an account as uncollectible when the specific charge-off method is used.

ACCOUNTING LANGUAGE

Allowance method of accounting for bad debts expense

Specific charge-off method of accounting for bad debts expense

© 2013 Cengage Learning. All Rights Reserved. May not be scanned, copied, duplicated, or posted to a publicly accessible website, in whole or in part.

Problem B-1

GENERAL JOURNAL   PAGE _____

	DATE		DESCRIPTION	POST. REF.	DEBIT	CREDIT	
1							1
2							2
3							3
4							4
5							5
6							6
7							7
8							8
9							9
10							10
11							11
12							12
13							13
14							14
15							15
16							16
17							17
18							18
19							19
20							20
21							21
22							22
23							23

© 2013 Cengage Learning. All Rights Reserved. May not be scanned, copied, duplicated, or posted to a publicly accessible website, in whole or in part.

Problem B-2

GENERAL JOURNAL   PAGE _____

	DATE		DESCRIPTION	POST. REF.	DEBIT	CREDIT	
1							1
2							2
3							3
4							4
5							5
6							6
7							7
8							8
9							9
10							10
11							11
12							12
13							13
14							14
15							15
16							16
17							17
18							18
19							19
20							20
21							21
22							22
23							23

© 2013 Cengage Learning. All Rights Reserved. May not be scanned, copied, duplicated, or posted to a publicly accessible website, in whole or in part.

Problem B-3

GENERAL JOURNAL   PAGE _____

	DATE		DESCRIPTION	POST. REF.	DEBIT	CREDIT	
1							1
2							2
3							3
4							4
5							5
6							6
7							7
8							8
9							9
10							10
11							11
12							12
13							13
14							14
15							15
16							16
17							17
18							18
19							19
20							20
21							21
22							22
23							23

© 2013 Cengage Learning. All Rights Reserved. May not be scanned, copied, duplicated, or posted to a publicly accessible website, in whole or in part.

Inventory Methods

LEARNING OBJECTIVES

1. Determine the amount of the ending merchandise inventory by the weighted-average-cost method.

2. Determine the amount of the ending merchandise inventory by the first-in, first-out (FIFO) method.

3. Determine the amount of the ending merchandise inventory by the last-in, first-out (LIFO) method.

ACCOUNTING LANGUAGE

First-in, first-out (FIFO) method
Last-in, first-out (LIFO) method
Weighted-average-cost method

© 2013 Cengage Learning. All Rights Reserved. May not be scanned, copied, duplicated, or posted to a publicly accessible website, in whole or in part.

Problem C-1

_____	cu. yds. @ _____ per cu. yd.	=	
_____	cu. yds. @ _____ per cu. yd.	=	
_____	cu. yds. @ _____ per cu. yd.	=	
_____ _____	cu. yds. @ _____ per cu. yd.	=	_____
Total units available _____			_____

_____   =   average cost per cu. yd. (rounded)
_____

_____ cu. yds.   ×   _____   =   _____

Problem C-2

	cu. yds. @ _____ per cu. yd.	=	
_____	cu. yds. @ _____ per cu. yd.	=	_____
_____	cu. yds.		

Problem C-3

_____ cu. yds. @   _____ per cu. yd.   =   _____

© 2013 Cengage Learning. All Rights Reserved. May not be scanned, copied, duplicated, or posted to a publicly accessible website, in whole or in part.

The Statement of Cash Flows

LEARNING OBJECTIVES

1. Classify cash flows as Operating Activities, Investing Activities, and Financing Activities.

2. Prepare a statement of cash flows.

ACCOUNTING LANGUAGE

Cash equivalents
Financing activities
Investing activities
Operating activities
Statement of cash flows

© 2013 Cengage Learning. All Rights Reserved. May not be scanned, copied, duplicated, or posted to a publicly accessible website, in whole or in part.

Problem D-1

© 2013 Cengage Learning. All Rights Reserved. May not be scanned, copied, duplicated, or posted to a publicly accessible website, in whole or in part.

Problem D-2

© 2013 Cengage Learning. All Rights Reserved. May not be scanned, copied, duplicated, or posted to a publicly accessible website, in whole or in part.

Problem D-3

© 2013 Cengage Learning. All Rights Reserved. May not be scanned, copied, duplicated, or posted to a publicly accessible website, in whole or in part.

Problem D-4

© 2013 Cengage Learning. All Rights Reserved. May not be scanned, copied, duplicated, or posted to a publicly accessible website, in whole or in part.

Extra Form

© 2013 Cengage Learning. All Rights Reserved. May not be scanned, copied, duplicated, or posted to a publicly accessible website, in whole or in part.

E

Departmental Accounting

LEARNING OBJECTIVES

1. Compile a departmental income statement.

2. Understand departmental margin.

ACCOUNTING LANGUAGE

Apportionment of expenses
Departmental margin
Direct expenses
Indirect expenses

© 2013 Cengage Learning. All Rights Reserved. May not be scanned, copied, duplicated, or posted to a publicly accessible website, in whole or in part.

Problem E-1

	BOOK DEPARTMENT		
1			
2			
3			
4			
5			
6			
7			
8			
9			
10			
11			
12			
13			
14			
15			
16			
17			
18			
19			
20			
21			
22			
23			
24			
25			
26			
27			
28			
29			
30			
31			
32			
33			
34			
35			
36			
37			
38			
39			
40			
41			
42			

© 2013 Cengage Learning. All Rights Reserved. May not be scanned, copied, duplicated, or posted to a publicly accessible website, in whole or in part.